A Feminist Companion to Matthew

Feminist Companion to the New Testament
and Early Christian Writings, 1

A Feminist Companion to Matthew

edited by
Amy-Jill Levine
with Marianne Blickenstaff

Sheffield Academic Press
www.SheffieldAcademicPress.com

Copyright © 2001 Sheffield Academic Press

Published by Sheffield Academic Press Ltd
Mansion House
19 Kingfield Road
Sheffield, S11 9AS
England

in Great Britain
by Cromwell Press
Trowbridge, Wiltshire

British Library Cataloguing-in-Publication Data

A catalogue record for this book is available
from the British Library

ISBN 1-84127-211-6

CONTENTS

Preface	7
Acknowledgments	8
Abbreviations	9
List of Contributors	11
AMY-JILL LEVINE Introduction	13
JANICE CAPEL ANDERSON Matthew: Gender and Reading	25
JULIAN SHEFFIELD The Father in the Gospel of Matthew	52
AMY-JILL LEVINE Discharging Responsibility: Matthean Jesus, Biblical Law, and Hemorrhaging Woman	70
CELIA DEUTSCH Jesus as Wisdom: A Feminist Reading of Matthew's Wisdom Christology	88
GAIL R. O'DAY Surprised by Faith: Jesus and the Canaanite Woman	114
ELAINE M. WAINWRIGHT Not Without my Daughter: Gender and Demon Possession in Matthew 15.21-28	126
STEPHENSON HUMPHRIES-BROOKS The Canaanite Women in Matthew	138
ANTHONY J. SALDARINI Absent Women in Matthew's Households	157

MARIE-ELOISE ROSENBLATT
   Got into the Party after All:
   Women's Issues and the Five Foolish Virgins   171

THOMAS R.W. LONGSTAFF
   What Are Those Women Doing at the Tomb of Jesus?
   Perspectives on Matthew 28.1   196

CAROLYN OSIEK
   The Women at the Tomb: What Are They Doing There?   205

Bibliography   221
Index of References   235
Index of Authors   245

PREFACE

A Feminist Companion to Matthew inaugurates a new series, but one with excellent precedent. This volume, and the volumes to follow on the texts and history of Christian Origins, adopt the model established by Athalya Brenner, editor of the enormously successful Feminist Companion to the Bible. This sister to FCB marks an important new dimension in Sheffield Academic Press's list of titles in the areas of feminist hermeneutics and theology, and its content will underline the extent to which feminist critique is established as a core discipline of biblical, historical and theological research.

The new series, like FCB, contains contributions by beginning as well as established scholars; it presents both previously published work (primarily from sources either out of print or difficult to find) and new essays. In some cases, scholars have been invited to re-visit their earlier work to examine the extent to which their arguments and approaches have changed; in others, they have sought to apply their earlier insights to new texts.

We wish to thank Marianne Blickenstaff for her numerous organizational contributions as well as her discerning insights and Kathy Williams for help with proofreading. We also wish to thank the Carpenter Program in Religion, Gender, and Sexuality at Vanderbilt Divinity School for financial and technical support.

This series seeks international representation; to this end, gratitude is due as well to Vanderbilt Divinity School, which has provided funding for translating into English both previously published work and new articles.

It is our hope that this new series will quickly establish itself as a standard work of reference to scholars, students and also to others interested in the New Testament and Christian Origins.

Amy-Jill Levine, Vanderbilt Divinity School
Philip R. Davies, Sheffield Academic Press

ACKNOWLEDGMENTS

The editors and publisher are grateful to the following for permission to reproduce copyright material: Scholars Press for 'Discharging Responsibility: Matthean Jesus, Biblical Law, and the Hemorrhaging Woman', by Amy-Jill Levine, from *Treasures New and Old: Recent Contributions to Matthean Studies*; *Listening/Journal of Religion and Culture*, for 'Surprised by Faith: Jesus and the Canaanite Woman', by Gail R. O'Day, from *Listening/Journal of Religion and Culture* 24; *Ex Auditu*, for 'The Women at the Tomb: What are They Doing There?', by Carolyn Osiek, from *Ex Auditu* 9; *Continuum*, for 'Got Into the Party After All: Women's Issues and the Five Foolish Virgins', by Marie-Eloise Rosenblatt, from *Continuum* 3.

ABBREVIATIONS

AB	Anchor Bible
ABD	David Noel Freedman (ed.), *The Anchor Bible Dictionary* (New York: Doubleday, 1992)
AJA	*American Journal of Archaeology*
AnBib	Analecta biblica
ANRW	Hildegard Temporini, Joseph Vogt and Wolfgang Haase (eds.), *Aufstieg und Niedergang der römischen Welt: Geschichte und Kultur Roms im Spiegel der neueren Forschung* (Berlin: W. de Gruyter, 1972-)
ATRSup	*Anglican Theological Review Supplementary Series*
BA	*Biblical Archaeologist*
BAG	Walter Bauer, William F. Arndt and F. William Gingrich, *A Greek-English Lexicon of the New Testament and Other Early Christian Literature* (Chicago: University of Chicago Press, 1952)
BAGD	Walter Bauer, William F. Arndt, F. William Gingrich and Frederick W. Danker, *A Greek-English Lexicon of the New Testament and Other Early Christian Literature* (Chicago: University of Chicago Press, 2nd edn, 1958)
BASOR	*Bulletin of the American Schools of Oriental Research*
BDF	Friedrich Blass, A. Debrunner and Robert W. Funk, *A Greek Grammar of the New Testament and Other Early Christian Literature* (Cambridge: Cambridge University Press, 1961)
Bib	*Biblica*
BibOr	Biblica et orientalia
BibRes	*Biblical Research*
BJS	Brown Judaic Studies
BR	*Bible Review*
BTB	*Biblical Theology Bulletin*
BZ	*Biblische Zeitschrift*
BZNW	Beihefte zur ZNW
CBQ	*Catholic Biblical Quarterly*
CBQMS	*Catholic Biblical Quarterly*, Monograph Series
CSCJA	Center for the Study of Judaism and Christianity in Antiquity
CSRBull	*Council on the Study of Religion Bulletin*
CTM	Calver Theologische Monographien
EJ	*Encyclopedia Judaica*
ETL	*Ephémérides theologicae lovanienses*
EvT	*Evangelische Theologie*
ExpTim	*Expository Times*
HR	*History of Religions*

HTR	*Harvard Theological Review*
IB	*Interpreter's Bible*
IBT	Interpreting Biblical Texts
ICC	International Critical Commentary
IEJ	*Israel Exploration Journal*
Int	*Interpretation*
JBL	*Journal of Biblical Literature*
JES	*Journal of Ecumenical Studies*
JFSR	*Journal of Feminist Studies in Religion*
JJS	*Journal of Jewish Studies*
JNSL	*Journal of Northwest Semitic Languages*
JSNT	*Journal for the Study of the New Testament*
JSNTSup	*Journal for the Study of the New Testament*, Supplement Series
LTP	*Laval Théologique et Philosophique*
MNTC	Moffatt NT Commentary
NEB	New English Bible
NovT	*Novum Testamentum*
NTAbh	Neutestamentliche Abhandlungen
NTS	*New Testament Studies*
RB	Revue biblique
Rel	*Religion*
RSV	Revised Standard Version
RTP	*Revue de théologie et de philosophie*
SANT	Studien zum Alten und Neuen Testament
SBLSP	*Society of Biblical Literature Seminar Papers*
SBT	Studies in Biblical Theology
SJCA	*Studies in Judaism and Christianity in Antiquity*
SJT	*Scottish Journal of Theology*
SNTSMS	Society for New Testament Studies Monograph Series
Str–B	[Hermann L. Strack and] Paul Billerbeck, *Kommentar zum Neuen Testament aus Talmud und Midrasch* (7 vols.; Munich: Beck, 1922–61)
TDNT	Gerhard Kittel and Gerhard Friedrich (eds.), *Theological Dictionary of the New Testament* (trans. Geoffrey W. Bromiley; 10 vols.; Grand Rapids, MI: Eerdmans, 1964–)
TS	*Theological Studies*
USQR	*Union Seminary Quarterly Review*
VC	*Vigiliae christianae*
WBC	Word Biblical Commentary
ZAW	*Zeitschrift für die alttestamentliche Wissenschaft*
ZNW	*Zeitschrift für die neutestamentliche Wissenschaft*

LIST OF CONTRIBUTORS

Janice Capel Anderson, Department of Philosopy, University of Idaho, Moscow, Idaho, USA

Celia Deutsch, Barnard College, New York, New York, USA

Stephenson Humphries-Brooks, Religious Studies Department, Hamilton College, Clinton, New York, USA

Amy-Jill Levine, E. Rhodes and Leona B. Carpenter Professor of New Testament Studies, Vanderbilt University, Nashville, Tennessee, USA

Thomas R.W. Longstaff, Crawford Family Professor of Religious Studies, Colby College, Waterville, Maine, USA

Gail R. O'Day, A.H. Shatford Professor of New Testament and Preaching, Emory University, Atlanta, Georgia, USA

Carolyn Osiek, Professor of New Testament, Catholic Theological Union, Chicago, Illinois, USA

Marie-Eloise Rosenblatt, Lincoln Law School, San Jose, California, USA

Anthony J. Saldarini, Professor of Theology, Boston College, Chestnut Hill, Massachusetts, USA

Julian Sheffield, Union Theological Seminary, New York, New York, USA

Elaine M. Wainwright, Catholic Theological College, Banyo, Australia

INTRODUCTION

Amy-Jill Levine

Over a quarter-century ago, a few feminist readers—all possessing doctoral degrees, and all working within the dual contexts of academy and church—bravely set out along the road earlier traveled by Anna Julia Cooper, Matilda Joslyn Gage, Angelina and Sarah Grimké, Elizabeth Cady Stanton, Sojourner Truth, Frances Willard, and others. Their goal was to discover both women's contributions to the development of Christianity and a reading strategy that would name and interrogate canonical materials used against women in order to silence, disenfranchise, and constrain. These feminist pioneers did more than change the study of Christian origins, itself a remarkable feat. They began a process that continues to affect the academy, the church, and, increasingly, global societies.

Feminist analyses of early Christian literature and history, undertaken by those both inside and outside the church, have entered the secular classroom and thereby created new interests in the ancient materials. Given its interdisciplinary foci, feminist biblical and historical work has enhanced the study not only of Christian origins narrowly defined, but also of Classics, of Early Judaism, and of Mediterranean archaeology. Moreover, the various hermeneutical lenses that provide clarity to feminist analysis have enabled the approach to profit from as well as to contribute to advancements in literary and cultural studies.

Inside the church, feminist-critical work has inspired countless women to find their own place in the canon; it has reconfirmed the religious commitments of some, enabled others to name the sources of their disaffection, provoked yet others to seek changes to ecclesial practices and polities. Politically, the recovery of early Christian women's diverse literary representations and social roles—and the concomitant attention to constructions of gender and sexuality—has bolstered arguments for greater incorporation from the pulpit and in church educational programs of women's presence and voice.

Thus, feminist historiography, exegesis, and hermeneutics have been and continue to be a major force in the opening of both academy and church to include the presence and voices of those both in antiquity and today who because of gender expectations have been ignored, marginalized, or excluded. In turn, they have provided one of the models for, even as they have learned from, those who struggle to overcome silencing based on such factors as sexual orientation, race, ethnicity, and religious views.

Feminist approaches appear today in prestigious journals and award-winning books; they are topics for sessions and major addresses at Society of Biblical Literature and Catholic Biblical Association meetings; they have found their way into growing numbers of classrooms and curricula, both confessional and secular. It remains the case however that in some church and academic circles feminist readings are met with dismissal and disparagement, with labels ranging from 'bad scholarship' to 'heresy'; in other contexts, they are lumped together with studies reflecting the experiences and reading strategies of non-Western interpreters and then presented as alternatives to the way 'we normally do things'. Nevertheless they inexorably continue to challenge their detractors even as they to grow in sophistication and diversity.

As feminist readers recognize the effects of their work and meet the criticisms of their analyses brought by feminists and non-feminists alike, our interpretive processes mature and expand. Today there are countless readings that could be labeled feminist, even as there are countless ways that the term has been and can be defined. The feminist choir no longer sounds the single note of white, Western, middle-class, Christian concerns; 'feminist biblical studies' is now a symphony. It acknowledges the different concerns social location and experience bring to interpretation and recognizes the tentativeness and partiality of each conclusion: no instrument alone is complete; no two musicians play the music exactly alike. Feminist readers of Christian origins are so diverse in terms of approach (literary, historical, sociological, text-critical, ideological, cross-cultural...), focus (imagery, characterization, genre, plot, Christology, ethics, politics, polemic...), hermeneutics (of suspicion, of recovery...), identity (Womanist, Latina, African, Evangelical, lesbian, Jewish, Catholic...) and conclusions— namely, it is just like most biblical studies and indeed like most academic disciplines in the humanities and social sciences—that any single definition of what constitutes a 'feminist reading' is necessarily reified.

Finally, feminist biblical analysis now has its own history, its own repository of earlier work. Studies that were earlier limited to citations of those scholars who had never heard of or never engaged in feminist analysis now exhibit interaction with other feminist work. In part because of this flourishing of feminist studies, and in part because of their continual engagement with the methods of other disciplines, essays are becoming more detailed. Originally, this volume had been planned to include essays on the Gospels of both Matthew and Mark. Yet when the collected papers went to press, the page count far exceeded Sheffield Academic Press's—or my—expectations. Consequently, the 11 essays on Mark originally planned for this volume are presented under their own cover. Together, these studies, and the essays and volumes to follow, represent only a sampling of the blossoming field.

A major contribution to this field, and one that first brought feminist insights to the attention of many biblical scholars, occurred in 1983 when Mary Ann Tolbert edited an issue of *Semeia*, a journal devoted to 'experimental' biblical studies, entitled *The Bible and Feminist Hermeneutics*. Its lead article by Janice Capel Anderson, which is the opening article of this volume, epitomized the journal's mission. Capel Anderson's 'Matthew: Gender and Reading' introduced many students of the Bible to Fetterley's 'resisting reader' and Iser's 'implied reader', concepts which are today in some circles more familiar than the Griesbach hypothesis or Codex Bezae. More, it offered a feminist reading of Matthew so well grounded in critical theory and rigorous exegesis that no one could accuse the article, or the volume, of being even remotely irrelevant or precious (both strong possibilities in the early 1980s, when feminist biblical criticism still remained a frequent target of attack, especially by those who *presumed* to know what it was).

Capel Anderson begins by observing points of contact between feminist literary criticism and fledgling feminist biblical criticism. These include the highlighting of androcentric expressions and attitudes, attempts to recover positive female images, interest in women's experience, attention to the symbolic significance of gender, and a focus on the reader. This detailed opening leads to one of the earliest articulations of feminist biblical hermeneutics' distinctions from (secular) criticism, including in particular the negotiations women undertake in order to read androcentric Scripture as authoritative for their own experience.

To begin a response to this complex situation, Capel Anderson approaches the Gospel of Matthew first through its depiction of gender's symbolic significance and then through the lens of the 'implied reader'. She describes how the narrative's androcentrism permeates its assumptions, expressions, and depictions of power—an approach quite new in the early 1980s but one that has now found a new home in 'ideological criticism'—and how this pervasiveness constructs the reader. Her feminist interrogation embraces the Matthean genealogy's treatment of 'female difference', the role of women characters as both models of faith and signifiers of the powerless, and the means by which gender situates the women at Bethany, Golgotha, and the Tomb as foils to the male disciples without threatening their authoritative role.

Similarly attentive to androcentric language, Julian Sheffield recognizes how the Gospel of Matthew shapes the term 'father' to displace earthly fathers, against whom the text displays some animosity. As Sheffield demonstrates, this usage both relativizes patriarchal privilege within the discipleship community and justifies the replacement of the natal family with a new kinship group. Her detailed analysis then leads her to examine other familial expressions and characterizations, including the role of the women in the genealogy as well as throughout the gospel, as *mothers*. From her examination of parental language and roles, Sheffield is able to draw tentative conclusions about women's activity and authority in the Matthean community.

By conjoining traditional exegetical approaches, such as statistical models and redaction criticism, and newer rubrics such as the 'fictive kinship group' developed in social-scientific circles, Sheffield offers new insight into both the possible roles of women within Matthew's community and the functions of their representation in the gospel. The reading in turn has substantial implications for not only history and exegesis, but also theology, Christology, politics, and Jewish/Christian relations.

My own 'Discharging Responsibility' was prompted precisely by a concern for Jewish/Christian relations, specifically, the means by which scholars have constructed an often negative picture of Judaism within which to set Matthew's complementarily constructed positive treatment of women. The article argues against the claims, first, that women were marginalized in Matthew's Jewish environment because of purity codes and, second, that the conjoined story of the hemorrhaging woman and the dead girl demonstrates Jesus' dismantling of ritual barriers to the formation of an egalitarian community. By noting what the pericope does say (e.g. women suffer, they are healed, they are revivified) and what it doesn't say (e.g. anything about purity, ritual law, women's subordination)—and at what commentators have both ignored and imported—I seek to demonstrate a means by which readers interested in the representation of women, women's discipleship, and women as theological models can appropriate this story without resorting to incomplete and false comparisons, artificial dualisms, and supersessionist perspectives.

In this process, I found myself in dialogue not only with traditional commentaries but also with feminist work, including my own earlier writing, and I found myself having to recant what I had previously written. In this respect, I am in a position similar to Sharon Ringe, whose re-reading of Mark's Syro-Phoenician woman appears in the second volume of this Feminist Companion series. We learn as we heed more voices, find wider circles within which to dialogue, and, especially for this piece, come to trust our personal insights. I, like most biblicists who did graduate work in the late 1970s and early 1980s, found no problem with claims such as 'Jewish women were ostracized during their menstrual cycle' and 'Jewish purity codes served to oppress women'. Although I had never seen conclusive evidence for these claims, and although Matthew's Gospel never offered such a picture, I saw no reason to question what I had been taught. Even when I felt a nagging sense of discomfort about 'misogynistic Judaism', I dismissed it as biased personal apologetic. I thought I had been reading as a 'scholar' and a 'feminist', but each identity was skewed. My scholarship did not re-examine the primary sources of Hellenistic and early Rabbinic Judaism, and my feminism repressed my identity as a Jew. I am certainly biased in my argument and conclusions—as all exegesis has a subjective element—but to be biased does not necessarily make one wrong.

Celia Deutsch, well known for her work on Matthew's Wisdom Christology, offers in 'Jesus as Wisdom' a model for moving from literature to history, from metaphor to fact. Demonstrating how Matthew heightens the identification of Jesus with (Lady) Wisdom already present in the received tradition, Deutsch advocates caution in moving from representation to *realia*: female metaphors may not reflect women's religious experience in the Matthean church; they may, to the contrary, serve to erase real women and so to subordinate them.

Following a discussion of the function of metaphor, Deutsch explores the permutations of the metaphor 'Lady Wisdom' through Jewish (postexilic, Second Temple [including Philo], and Tanaanitic) texts; the comparison to Matthew's usage demonstrates how, in the gospel, the metaphor's female aspect all but vanishes. The evangelist transforms Lady Wisdom into Jesus-Wisdom and thereby makes a female image male; Jesus is Wisdom because he does what Wisdom does, and not because of any gendered implications. Further, since Wisdom speculation is produced most often in scribal settings, themselves usually male enclaves, Deutsch proposes that Jesus-Wisdom serves to legitimate the teaching authority of a select group of men. Feminist criticism is thus not limited to recovering images and figures long absent from scholarly and ecclesial view, nor is it always the bearer of good news. Sometimes it offers a caution: female metaphors and imagery may stand for more, or less, than we might hope.

Just as Mark's account of the Syro-Phoenician woman is a center of feminist interpretation, as several of the articles in the next volume of this series demonstrate, so too is Matthew's parallel story, the account of the Canaanite woman in 15.21-28. In her 'Surprised by Faith: Jesus and the Canaanite Woman', originally published in *Listening/Journal of Religion and Culture* (1989), Gale O'Day unites expertise in exegesis and homiletics to bring to the pericope a sensitivity to textual construction, to *what* it says as well as *how* it communicates.

O'Day's creative analysis leads to surprising theological as well as pastoral conclusions. Her attention to form reveals the woman to be the protagonist, the 'lifeblood of the story'; rhetorical analysis shows the Canaanite's encounter with Jesus to be a 'narrative enactment of a lament psalm'. The woman's actions and words thus do not indicate submission or hysteria, as is often argued; to the contrary, they reflect the robust faith of Israel's psalms. Moreover, just as Jewish tradition holds the Deity accountable to the covenant community—the covenant has two parties—so the Canaanite woman reminds Jesus of his mission of fullness. Her persistence and self-confidence thereby make her a model for all readers of the gospel as they hold faith in divine promise.

Elaine M. Wainwright is also drawn to Mt. 15.21-28, but her study addresses two subjects rarely if ever considered in interpretation of the story: the role of the daughter and the connotations of demon possession. Adopting for the woman the name Justa (her identification in the *Pseudo-Clementine Epistles*), Wainwright first seeks to facilitate a means by which this Cannanite mother can be remembered and made prominent in Christian tradition. She then explores the neglect of both Justa's daughter—as Wainwright notes, scholarship has given more attention to the metaphorical dogs than the ailing girl—and Jesus' role as exorcist, a topic rarely addressed because, perhaps, it causes contemporary scholars some embarrassment.

In Matthew's Gospel, Justa's daughter is the only female afflicted by possession and the only demon-possessed person about whom neither exorcism nor reaction to her healing is presented, but these anomalies have also been ignored rather than analyzed; it is not difficult to ignore an unnamed and undescribed character, even if her plight drives the story. To rectify this exegetical gap, Wainwright employs a cross-cultural, anthropological model of healing. In disclosing through her analysis the interrelationship among gender, ethnicity, and disease in Matthew's text, she accents the problems a singular focus produces. Her reclamation of the daughter demonstrates that for all the feminist attention to the marginalization of the Canaanite woman, her daring ripostes to Jesus, and her tenacity and her faith, her prominence comes at several costs to the reader. Further, the focus on Justa's plight ironically serves to push to the margins both her child and even Jesus, whose power as an exorcist who reintegrates individuals into society is erased.

Ethnicity, gender, and Justa are also of principal interest to Stephenson Humphries-Brooks, but his interpretive lens is much different than Wainwright's. While Wainwright compares Justa and her daughter to Matthew's Jewish women and Jews both male and female in need of healing, Humphries-Brooks investigates the three 'Canaanite Women in Matthew'. First is Rahab, the ancestor of Jesus according to the genealogy and the prostitute from Jericho according to the book of Joshua; next is the Canaanite mother of Mt. 15, who becomes the teacher to the Son of David and the only character in the gospel tradition to best Jesus in a theological argument. The third 'Canaanite' woman is, unlike the first two, unexpected in this category: Herodias, the wife of Herod Antipas and the cause of the Baptist's death. Humphries-Brooks argues that her characterization in Matthew's Gospel reflects the portrait in 1 Kings of Jezebel, the Canaanite queen of Israel.

Querying their literary histories as well as their individual portraits and comparative roles in the gospel narrative, Humphries-Brooks demonstrates how for all three Canaanite women, ethnicity, class, and gender play integral parts. While readers may celebrate the success of Rahab, who saves her family, joins the covenant community, and finds her way into Jesus' ancestry, and the success of the Canaanite mother, who obtains an exorcism for her daughter while providing an arresting example of faith and tenacity, we might also recognize that Herodias too is successful: the Baptist is executed, and, at least for the duration of Matthew's text, she and her husband retain their thrones. For Humphries-Brooks, Herodias's success is a stand against prophetic extremism; she represents the end of an earlier system of monotheistic absolutism that results in holy war and genocide. Although I substantially disagree with this particular conclusion (both in terms of how class functions and in terms of how monotheism is construed), I am persuaded by numerous other observations in this essay, including Humphries-Brooks's argument that a study of the Canaanite women together—not just because they are women, and not just because they are Canaanites, but because they are Canaanite women—reveals striking components of the gospel. As Jesus himself recognizes, we ignore Matthew's Canaanite women at our own peril: they may have something of major import to teach us.

To this point in the collection, all the essays are written by individuals known to have explicitly feminist concerns or interests in female characters. The following piece extends the authorial assemblage. One of the goals of this series of Feminist Companions is to encourage established scholars who have not entered into extensive, or even any, conversation with feminist readings to familiarize themselves with this literature and, if they can be convinced, tempted, or even (gently) coerced, to respond to it or incorporate it into their own work. Such is the case with Anthony J. Saldarini, who has worked extensively on Matthew's social setting and who has sponsored feminist dialogues at the Catholic Biblical Association, but who has not, until now, explicitly addressed feminist approaches to and conclusions about the first gospel.

Saldarini's 'Absent Women in Matthew's Households' begins, appropriately for a feminist-inspired analysis, with the work of Elaine Wainwright, and her criticism of his failure to listen 'for the voices of resistance' within the developing Matthean community. But criticism can and sometimes should work in both directions: acknowledging Wainwright's point, Saldarini also notes that to make her own case, she must 'read against the grain' of Matthew's narrative, for the gospel conceals the presence of women in the community. Chapters 18–20 then provide Saldarini a test-case for examining how Matthew conceals women, and why.

Although Mt. 18-20 attends to family-based household structures and enjoins the abandoning of the father's patriarchal privilege, the gospel only presumes the presence of women in the household. For Saldarini this absence of explicit reference is consistent with the evangelist's principal concern: the instruction of men with social power. Thus, any reconfiguration of Matthean households remains an act of male power; the men may adopt the low social status symbolized by children and slaves, even as the parables in ch. 18 offer only male models of humility and forgiveness, but there is no complementary attention paid to women's representation, needs, or experiences.

Returning to Wainwright at the article's end, Saldarini agrees with her call for imaginative, new ways of reading. He observes that while a feminist reading may assert women's participation in the process of community development and their benefits obtained from the new social roles men in the group adopted, the assertion is based not in what Matthew explicitly says, but in the creative constructions of the reader.

Although absent in the parables of chs. 18–20, women make a striking appearance in Mt. 25.1-13, the story of the 10 virgins. Marie-Eloise Rosenblatt's 'Got Into the Party After All: Women's Issues and the Five Foolish Virgins' (originally published in *Continuum* in 1993) begins with an equally striking confession: 'I never liked the story of the ten virgins as it occurs in Matthew's Gospel'. This reaction should not surprise; the parable could easily be construed as teaching that the Kingdom of Heaven is 'about women at war with each other over oil'. Certainly it is an odd parable: unique to Matthew, featuring women, presenting a groom but not a bride, manifesting a seemingly trivial concern for oil, apparently advocating lack of generosity, barring the door to those seeking entry.

Rosenblatt's continued wrestling with the parable eventually caused her to modify her earlier view as it led her to conclude that the parable contains two stories: one celebratory and one polemical. So, seeking scholarly support for this observation—the academy does have its requirements—she turned to the literature on parables, only to discovered an absence. The virgins have not caught scholars' attention, or have been deliberately ignored, with some consistency. And this absence in libraries is matched by the virgins' near-absence from the Roman Catholic lectionary. The few interpretations the parable has received are decidedly conventional (e.g. as depicting eschatological urgency, as exhorting characteristics of watchfulness and preparation, as conforming to first-century wedding practices). It is in painted, sculpted, and poetic retellings of the parable that Rosenblatt finds confirmation of her thesis; what traditional biblical scholarship is not trained to see is precisely what artists find fascinating. Some highlight the joy of those who enter with the groom; others depict the despair of the five left outside.

Behind the parable's condemnation of the foolish virgins and their exclusion from the wedding feast, Rosenblatt suggests, may lie a rift within the community. From the perspective of the gospel writer, certain women were foolish in their rejection of the (male) leaders' teaching and authority; perhaps the women these virgins represent would have told a much different story. This 'redemptive reading' does not ignore the parable's oppressive potential, but it nevertheless celebrates women's self-determination.

Along with asking established scholars not typically associated with feminist concerns to explore how feminist studies might impact their readings, this series also invites such scholars to revisit earlier articles in light of new feminist research. Responding to this invitation, Thomas R. W. Longstaff revises his 1981 article in *New Testament Studies* to ask, again, 'What are Those Women Doing at the Tomb of Jesus?'

Presupposing Matthean rather than Marcan priority Longstaff forgoes the more typical approaches to Matthew's final chapter, source and redaction criticism, to focus instead on internal evidence. While several scholars have found Matthew's depiction of the women at the tomb incredible or incomprehensible (why would they go just to 'look'?), Longstaff argues that the account must have been credible to the evangelist and the gospel's initial audience. Freed from the constraints of the two-document hypothesis and modern aesthetic projections onto the text, Longstaff profitably explores the Matthean scene through its connections to early Jewish burial practices. By combining his earlier archaeological and rabbinic studies with Kathleen Corley's newer work on women's mourning practices (some of which appears in her contribution to the second volume in this series), he develops a clearer picture of the central role women play in rituals associated with death and burial as well as demonstrates how, in Matthew's Gospel, the women are not doing anything incomprehensible. They are, rather, doing precisely what faithful disciples might be expected to do: watch the tomb.

Carolyn Osiek's 'The Women at the Tomb: What are They Doing There?' previously published in *Ex Auditu* (1993), shares with Longstaff's essay the same question, although her methodology and interests differ: Osiek analyzes the Matthean account along with Mk 16, Lk. 24, Jn 20, and the presentation of the scene in later apocryphal gospels, and her focus is the resurrection kerygma. Among her concerns are several which return the reader of this volume to its other essays even as they point forward to essays in the forthcoming collection on Mark's Gospel. These concerns include how the silence of the women in Mark (the forthcoming essay by Victoria Phillips) affects their credibility as witnesses; Matthew's emphasis on the women's goal of 'seeing' the tomb (Longstaff); the comparison of the scene to Greco-Roman apotheosis accounts (in the next volume the articles by Dennis R. MacDonald, Wendy Cotter, and Marianne Sawicki), the role gender plays in mourning and burial practices (Sawicki as well as Corley in the next volume), and the common scholarly insistence that the women are not believed because 'Jewish tradition' did not permit them any public role, an argument derived from one remark by Josephus (my essay in this volume; Joanna Dewey's in the next).

Osiek concludes both that behind the disparate gospel versions is an initial account of Mary Magdalene's visit to a tomb she found empty and that the stories derive from the experiences and memories of women. Kerygmatically, they reveal how the 'least significant members of the community' were first entrusted with the good news of the resurrection. The story remained in the tradition, despite its absence from Paul and Acts, because the memory of the women's role was too persistent, and this, Osiek claims, indicates that 'something' actually happened Easter morning at the tomb.

The term 'companion' comes from the Latin *com-panis*, 'with bread'. There may not be a more appropriate term for a collection of feminist interpretations of the New Testament and early Christian literature, where the symbolism of 'bread' abounds. The piquant essays in this volume and those to follow — on the other gospels and Acts, the Pauline literature and the catholic epistles, apocalyptic visions and apocryphal recreations, 'orthodox' reflections and 'heretical' views — provide opportunities to relish again the savor of favorite foods, recreate old recipes with healthier ingredients, introduce new flavors and chefs, and, most important, provide sustenance. Even the bitter taste sometimes conveyed may well prove salutary for various bodies, religious, academic, and otherwise. The invitation to the banquet is open to all, there is no casting into outer darkness, and the only 'garment' one needs to enter is an open mind.

MATTHEW: GENDER AND READING*

Janice Capel Anderson

Feminist Literary Criticism and Feminist Biblical Criticism

There are a number of interesting parallels between feminist literary criticism and feminist biblical criticism. The first steps in both fields included (1) the highlighting of androcentrism in canonical texts and the interpretations of those texts and (2) attempts to recover positive images of women and attitudes toward women in the texts along with revisions of previous androcentric exegesis.[1] In feminist literary criticism a third direction has also been pursued. Women writers have become a center of attention:

> Female experience displaced male bias as the center of analysis; female literary genealogies jostled male traditions. Literary studies emphasized the distinctive features of female texts and traced lines of influence connecting women in a fertile and partially autonomous tradition.[2]

This focus has included examination of the ways women writers have responded to androcentric literary tradition and conventions, translating 'sexual difference into literary differences of genre, structure, voice and plot', and revising 'prevailing themes and styles'.[3] As a result there has been a renewed interest in how sexual difference has

---

* Originally published in Mary Ann Tolbert (ed.), *The Bible and Feminist Hermeneutics, Semeia* 28 (1983), pp. 3-27. Reprinted by permission.
 1. For biblical criticism see C. Christ, 'Women's Studies in Religion', *CSRBull* 10 (1979), pp. 3-5 (3). Christ offers representative examples. See also P. Trible, 'Feminist Hermeneutics and Biblical Studies', *Christian Century* (February 1982), pp. 116-18 and K. Doob Sakenfeld, 'Response to Ruether's "Christology and Feminism: Can a Male Savior Help Women?"' (paper circulated to SBL/AAR Liberation Theology Working Group, April, 1981), pp. 3-7. For literary criticism see E. Abel, 'Editor's Introduction', *Critical Inquiry* 8 (1981), pp. 179-84. For parallel developments in history, see J. Kelly-Gadol, 'The Social Relations of the Sexes: Methodological Implications of Women's History', *Signs* 1 (1976), pp. 809-24.
 2. Abel, 'Editor's Introduction', pp. 173-74.
 3. Abel, 'Editor's Introduction', p. 174.

influenced male texts: 'Women emerge in these analyses no longer as the passive victims of male authorial desire but rather as powerful figures that elicit texts crafted to appropriate or mute their difference'.[4] In literary history it has become important to ask: '...1) How do contemporary women's lives, women's concerns, or concerns about women constitute part of the historical context of this work? and 2) What is the symbolic significance of gender in this text?'[5] Interpreters must take seriously not only language, class, ethnic, and other analytic categories, but also gender.

Corresponding to the focus on the author and text in various types of feminist literary criticism there has been a focus on the reader. Judith Fetterley in *The Resisting Reader*, for example, concentrated on the way in which women readers are often forced to read as males in American literature.[6] Annette Kolodny in a stimulating article, 'A Map for Rereading: Or, Gender and the Interpretation of Literary Texts' argued for '...the crucial importance of the *sex* of the "interpreter" in that process which Nelly Furman has called "the active attribution of significance to formal signifiers."'[7] She used two short stories, Charlotte Perkins Gilman's 'The Yellow Wallpaper' and Susan Keating Glaspell's 'A Jury of Her Peers', as paradigms. In Glaspell's story men and women look for clues to the motive for a woman's murder of her husband. Only the women are able to see the clues because the men are unable to 'read' the importance and significance of the women's arena of activity and meaning. Men and women can learn to read and understand each other's texts, she argues. However, they must be aware of 'the fundamental problem of "reading correctly within cohabiting but differently structured worlds."'[8] Such an awareness requires a 'revisionist rereading' of the literary canon and the expansion of that canon to include the work of women writers. This, in turn, offers 'us all a potential enhancing of our capacity to read the world, our literary texts, and even one another, anew'.[9]

---

4. Abel, 'Editor's Introduction', p. 174.
5. A. Kolodny, 'Turning the Lens on "The Panther Captivity": A Feminist Exercise in Practical Criticism', *Critical Inquiry* 8 (1981), pp. 329-45 (345).
6. *The Resisting Reader: A Feminist Approach to American Fiction* (Bloomington, IN: Indiana University Press, 1978).
7. Nelly Furman, 'The Study of Women and Language: Comment on Vol. 3, No. 3', *Signs* 4 (1978), p. 184, quoted in Annette Kolodny, 'A Map for Rereading: Or, Gender and the Interpretation of Literary Texts', *New Literary History* 11 (1980), pp. 451-67 (460).
8. Kolodny, 'A Map for Rereading', p. 464.
9. Kolodny, 'A Map for Rereading', p. 465.

In religious studies there has been a parallel concern for women's experience and women's texts.[10] However, in biblical studies scholars have had to try to recover repressed women's traditions within and without the canon. There are few Jewish or Christian texts known to have been produced by women prior to the modern period. As theologians have sought to develop a feminist hermeneutic, complex questions concerning the nature and authority of Scripture and canon have been raised.[11] Are only non-androcentric Scriptural traditions authoritative? What is the status of marginalized or 'heretical' texts which preserve women's traditions and experiences absent or muted in canonical texts? What attitude should be taken toward androcentric traditions of interpretation? These questions have their counterparts in literary studies,[12] but take on unique dimensions in the context of Jewish or Christian theology and praxis. Two directions that have not been explored fully are (1) how patriarchal biblical texts embody responses to female difference, and (2) how the sex of woman reader/ interpreters influences their readings of male texts. These directions, suggested by feminist literary criticism, bear investigation. Not only would exegeses which ask these questions be interesting in their own right, they would also contribute to the discussion of difficult issues raised in feminist hermeneutics. For example, how has it been or could it be possible for women *positively* to appropriate androcentric texts as authoritative texts for their religious experience?

This article attempts to move in the two directions mentioned above. First, it begins to explore the symbolic significance of gender in the Gospel of Matthew. Second, it looks at the role of the implied reader[13] in relationship to a feminist's reading of the gospel. These analyses are experimental and limited in a number of ways. Literary methods

---

10. Christ, 'Women's Studies in Religion', p. 3.

11. For two articles which raise these issues sharply see E. Schüssler Fiorenza, 'Toward a Feminist Biblical Hermeneutics: Biblical Interpretation and Liberation Theology', in B. Mahan and L.D. Richesin (eds.), *The Challenge of Liberation Theology: A First World Response* (Maryknoll, NY: Orbis Books, 1981), pp. 91-112; and R. Radford Ruether, 'Feminist Theology: Methodology, Sources, and Norms', in *eadem, Sexism and God-Talk: Toward a Feminist Theology* (Boston: Beacon Press, 1983), pp. 1-46.

12. For example: Should blatant chauvinists such as Norman Mailer continue to be part of the literary canon? Do the early female Gothic novelists belong alongside the male authors now accepted as significant for their period? Is anything to be gained by adapting admittedly male-biased methods such as Freudianism or New Criticism?

13. For a definition of the implied reader see n. 19 below.

alone, primarily rhetorical criticism, are used.[14] The gospel as a narrative whole is the context for interpretation. Neither source nor redaction criticism is employed. Only the most basic competence in the text's linguistic, historical, and social codes is assumed. The full historical dimensions of the questions posed are not explored. This is due partly to the limitations of space and expertise and partly to the fact that we have a limited knowledge of the social world(s) of early Christianity.[15] The examination of the interplay between the representation of gender in New Testament texts and the actual roles of men and women in various early Christian communities awaits further study. Similarly, the response of actual first-century women reading or listening to the Gospel of Matthew remains an area of conjecture. Furthermore each reader, male or female of whatever historical matrix, will have a unique response to the gospel. This article only focuses on the role of the implied reader and possible feminist responses to that role. Finally, although it is an exercise in feminist biblical criticism there is no attempt to articulate a nuanced feminist position. The article operates within a broad definition of feminism as beliefs and actions which support the possibility of authentic existence for both females and males and oppose the oppression of either sex by the other.

Gender in Matthew

The first question to be approached is the symbolic significance of gender in the text. This, as noted above, is an important approach in feminist literary criticism. As Annette Kolodny has written, this approach is crucial:

> because it acknowledges the often subtle distinction between the depiction of male or female characters for their recognizable gender behaviors and the manipulation of gender for symbolic purposes that may have only incidental relation to actual contemporary sex roles. Pursuing this second concern thus sometimes reveals little about the authentic

---

14. For a definition of rhetorical criticism see M.H. Abrams, *A Glossary of Literary Terms* (New York: Holt, Rinehart & Winston, 4th edn, 1981), pp. 160-61. The term is used as in literary studies. It should be distinguished from Old Testament Rhetorical Criticism inspired by James Muilenburg ('Form Criticism and Beyond', *JBL* 88 [1969], pp. 1-18) although their interests are related.

15. We simply cannot yet discuss with depth 'the significance of the presence of women (as readers, writers, and as societal participants)' when dealing with the historical contexts of New Testament texts as Kolodny does when she turns her lens on 'The Panther Captivity', p. 339.

reality of men and women but much about the symbolic terms through which a given cultural group struggles to define the meaning of its most perplexing dilemmas.[16]

Although gender roles are not a major theme in the Gospel of Matthew, its norms and values incorporate attitudes toward gender. The narrator, Jesus, and other characters speak about men and women. Women and men also appear as characters.[17] In this section the overall androcentric perspective of the gospel will be briefly established. Then several passages which deal with women will serve as examples of ways in which the gospel treats gender. These passages include the genealogy (1.1-17); two scenes concerning the faith and initiative of marginal women characters (the woman with the hemorrhage, 9.20-22; and the Canaanite woman, 15.21-28) and passion and resurrection scenes involving women characters (the woman at Bethany, 26.6-13; the women at the cross, 27.55-56; and the two Marys, 27.61; 28.1-10).

The Androcentric Perspective of the Gospel
There is no doubt that the author of the Gospel of Matthew wrote from an androcentric perspective. Whether the author was male or female, the story world embodies patriarchal assumptions. There are many examples which illustrate the pervasive androcentrism. The opening genealogy is patrilineal and the birth story centers on Joseph. Positions of power and status including those of the Jewish leaders and the disciples are male. God is repeatedly pictured as Father.[18] Patriarchal marriage and inheritance practices are assumed (1.18-25; 5.31-32; 19.1-12; 21.33-43; 22.23-33, etc.). The narrator speaks in a brief but telling phrase of 'four thousand (five thousand) men besides women and children' (14.21; 15.38) in the feeding stories. Even Jesus' teaching often assumes a male audience. In the Sermon on the Mount Jesus warns 'everyone who looks on a woman with desire' and 'everyone divorcing his wife apart from a matter of unchastity' (5.28, 32).

The Genealogy
The narrator begins the Gospel of Matthew with a superscription and genealogy (1.1-17). This passage is a form of direct commentary to the

16. Kolodny, 'The Panther Captivity', p. 339.
17. For a list of references to women in the Gospel see the Appendix.
18. Although God is imaged as a woman in 13.33 and 23.37. The fatherhood of God may also be seen as a challenge to a patriarchal worldview. Elisabeth Schüssler Fiorenza ('Luke 2:41-52', *Int* 36 [1982], pp. 399-403 [403]) argues that the father symbol for God in the gospels 'relativizes all claims of earthly fatherhood and rejects all power of a patriarchally institutionalized society'.

narratee. Since the implied author and narrator and the implied reader and narratee are virtually identical in Matthew,[19] direct commentary guides the reading process. It may explain or call attention to the significance of a narrative element, provide criteria for evaluation, etc. Actual readers are free to accept or reject this guidance but must respond to it as they read. The superscription and genealogy set the stage for reading the rest of the gospel.[20] They establish the implied reader's initial understanding of Jesus' identity. The heading characterizes Jesus as the Christ, the Son of Abraham, and the Son of David. The genealogy begins to supply clues to the content of these titles. The expectations or associations evoked in actual readers will be confirmed or denied, expanded or narrowed as they read.

In terms of gender, the genealogy substantiates Jesus' patrilineal claim to the titles. It also locates him in the sweep of salvation history from Abraham to David, from David to the exile and from the exile to the Christ. This salvation history is viewed essentially as a male enterprise. The stereotyped pattern of the genealogy—male δὲ ἐγέννησεν τὸν ('begat') male(s)—repeats itself 39 times. The most striking break in this patriarchal pattern[21] is the inclusion of five female names in the line of descent, four of whom are named in another repeated pattern:

---

19. The term 'implied author' was coined by W. Booth in *The Rhetoric of Fiction* (Chicago: University of Chicago Press, 1961), pp. 70-76, 151. It refers to the 'creating person who is implied by the totality of a given work when it is offered to the world' (Booth, *Critical Understanding* [Chicago: University of Chicago Press, 1979], p. 269). This voice or persona is the authorial presence the reader experiences in the text. See also Abrams, *Glossary*, p. 126. The term 'implied reader' was coined by W. Iser who discusses it in *The Implied Reader* (Baltimore: The Johns Hopkins University Press, 1974) and *The Act of Reading* (Baltimore: The Johns Hopkins University Press, 1978). The implied reader is distinguished from the flesh-and-blood reader past and present because it includes the textual structure which must be realized as well as the structured act of realization. It is the role the real reader must play. It is *not*, however, an exact counterpart to Booth's implied author because the implied reader is not entirely within the text. The aspect of the implied reader contained within the text can be referred to as the inscribed reader. This is the counterpart of Booth's implied author.

20. This is true whether the superscription is understood as the heading of the entire gospel, the infancy narrative, or merely the genealogy.

21. There are a few other breaks. The labels 'David the King' in 1.6 and 'Jesus the one called Christ' in 1.16 and the references to the Babylonian exile in 1.11, 12 highlight the periods of time confirmed as divisions in 1.17. According to R.E. Brown (*The Birth of the Messiah: A Commentary on the Infancy Narratives in Matthew and Luke* [Garden City, NY: Doubleday, 1977], p. 71) the addition 'and his brothers' in 1.2 and 1.11 may accent points at which God exercised selectivity in carrying forward the messianic line.

ἐκ τῆς Θαμάρ   (by Tamar) (1.3)
ἐκ τῆς Ῥαχάβ   (by Rahab) (1.5a)
ἐκ τῆς Ῥούθ   (by Ruth) (1.5b)
ἐκ τῆς τοῦ Οὐρίου   (by the one of Uriah [i.e. Bathsheba]) (1.6)
Μαρίας ἐξ ἧς ἐγεννήθη
Ἰησοῦς   (Mary, of whom was born [begotten] Jesus) (1.16)

Why has the narrator included these women? What is the symbolic significance of these obvious breaks in an otherwise male genealogy? Raymond E. Brown summarized the three most common interpretations offered by actual readers over the years in *The Birth of the Messiah*. These are:

> (1) '...the four Old Testament women were regarded as sinners and their inclusion for Matthew's readers foreshadowed the role of Jesus as the savior of sinful men'.
> (2) '...the women were regarded as foreigners and were included by Matthew to show that Jesus, the Jewish Messiah, was related by ancestry to the Gentiles'. (This would not apply to Mary.)
> (3) The women share two things in common: '(a) there is something extraordinary or irregular in their union with their partners—a union which, though it may have been scandalous to outsiders, continued the blessed lineage of the Messiah; (b) the women showed initiative or played an important role in God's plan and so came to be considered the instrument of God's providence or of His Holy Spirit'.[22]

The variety of interpretations indicates the important part the reader plays in creating textual meaning. The first interpretation reads the first four women in terms of the Eve/Mary polarity. Women, sexuality, and sin are linked. The second ignores the fact that the four persons viewed as Gentiles are women and paradoxically thereby— perhaps—characterizes women as foreign. This interpretation, however, is supported by the identification of Bathsheba as the wife of the Gentile Uriah. It also takes into consideration the role of outsiders— the poor, blind, Gentiles, women, etc.—in the gospel. Justification of the mission to the Gentiles is a major theme. The key to the third interpretation is that it asks what Mary and the other four women have in common. This eliminates the first and second interpretations. Mary is neither a sinner nor a Gentile. The third interpretation also points to the unusual circumstance that Jesus has no male progenitor. The irregularities in the ways the first four women produced the male heirs prepare for the irregularity of Jesus' birth. The initiative of the

---

22. Brown, *Birth of the Messiah*, pp. 71-73.

women and the role of the Spirit have the same function. The difference between Mary and the others is also taken into account. The shift of the verbal pattern from '(male) begot child "out of" (woman's name)' to 'Mary, *of whom* was born Jesus' indicates this difference. There is no father. The genealogy raises the question about Jesus' birth and identity. Why does Jesus have no father? How can Jesus be the heir of Abraham and David with no father from whom he can trace his descent? The birth story begins to offer a more complete explanation. Jesus was conceived ἐκ πνεύματος ἁγίου ('of the Holy Spirit', 1.18, 20) and becomes Joseph's legal heir when Joseph names him. Jesus is thus both 'Son of God' and a Davidid.

In what way does the text deal with female difference? If the third reading is adopted, the patrilineal genealogy and the birth story's concentration on Joseph can be seen in part as attempts to come to terms with female difference. Birth belongs to the female sphere. Not only does Mary give birth to Jesus, she produces him without male assistance. The Holy Spirit employs no male partner. The gospel speaks of Mary as Jesus' mother, but never of Joseph as his father. Although in later passages the gospel views God as Jesus' ultimate Father (Jesus is the Son of God), this does not ameliorate the difficulty of a woman conceiving without a male. The text does not portray God or the Spirit as a male progenitor.[23] The genealogy and Joseph's role in the birth story incorporate Jesus back into the male sphere, the ordinary scheme of things. They place him within an androcentric perspective. From that perspective a genealogy traced through Mary would be of questionable validity. Yet the problem of the 'otherness' and divine mystery of Jesus' birth remains. The inclusion of the women in the genealogy foreshadows and explains Mary's role. It provides a means of pointing

---

23. See H.C. Waetjen, 'The Genealogy as the Key to the Gospel According to Matthew', *JBL* 95 (1976), pp. 220-30 (223-24). He argues that in Matthew the Spirit 'generates Jesus by a direct act of creation', p. 224. Waetjen notes that the aorist passive particle γεννηθέν used as a substantive in 1.20 contrasts with the 39 repetitions of ἐγέννησεν in the genealogy. The phrase ἐκ πνεύματος ἁγίου does not imply a male impregnator. Investigation of the LXX reveals that ἐκ only indicates a male agency with ἐν γαστρὶ λαμβάνεσθαι/συλλαμβάνεσθαι never with ἐν γαστρὶ ἔχειν as in Mt. 1.18b, 23. Γεννᾶν plus ἐκ πνεύματος ἁγίου is found only in Johannine tradition where it represents divine generation as opposed to human sexual generation. See also Brown, *Birth of the Messiah*, pp. 124-25, 137. He writes: 'There is never a suggestion in Matthew or in Luke that the Holy Spirit is the male element in a union with Mary, supplying the husband's role in begetting. Not only is the Holy Spirit not male (feminine in Hebrew; neuter in Greek), but also the manner of begetting is implicitly creative rather than sexual', p. 124.

to and at the same time coming to terms with the female production of the Messiah. God has acted in a radically new way—outside of the patriarchal norm. Although Jesus is Son of David through Joseph, he is Son of God through Mary.[24]

The Faith and Initiative of the Marginal
There are five major character groups in the Gospel of Matthew: the Jewish leaders, the disciples (οἱ μαθηταί), the crowds (οἱ ὄχλοι), the supplicants, and the Gentiles.[25] Each group is primarily characterized in terms of its relationship to Jesus, the protagonist. Their interactions with Jesus are compared and contrasted. They serve as foils for one another. To the extent that characters change in the course of the narrative they do so primarily in terms of their acceptance and/or understanding of Jesus and his mission. After the exposition, the plot moves forward as Jesus interacts with the various groups and the individuals who make them up. The most obvious conflict is, of course, with the Jewish leaders. Other tensions are apparent as well. Will the disciples come to full understanding and mature faith and thus fulfil their calling? Will the crowds side with Jesus or the Jewish leaders? Will Jesus' mission be extended to Jewish outcasts and Gentiles? The implied author guides the implied reader's response to each group by arranging the episodes to highlight the comparisons and contrasts between them. He or she also guides the implied reader's response by means of Jesus' reactions to each group. As the most central and

24. See Brown's comments on the 'who' and 'how' of Jesus' identity as Son of David and Son of God, *Birth of the Messiah*, pp. 133-43.
25. Although various sub-groups of the Jewish leaders are named, there are no sharp distinctions made and all function together as Jesus' opponents. See S. Van Tilborg, *The Jewish Leaders in Matthew* (Leiden: E.J. Brill, 1972), pp. 1-7. For recent articles on the disciples in Matthew see M. Sheridan, 'Disciples and Discipleship in Matthew and Luke', *BTB* 3 (1973), pp. 235-55; U. Luz, 'Die Jünger im Matthäusevangelium', *ZNW* 62 (1971), pp. 141-71. See also P.S. Minear, 'The Disciples and the Crowds in the Gospel of Matthew', *ATRSup* 3 (1974), pp. 28-44. Minear, however, treats the supplicants and Gentiles as members of the crowds. The view of this article is that Jesus and the Jewish leaders vie for the loyalty of the crowds until the crucial shift to ὁ λαός ' in 27.25. J.D. Kingsbury ('The Title "Son of David" in Matthew's Gospel', *JBL* 95 [1976], pp. 591-602 [599-600]) differentiates as I do between the crowds and the 'no-accounts'. Although the supplicants appear as individuals the similarity between them, especially in relationship to Jesus, justifies treating them as a group. The same is true of the Gentiles, although not to the same extent. There is some overlap between the supplicant group and the Gentiles. The Gentiles also can be considered a group because of the important role they play in the development of the theme of the justification of mission to the Gentiles.

consistently reliable character, his judgments are virtually equivalent to those of the implied author.[26]

The woman with the hemorrhage (9.20-22) and especially the Canaanite woman (15.21-28) play important roles in the narrative. Both are supplicants and members of marginal groups. The woman with the hemorrhage is ritually unclean.[27] The Canaanite woman is a Gentile. Both, of course, are also women. They appear alone with no indication of an embedded status in a patriarchal family. They way they are introduced emphasizes their double marginality:

> Καὶ ἰδοὺ γυνὴ αἱμορροῦσα δώδεκα ἔτη ὁρίων
> And behold a woman suffering a hemorrhage twelve years (9.20).
>
> Καὶ ἰδοὺ γυνὴ Χαναναία ἀπὸ τῶν ὁρίων ἔτη
> And behold a Canaanite woman from the area (15.22).

Both exhibit initiative and faith in their approach to Jesus. Jesus highlights their faith:

> Be of good cheer, daughter: Your faith has healed (σέσωκέν) you. (9.22a)
> O woman, great is your faith. (15.28b)

In both cases the healing takes place 'from that hour' (9.22b; 15.28c). Jesus' treatment of both explodes the boundaries of acceptable association. This is also true of other healing episodes with which these two scenes have links. Jesus responds positively to the blind, the lepers, women, etc. Jesus' healing of these outcasts characterizes him as the messianic salvation bringer.[28] The Jewish leaders, crowds, and disciples are characterized in contrast to these figures. Reactions to Jesus' healings are part of the developing plot.

The woman with the hemorrhage. The woman with the hemorrhage episode occurs early in the gospel. It forms part of the so-called Matthean 'Miracle Chapters', 8–9.[29] Scholars often subdivide chs. 8–9 themati-

---

26. For a discussion of the use of 'reliable' characters see Booth, *A Rhetoric of Fiction*, p. 18.

27. Lev. 15 deals with the status of male and female genital discharges. Lev. 15.25-39 seems to apply here.

28. According to Kingsbury ('Son of David', esp. pp. 598-99) this is underlined by the use of Son of David in connection with healing. D. Duling ('The Therapeutic Son of David: An Element in Matthew's Christological Apologetic', *NTS* 24 [1978], pp. 392-410) argues that in general Matthew's 'Messiah of Deed is primarily a therapeutic Messiah', p. 399), and that Son of David is used in conjunction with healing. See also Mt. 4.23-24; 8.16-17; 9.35; 11.4-6; 15.30-31.

29. For discussion of the miracle chapters see H.J. Held, 'Matthew as Interpreter of the Miracle Stories', in G. Bornkamm, G. Barth and H.J. Held (eds.),

cally.³⁰ The healings of 9.18-31—the ruler's daughter (9.18-19, 23-26), the woman with the hemorrhage (9.20-22), and the two blind men (9.27-31)—focus on the faith of the supplicant. These scenes form the immediate context for the hemorrhaging woman episode. It is intercalated into the healing of the ruler's daughter. This intercalation creates a suspenseful interlude between the ruler's request and the healing of his daughter. It also encourages the implied reader to read each story in the light of the other. The socially acceptable ruler³¹ publicly approaches, does obeisance to Jesus, and makes his request. The ritually unclean woman approaches Jesus from behind, hoping only to touch the fringe of his garment. The intercalation indicates that although not equal in status, they are equal in faith. If anything the intercalation emphasizes the faith of the doubly marginal woman. Her faith, which Jesus commends, also contrasts with the ridicule of the flute-players and the terrified crowd. She is healed (saved, σέσωκέν, ἐσώθη, 9.22) while they are cast out (ἐξεβλήθη, 9.25).³²

The healing of two blind men (9.27-31) immediately follows the combined ruler's daughter–hemorrhaging woman episodes. This juxtaposition underscores similarities between these scenes. The blind men are outcasts like the woman. They 'approach' Jesus as did the ruler and woman. Faith also plays a role in their cure. They are healed by physical contact. The report of their healing goes out as did that of the ruler's daughter 'in all that land' (9.26, 31). Yet the blind men differ from the ruler and the woman in at least two ways. First, they address Jesus as Son of David and Lord, recognizing him as the messianic healer.³³ Second, they receive and disobey a command to tell no one

---

Tradition and Interpretation in Matthew (Philadelphia: Westminster Press, 1963), pp. 165-299 [246-53]; W.G. Thompson, 'Reflections on the Composition of Matthew 8:1–9:34', *CBQ* 33 (1971), pp. 365-88; and J.D. Kingsbury, 'The "Miracle Chapters" of Matthew 8–9', *CBQ* 40 (1978), pp. 559-73.

30. Held, 'Matthew as Interpreter of Miracle Stories' (pp. 248-49) offers the following division: 8.2-17, Christology; 8.18–9.17, discipleship; 9.18-31, faith; and 9.32-34, conclusion to the whole composition. C. Burger offers a modification of Held discussed by Kingsbury ('Miracle Chapters', p. 562): 8.1-17, Christology; 8.18-34, discipleship; 9.1-17, separation of Jesus and his followers from Israel; and faith, 9.18-34.

31. The word ἄρχων (9.18) could designate either a Jew or Gentile, but most commentators argue that the presence of flute players (9.33) indicates a Jewish household.

32. Thompson, 'Reflections', pp. 381-82.

33. The significance of the use of Lord is a matter of dispute. G. Bornkamm ('End-Expectation and Church in Matthew', in Bornkamm, Barth and Held [eds.], *Tradition and Interpretation in Matthew*, pp. 41-43) associates the use of κύριε with a

of their cure. Despite their confession, the blind men's faith contrasts negatively with that of the woman. Jesus says to her, 'Your faith has healed [saved, σέσωκέν] you' (9.22). To the blind men he says somewhat ambiguously, 'According to your faith let it be to you' (9.29b). Their eyes are opened, but are they fully healed?

The stories which precede and follow 9.18-31 also cause the implied reader to compare and contrast the hemorrhaging woman and her fellow supplicants to the Jewish leaders, crowds, and disciples. Opposition between Jesus and the Jewish leaders figures strongly in the three previous scenes. The faith of the supplicants contrasts with the reactions of the Jewish leaders and the crowds in 9.1-8. The Jewish leaders think Jesus blasphemes by forgiving sins (9.3), while the crowds fear and glorify 'God who gives such authority to men' (9.8). In the next two episodes the leaders and even the disciples of John the Baptist challenge Jesus' and his disciples' violation of accepted norms. They associate with tax collectors and sinners (9.9-13) and do not fast (9.14-17). This prepares for Jesus' healings of the ritually impure in 9.18-31: a dead girl, a hemorrhaging woman, and two blind men. In fact, the ruler approaches Jesus while he is still speaking of putting new wine into new wine skins (9.18). Instead of challenging Jesus, the supplicants put their faith in Jesus. The final episode in the miracle chapters which immediately follows the healing of the two blind men summarizes the developing reactions of the Jewish leaders and the crowds. Jesus' healing of a dumb demoniac evokes two responses. The crowds marvel, 'Never was anything like this seen in Israel' (9.33b). The Pharisees condemn Jesus, 'By the ruler of demons, he casts out the demons' (9.34). In comparison to the woman with the hemorrhage and the other supplicants in 9.18-31, the Jewish leaders have no faith. They are Jesus' enemies. The crowds are amazed and perhaps can be led to faith. Indeed, following the transitional summary passage of 9.35, Jesus' compassion on the crowds leads to the missionary discourse of ch. 10. What of the disciples? In ch. 10 Jesus gives them the authority to undertake a preaching and healing mission to Israel, replicating many of his own activities. However, in at least one episode in

---

recognition of divine majesty and discipleship. J.M. Gibbs ('Purpose and Pattern in Matthew's Use of the Title "Son of David"', *NTS* 10 [1963–64], pp. 416-64 [450]) views the use of Lord by the blind men here and those in 20.29-34 as well as that of the Canaanite woman in this light. J.D. Kingsbury (*Matthew: Structure, Christology, Kingdom* [Philadelphia: Fortress Press, 1975], pp. 109-10) sees the use of κύριε as subordinate to the title Son of David in the blind men and Canaanite woman stories. The outcasts attribute to Jesus as Son of David a high status and the power to heal.

chs. 8 and 9 their faith is negatively contrasted to that of faithful supplicants like the hemorrhaging woman. In the stilling of the storm (8.23-27) instead of confidently trusting Jesus, they exhibit 'little faith'.

The woman with the hemorrhage rendered doubly marginal by her gender and gender-related affliction serves as an outstanding example of faith and initiative. Along with the characterization of Jesus as healer of the most marginal members of society, her faith is the focus of 9.20-22. This faith is contrasted with that of the Jewish leaders, crowds, and disciples in chs. 8 and 9.

The Canaanite woman. The Canaanite woman episode accomplishes many of the same objectives as that of the woman with the hemorrhage. She approaches Jesus as an unembedded female. However, she is a Gentile. Jesus' initial response to her verbally echoes his restriction of the disciples' mission in 10.6: 'I was sent only to the lost sheep of the house of Israel' (15.24). Her faith and persistence lead him to expand his mission and heal her daughter. Her confession of Jesus as Lord and Son of David casts the rejection of Jesus by the Jewish leaders and crowds in a dark light. Together with direct narratorial comments (4.14-16; 12.18-21) and the Magi (2.1-12) and Roman centurion (8.5-13) episodes, this episode makes a powerful argument justifying the mission to the Gentiles. This is an important theme in the gospel, coming to a climax in the Great Commission. Thus the Canaanite woman scene is more significant for the gospel as a whole than that of the hemorrhaging woman.

The significance of this pericope is reinforced structurally. It is the fulcrum of a chiastic pattern of nearly identical Matthean doublets:

> A Two Blind Men (9.27-31)
>   B Sign of Jonah (12.38-42)
>   C Feeding of 5,000 (14.13-21)
>   D Canaanite Woman (15.22-28)
>   C' Feeding of 4,000 (15.32-38)
>   B' Sign of Jonah (16.1-4)
> A' Two Blind Men (20.29-34) [34]

The Canaanite woman is included in this pattern because it forms a triad with the blind men doublets. It follows the same pattern as the

---

34. For a more complete discussion of this chiastic pattern see Janice Capel Anderson, 'Over and Over and Over Again: Studies in Matthean Repetition' (PhD dissertation, University of Chicago, 1983). The expanded doublets 8.23-27 = 14.22-23 and 9.32-34 = 12.22-37 are not included in this pattern since they are not as completely identical. The second member is expanded.

other two members: cry for help, (attempt to silence), renewed request
—questioning by Jesus, healing on the basis of faith. The supplicants
also offer word for word the same request for help:

> cried out saying: 'Have mercy on me Lord, Son of David' (15.22)
> cried out saying: 'Lord, have mercy on us, Son of David' (20.30)
> crying out and saying: 'Have mercy on us, Son of David' (9.27)
> 'Yes, Lord' (9.28).

The chiastic pattern draws sharp comparisons between character groups. The repetition with slight variation of similar episodes also causes the implied reader to read each member of a doublet in light of the other. The faith of the outcast supplicants—the blind men and the Gentile woman—contrasts with the sign seeking of the Jewish leaders who would reject them and with the wavering faith and understanding of the disciples in the feeding stories. The second sign of Jonah episode emphasizes the contrast with the Jewish leaders. There the Jewish leaders try to 'tempt' Jesus. If their first request is genuine, their second is not. The second episode also serves as a transition to Jesus' condemnation of the leaven of the Pharisees and Sadducees in 16.5-12. It recalls Jesus' condemnation of their teaching on defilement (15.1-20) which immediately precedes the Canaanite woman scene. The second feeding episode underlines the disciples' failure in understanding. Why do the disciples wonder where the loaves to feed the crowd will come from when they have so recently participated in the first feeding? The motif of bread introduced by the first feeding ties together a number of episodes. Since the feeding of the four thousand immediately follows the Canaanite woman episode, the contrast between the disciples and the woman who is willing to receive '*bread crumbs*' is strong. It is also highlighted by the disciples' subsequent difficulty in understanding Jesus' teaching about the *leaven* of the Pharisees and Sadducees (16.5-12). They do not understand until Jesus reminds them of the *loaves* involved in the two feedings.

The faith of the Canaanite woman also contrasts with the faith of her fellow outcasts in the blind men episodes. As noted above, the first pair of blind Jewish men are healed according to their faith (9.29) but immediately disobey Jesus. She calls Jesus Lord three times and worships (προσκυνεῖν) him.[35] Jesus declares her faith to be great. He heals

---

35. προσκυνεῖν appears in Mt. 2.2, 8, 11; 8.2; 9.18; 14.33; 15.25; 18.26; 20.20; 28.9, 17. BAG lists Mt. 2.2, 8, 11; 8.2; 9.18; 14.33; 15.25; Jn 9.38; Mt. 20.20 as examples of its use where Jesus is 'revered and worshipped as Messianic King and Divine Helper'. It lists Mt. 28.9, 17 as examples of worship of the risen Lord. W.G. Thompson (*Matthew's Advice to a Divided Community* [AnBib, 44; Rome: Biblical

her daughter 'from that hour'. In comparison to the second pair, who overcome the objections of the crowds (20.31), she must overcome objections from the disciples (15.23) and Jesus himself (15.24).

What is the significance of gender in the hemorrhaging woman and Canaanite woman scenes? Female gender is paradoxically a strength and weakness. Gender makes these women doubly marginal, heightening their accomplishments. It creates a greater contrast between their model faith and the failings of those more privileged such as the Jewish leaders and disciples. Gender is not a barrier to faith. Indeed, these women unembedded in any patriarchal family structure show great initiative and are rewarded. Yet their roles are limited. The episodes involving these women are isolated and self-contained. The women never reappear in the narrative nor become members of the inner circle of disciples. This is also true of other outcast supplicants.

As noted above, the supplicant episodes characterize Jesus as the messiah who heals the outcast. They illustrate the theme of God's concern for all and provide the occasion to show various reactions to Jesus and his ministry. The supplicants serve as models of faith and foils for other character groups. Nevertheless, they do not have a continuing narrative role in the same way as the Jewish leaders, disciples, or crowds.[36] Although some commentators argue the blind men's and the Canaanite woman's confessions of Jesus as Lord and Son of David,[37] or the blind men's following (ἀκολουθεῖν) in 20.34[38] indicate discipleship, other commentators deny this. The difference in evaluation depends on whether 'discipleship' is viewed as membership in the character group 'the disciples' or as the proper response to belief in Jesus. If the first definition is adopted, none of these supplicants is a disciple. They are never pictured as members of 'the disciples' as a character group. Although in contrast to Jesus' enemies who call Jesus

---

Institute Press, 1970], pp. 214-15 n. 62) follows J. Horst in distinguishing Matthew's use of προσκυνεῖν in the imperfect as supplication (8.2; 9.18; 15.25; 18.26) and in the aorist as worship/adoration (2.11; 14.33; 28.9, 17).

36. See R. Tannehill's description of the supplicants in Mark ('The Gospel of Mark as Narrative Christology', *Semeia* 16 [1979], pp. 57-95 [67-68]).

37. See n. 33 above.

38. J.D. Kingsbury ('The Verb *Akolouthein* ["to follow"] as an Index of Matthew's View of His Community', *JBL* 97 [1978], pp. 56-73 [57]) lists eight who hold this view; to which add Gibbs ('Purpose and Pattern', pp. 454-55, 460). If so, then they have gone beyond the first pair who disobey Jesus and perhaps the Canaanite woman who does not 'follow' Jesus. However, if the confession Lord and Son of David is taken as an indication of discipleship then a distinction between the woman and the second pair is less likely.

rabbi or teacher, certain supplicants and disciples call Jesus Lord, the disciples never call Jesus Son of David. In addition to God and the Roman centurion in 27.54, only they call Jesus Son of God. Finally, 'following' often refers metaphorically to a disciple or discipleship in Matthew. J.D. Kingsbury, however, argues it does so only when Jesus speaks and not in the narrator's voice[39] as in 9.27 or 20.34. Kingsbury has also argued that two factors are always present when ἀκολουθεῖν is to be understood metaphorically: 'personal commitment', where Jesus summons disciples or addresses those who are already disciples; and 'cost', where following involves sacrifice or leaving one's former life.[40] With these two factors as criteria, Kingsbury limits himself almost entirely to contexts involving members of the character group.[41] One might add that the supplicants' function as foils would be limited if they became disciples.

The dispute over the 'discipleship' of supplicants including women points beyond itself to the reading experience. What role do the supplicants and the disciples play in the rhetoric of the gospel? Does the implied reader identify with both groups, with one, with neither? How do actual readers respond? Do they view any of the character groups as role models? The questions of gender and discipleship and the reading experience emerge also in the next set of passages.

The Women at Bethany, the Cross, and the Tomb
The final set of passages to be examined is associated with the passion and resurrection narratives. The woman at Bethany (26.6-13) and the women at the cross and tomb (27.55-56, 61; 28.1-10) serve as foils for the disciples and play important roles the disciples should have played.[42] They also are the means by which the disciples are reunited with Jesus and receive the Great Commission. Their gender allows them to take on these functions without supplanting the disciples.

The woman at Bethany. As the passion narrative begins a woman anoints Jesus at Bethany (26.6-13). She is described only as 'a woman (γυνή) having an alabaster vial of very expensive ointment' (26.7). She anoints Jesus' body beforehand for burial, possibly with messianic overtones.

39. Kingsbury, '*Akolouthein*', pp. 58, 61.
40. Kingsbury, '*Akolouthein*', p. 58.
41. With the exception of 8.19 and 19.20-22.
42. Norman Perrin (*The Resurrection According to Matthew, Mark and Luke* [Philadelphia: Fortress Press, 1977], pp. 29-31) makes the observation that the women in Mark's passion narrative take the place of the disciples.

The disciples protest her action. They do not understand its significance although Jesus has just uttered the final preparatory passion prediction in 26.2. Judas, 'one of the Twelve', leaves the scene to make his bargain with the chief priests. The failure of the disciples, but also their reconciliation with Jesus, is highlighted by Jesus' concluding declaration foreshadowing the Great Commission. The woman is to be memorialized 'wherever this gospel is proclaimed in all the world' (26.13).

This unembedded woman succeeds where the disciples fail. Her gender highlights their failure. Her actions honor her and shame them. Nonetheless, the woman's gender and limited role prevent her from becoming a rival despite her 'good work' (26.10).

The women at the cross and tomb. As the woman at Bethany provides a non-threatening contrast with the disciples so do the women at the cross and tomb. The women at the cross (27.55-56) stand with Jesus in the hour of his passion when the disciples have forsaken him and fled. Two of them, Mary Magdalene and Mary the mother of James and Joseph, watch over his burial (27.61). Later the two Marys are the first to learn of Jesus' resurrection. They receive an angelic commission to tell the disciples of Jesus' resurrection and future appearance in Galilee (28.1-7). As they run to tell the disciples, the resurrected Jesus appears to them and reiterates the angel's commission (28.8-10). These women, not the disciples, are 'last at the cross and first at the tomb'. They remain faithful to Jesus, and their faith enables the disciples to be reunited with Jesus. Details of the resurrection appearances also underscore a contrast with the disciples. When the women meet Jesus they hold his feet and 'worship [προσεκύνησαν]' him (28.9), a favorite Matthean term indicating the proper attitude toward Jesus.[43] When Jesus appears to the Eleven, some 'worship' Jesus, but some doubt (28.17).[44]

What is the status of these women? Why do they pose no threat to the disciples? The women at the cross are described as women 'who followed [ἠκολούθησαν] Jesus from Galilee serving [διακονοῦσαι] him; among whom was Mary the Magdalene, and Mary the mother of James and Joseph, and the mother of the sons of Zebedee' (27.55-56). Some

---

43. See n. 35 above.
44. Despite the efforts of some commentators to make v. 17 include disciples other than the Eleven, v. 16 unambiguously indicates that the characters present are the Eleven.

commentators treat the women as disciples.[45] Four pieces of evidence shape this interpretation. One is the verb 'followed', often indicative of discipleship in Matthew. Second is the verb 'serving' or 'ministering'. Third is the phrase ὅς καὶ αὐτὸς ἐμαθητεύθη τῷ Ἰησοῦ ('who also himself had become a disciple [or was discipled] to Jesus'), used to describe Joseph of Arimathea in 27.57. Fourth is the character of the women's actions. Other interpreters do not raise the issue or deny that the women are disciples. Kingsbury argues that ἠκολούθησαν does not characterize the women as disciples.[46] As with the two blind men in 20.34 (discussed in the previous section), the word 'to follow' appears in the narrator's voice and the criteria of 'personal commitment' and 'cost' are absent. He adds, 'The appended notation that they were 'waiting on him' is not meant to characterize them as disciples of Jesus in the strict sense of the word but instead explains why they had been in his company'.[47] An examination of Matthew's use of διακονέω ('wait on, serve, minister to') supports Kingsbury's contention. In 4.11 the angels minister to Jesus following the temptation. In 8.15 Peter's mother-in-law ministers to Jesus after he enters Peter's house and cures her fever. In 25.44 those on the left in the parable of the sheep and goats say, 'Lord, when did we see you hungering or thirsting or a stranger or naked or ill or in prison and did not minister to you?' In 20.25b-28 Jesus responds to the anger of the Ten at the sons of Zebedee:

> You know that the rulers of the Gentiles lord it over them and great ones have authority over them. It is not so among you; but whoever among you wishes to become great, will be your servant [διάκονος], and whoever among you wishes to be first, he shall be your slave; as the Son of Man came not to be served [or ministered to, διακονηθῆναι], but to serve [or minister, διακονῆσαι] and to give his life as a ransom for many.

In the first three cases 'ministering' or 'serving' connotes caring for primarily physical needs. In the last instance, 'service' involves taking on the role of a slave and dying for others. The Twelve never serve in this fashion in the narrative nor are they ever described as 'ministering' or 'serving'. Thus the description of the women at the cross as 'ministering to Jesus' seems to indicate that they cared for Jesus'

---

45. For example, R. Gundry, *Mathew: A Commentary on his Literary and Theological Art* (Grand Rapids: Eerdmans, 1982), pp. 578-79; E. Schweizer, *The Good News According to Mark* (trans. D.H. Madvig; Richmond, VA: John Knox Press, 1970), pp. 517-18; A.H. McNeile, *The Gospel According to St. Matthew* (repr.; Grand Rapids: Baker Book House, 1980 [1915]), p. 426.
46. Kingsbury, 'Akolouthein', p. 61.
47. Kingsbury, 'Akolouthein', p. 61.

needs on the journey from Galilee. That women would perform these tasks is not unusual given the narrative's social world. The use of διακονέω perhaps also characterizes the women as servants, the role that the disciples should have pursued. As with the discussion of whether or not certain supplicants are disciples, the difference between 'discipleship' and being a member of the character group 'the disciples' influences interpreters' readings.

The same is the case with various interpretations of 27.57. Joseph is described as 'a rich man from Arimathea who also was discipled (ἐμαθητεύθη) to Jesus'.[48] Does μαθετεύω indicate that Joseph is one of 'the disciples'? Does ὃς καί indicate that in addition to being a rich man from Arimathea Joseph was discipled to Jesus, or that 'he, as well as the women, had become a disciple'?[49] No critical consensus has emerged in answer to these questions.[50] The phrase 'who was also discipled to Jesus' may explain why this particular rich man would want to bury Jesus. It also prevents a negative comparison between Jesus and John the Baptist whose disciples retrieve and bury the body of their master in 14.12. Certainly neither the women nor Joseph are members of the Twelve, the disciples who fail and (with the exception of Judas) are reunited with Jesus in the passion and resurrection scenes.

Although the women play an important part in the narrative, gender seems to prevent their identification as disciples. They are an auxiliary group which can conveniently stand in for the disciples. Their presence at the cross is explained in terms of caring for Jesus' needs on the journey to Jerusalem. One of the three women named in 27.56 is identified as the mother of the sons of Zebedee, two of the Twelve. Earlier in the gospel she accompanied Jesus and the Twelve on the way to Jerusalem (20.20). This accords with the description of the women in 27.55-56. She accompanied them but was not privy to the private instruction given the Twelve. She approached Jesus after he took the

---

48. μαθετεύω appears two other times in Matthew. In 13.52 Jesus speaks of 'every scribe made a disciple (μαθητευθείς) to the kingdom of heaven'. In 28.19 Jesus commands the Eleven to 'make disciples (μαθητεύσατε) of all the Gentiles...'

49. McNeile, *Matthew*, p. 426.

50. These questions are related to the broader question of whether 'the disciples' are limited to the Twelve. See Luz, 'Die Jünger', pp. 141-52; Minear, 'The Disciples', p. 27; Sheridan, 'Disciples and Discipleship in Matthew and Luke', pp. 235-40; Thompson, *Advice*, pp. 71-72. In these discussions confusion exists between the disciples as a character group and the way in which a reader or listener responds to the gospel.

disciples aside to predict the passion and resurrection in 20.17-19. The only role of this mother was to request places of honor for her sons. Like Peter's mother-in-law, who, like the women at the cross, 'ministers' to Jesus, her relationship to Jesus is related to that of her sons.

Perhaps most telling are the references to 'the disciples' after the resurrection. These references clearly distinguish the women from the disciples. The angel commands the two Marys to 'tell *his disciples*' of Jesus' resurrection and appearance in Galilee (28.7). The narrator describes them running to tell *'his disciples'* (28.8). Jesus commands them to 'tell *my brothers* to go to Galilee' (28.10). When they obey, *'the eleven disciples'* go to Galilee, 'to the mountain where Jesus appointed them' (28.16). The women are not strangers or outsiders, but neither are they among the inner circle of disciples.

As with the supplicants discussed in the previous section, interpreters' readings of the women as disciples are influenced by whether they define discipleship as membership in the character group or the proper relationship to Jesus. Attitudes toward gender also influence various readings. Although it has been argued here, some interpreters simply assume that the women are not 'disciples'. Other interpreters assume women can be 'disciples' or that 'discipleship' is not a gender-related category. When an interpreter reads 'the disciples' as allegorical representations of church leaders, his or her view of gender requirements for church leaders may also influence interpretation. Patriarchy has sometimes perpetuated itself by insisting female readers are to see themselves only in the women of the gospel.

Tensions in Matthew
The exploration of the symbolic significance of gender has revealed tensions in Matthew. There is a tension between the treatment of female gender as a positive attribute or irrelevant in comparison to other values and its treatment as a mark of subordinate status. Women are not characterized as deficient in faith, understanding, or morality due to gender. In fact, with the exception of Herodias and her daughter in 14.1-12 and Jesus' family in 12.46-50, women are portrayed favorably. The important roles of women and Jesus' response to women supplicants strain the boundaries of the gospel's patriarchal worldview. Yet female gender renders the exemplary behavior of women as more of an achievement and heightens contrasts with male characters. It ensures for women subordinate and auxiliary positions. Mary's extraordinary role is contained by a patrilineal genealogy and birth story. The important roles of the female supplicants and the

women at Bethany, cross, and tomb are contained within a model that assumes male gender as a requirement for becoming a disciple.

The exploration of the symbolic significance of gender has also revealed how these tensions in Matthew have evoked various responses in readers. Interpretations are affected not only by the treatment of gender in the gospel, but by the ways interpreters are predisposed to view gender as they approach the text. The presence of the women in the genealogy has led to at least three different readings. Various interpretations of the status of women as 'disciples' have emerged.

Gender and the Implied Reader

Two aspects of the role of the implied reader in Matthew begin to shed light on how actual women readers may respond to that role and how different readings of gender in the text arise. Both involve point of view. One is the effect of the ideological alignment of the points of view of the narrator and Jesus on the implied reader. The other is the frequent alignment of the temporal perspectives of the narrator, Jesus, and the implied reader.

The implied author of the Gospel of Matthew shapes the role of the implied reader in many ways. Among them are direct commentary, the arrangement of episodes, the use of characters as foils, etc. Examples of these were seen in the exegeses above. Real readers respond to the role of the implied reader as they read. Part of this role is internal to the text and is sometimes called the inscribed or ideal reader. Part is external, the vantage point outside the text from which textual structures are actualized. To oversimplify, the implied reader is a set of instructions for reading the text. That set of instructions, however, includes gaps and areas of ambiguity. Real readers do not create identical readings of a text. The crucial question is often whether a particular reading violates or ignores textual instructions or whether it is a legitimate actualization.

Point of view is one of the most important means of shaping the role of the implied reader and determining actual readers' responses. Point of view involves the perspectives from which a narrative is presented and viewed. Narrator, narratee, and characters have various interrelated points of view. Boris Uspensky has proposed a helpful typology of point of view.[51] It includes four levels or planes: (1) the

---

51. B. Uspensky, *A Poetics of Composition* (Berkeley: University of California Press, 1973).

ideological, 'the system of ideas which shape the work';[52] (2) the phraseological, speech characteristics which indicate point of view; (3) the temporal and spatial, position in and view of time and position in space; and (4) the psychological, the subjective perspective inside a mind.

Ideological Alignment of Points of View
In Matthew one of the most significant factors in shaping the implied reader is the alignment of the ideological points of view of the narrator and Jesus. This alignment is supported by the partial alignments of their points of view on the other planes.[53] Among other things Jesus and the narrator share certain speech characteristics such as the use of the phrase 'in their synagogues' (4.23; 9.35; 10.17; 12.9, into; 13.54; and 23.34, in *your* synagogues). For most of the narrative their spatial positions are nearly identical. The narrator follows Jesus in much the same way as a movie camera. The narrator offers frequent sympathetic inside views of Jesus. Like the narrator, Jesus possesses a certain degree of omniscience. From time to time he correctly reads the minds of other characters and predicts the future. The implied author also accomplishes the ideological alignment of Jesus and the narrator by bestowing upon Jesus the 'badge of reliability'.[54] The heading and genealogy, the birth story, and the baptism and temptation scenes establish Jesus' identity and reliability before his ministry begins. Since their ideological points of view are aligned, the narrator and Jesus serve as reinforcing vehicles for the implied author's norms and values — the norms and values he or she imposes on the implied reader.[55]

What is the significance of the alignment of the ideological viewpoints of Jesus and the narrator for a female reader? On the one hand responding to them is negative. If the actual reader uncritically adopts the patriarchal worldview represented by the narrator and Jesus, she assumes a worldview which abridges the full humanity of female and male. The reading experience is destructive.

52. Uspensky, *A Poetics of Composition*, p. 8.
53. For a more detailed discussion of the basis of these claims see N. Petersen, 'Point of View in Mark's Narrative', *Semeia* 12 (1978), pp. 97-121; and J. Capel Anderson, 'Point of View in Matthew: Evidence' (paper delivered at SBL Symposium on the Literary Analysis of the Gospels and Acts, December, 1981).
54. Booth, *Rhetoric*, p. 18.
55. The narrator is undramatized, reliable, omniscient, and intrusive. He or she, in effect, serves as the implied author's voice. For all practical purposes their ideological viewpoints are identical. The narrator is one device the implied author uses to shape the reader's response.

On the other hand the fact that both the narrator and Jesus serve as vehicles for the ideology of the implied author is constructive. The narrator provides the implied reader with knowledge unavailable to characters within the narrative. He or she does this, for example, through the use of direct commentary and the provision of privileged inside views of characters including Jesus. In the case of the genealogy the implied reader has a superior knowledge of Jesus' identity, an identity which includes his being the Son of God through Mary. In addition to standing with the narrator, the implied reader also stands with Jesus as he evaluates characters and events. The implied reader evaluates characters regardless of ordinary status markers. Wealth, occupation, purity, ethnicity, and family ties are less important than the stance characters take in relationship to Jesus. The Jewish leaders, the story world's male establishment, are judged negatively; the male disciples positively and negatively, and so on. While it is true that the disciples become the new establishment with special teaching and governance responsibilities (16.18-19; 18.15-20; 28.19-20), their strengths and weaknesses are revealed. This reinforces anti-hierarchical aspects of Jesus' teachings on discipleship such as 20.25-28 and 23.8-12. Marginal characters including women receive fairly positive evaluations.

In accepting the role of the implied reader, then, an actual female reader is free to judge the ideological stances of the various character groups, male and female. In following the guidance of the narrator and Jesus, the actual reader may also be led to judge some of the patriarchal assumptions implicit in their ideological viewpoints.

Since the norms and values of the implied author are lodged with the narrator and Jesus, the implied reader is also directed to see in various characters traits to be prized or eschewed. No one group embodies the implied author's ideology nor serves as a single role model. This explains why some actual readers call characters like the Canaanite woman and the women at the cross and tomb disciples. If 'discipleship' is defined as the norms and values the implied author wishes the implied reader to adopt rather than as membership in the character group, then various male and female characters embody aspects of discipleship. The superiority of the implied reader to all character groups also gives the lie to any interpretation which insists certain readers must identify with certain character groups. Although actual readers—male or female—may identify with the points of view of various character groups ultimately they must judge all of them. A single reader might see his or her own worldview partially embodied in the Jewish leaders, the crowds, the disciples, or any combination of character groups. If an actual reader assumes the role of the implied reader, he or she will evaluate all ideological points of view from the aligned perspectives of the narrator and Jesus.

Alignment of Temporal Perspectives

Another important aspect of Matthew's implied reader is the occasional alignment of the temporal position of the implied reader with those of the narrator and characters, especially Jesus.[56] Most of the narrative takes place in the narrator's and reader's past. This is marked by the past tense. However, at important junctures their temporal positions are synchronized with that of Jesus. This is accomplished through the narrator's use of the historical present,[57] extended speeches by Jesus, and the introduction of direct discourse with the present participles of λέγειν ('to say').

A typical example of the narrator's use of the historical present is Mt. 22.41-46:

> When the Pharisees were assembled, Jesus questioned them saying: 'What does it seem to you concerning the Christ? Whose son is he?' *They say* to him: 'of David'. *He says* to them: 'How then does David call him lord in the spirit saying: 'The Lord said to my lord: Sit on my right until I put thy enemies underneath thy feet?' If then, David calls him lord, how is he his son?' And no one was able to answer him a word nor dared anyone from that day to question him any more.

The introduction and conclusion in the past tense frame the central conversation. The characters, the narrator, and the implied reader are contemporaneous during that exchange. This means that the characters' words are addressed to the implied reader as well as each other. This example is typical because the narrator overwhelmingly uses the historical present in conjunction with Jesus' speech.[58]

---

56. For a more detailed examination see Capel Anderson, 'Point of View', pp. 10-14.

57. J.C. Hawkins (*Horae Synopticae* [repr.; Oxford: Clarendon Press, 1968 (1909)], pp. 148-49) offers a list of Matthew's historical presents. To which add by narrator 2.22 βασιλεύει; 21.45 and 26.25b, λέγει; and by Jesus 11.17, 18, 19; 12.44, 45 (4 times) and 26.18. The function of the historical present is discussed by BDF §321; Uspensky, *A Poetics of Composition*, p. 71; A.A. Mendilow, *Time and the Novel* (New York: Humanities Press, 1965), p. 98; and in regard to Matthew, Thompson, *Advice*, p. 219.

58. Of the narrator's 80 uses of the historical present λέγει occurs 46 times (with Jesus as subject 43 times); λέγουσιν, 14 times (13 times when the subjects are speaking to Jesus); and φησίν, once.

Obvious examples of extended direct discourse are Jesus' five major discourses. Dialogue produces 'the illusion of immediacy and presentness in the reader'.[59] The length of Jesus' uninterrupted discourses enhances this effect greatly. It is as if Jesus speaks in the implied reader's present. The discourses, then, become addresses to the implied reader as well as the audiences designated in the narrative.

Three of the five major discourses as well as the woe discourse of ch. 23 are introduced with a present participle of 'to say' (5.2; 10.5; 13.3; 23.1-2). This is true of shorter sections of direct discourse as well such as Jesus' speech in 22.41-42 above. This device reinforces the temporal alignment of narrator, characters, and implied reader. The action denoted by the present participle, speech, occurs at the same time as the action denoted by the main verb. Thus the main verb freezes the moment of action and the participle indicates what was said at that moment as if it were being spoken in the present. Thus λέγων is often translated as 'saying' even though the main verb is an aorist.

The importance of the frequent synchronization of the temporal perspectives of narrator, implied reader, and characters associated with Jesus' speech is that Jesus' speeches are addressed to the implied reader as well as characters. Through the medium of Jesus the implied author presents his or her ideology in the moment of reading. Actual male or female readers 'hear' the Sermon on the Mount with its two-level narrative audience of crowds and disciples as well as privileged instructions such as the Missionary Discourse or the Great Commission. Although no women are portrayed as disciples, women readers are addressed as 'disciples'. Even though Jesus' speeches are colored by androcentrism, actual women readers have read 'Blessed are the peacemakers, for they shall be called sons of God' (5.9) inclusively and have responded to the Great Commission. Such readings could be destructive if women thus adopt an anti-female perspective and deny their own. However, since the androcentrism of Jesus' speeches consists for the most part in using non-inclusive language and he often attacks oppressive norms, this is not necessarily the case. The speeches often reflect tension between patriarchal and non-patriarchal values.

The reception by the implied reader of speeches addressed to the disciples also challenges certain interpretations of the gospel. Some interpreters limit the ultimate addresses of such discourses to male church leaders or members—either in Matthew's community or in

---

59. Mendilow, *Time and the Novel*, p. 112.

any age. In addition to committing the referential fallacy[60] by positing a *direct* correlation between the disciples and persons in the real world, they ignore the fact that a variety of actual readers may assume the role of implied reader.

Conclusion

This article has tentatively explored the symbolic significance of gender and the reading process in Matthew from a feminist perspective. More questions are raised than answered. It can only be hoped that readers will be stimulated to offer criticism and proposals of their own.

APPENDIX

Verses Concerning Women in Matthew
(There is some overlap between categories.)

Women Characters

Mary, Jesus' mother	birth narrative 1.18–2.23, see especially 1.18-25; 2.13, 19-21
mother and brothers	12.46-50
Mary, brothers and sisters	13.53-58
Peter's mother-in-law	8.14-17
Ruler's daughter	9.18-19, 23-26
Woman with hemorrhage	9.20-22
Herodias and daughter	14.1-12
4,000 (5,000) men besides women and children	14.21; 15.38
Canaanite woman	15.21-28
Mother of the sons of Zebedee	20.20; 27.56
Woman at Bethany	26.6-13
Pilate's wife	27.19
Maid who confronts Peter	26.69
Women at the cross and tomb	27.55-56, 61; 28.1-10 including Mary the mother of James and Joseph, Mary Magdalene and the mother of the sons of Zebedee

---

60. N. Petersen, *Literary Criticism for New Testament Critics* (Philadelphia: Fortress Press, 1978), p. 40.

Women in Jesus' Teaching

Lust	5.27-30
Divorce and Marriage	5.31-32; 19.1-12
Enmity in families	10.21, 35-39; 19.29
Children in Marketplace	11.16-17
Wisdom	11.19
Queen of the South	12.42
True family	12.46-50
Woman and leaven	13.33
Honoring father and mother	15.1-19; 19.19
'with his wife and children'	18.25
Tax collectors and harlots	21.31, 32
Controversy with Sadducees involving Levirite marriage	22.23-33
Jerusalem, hen, brood	23.37-39
Birth pangs of new age	24.8
Those who give suck and are with child	24.19
Two women grinding	24.41
Wise and foolish maidens	25.1-13

Female Imagery

Woman (Rachel) represents Israel	2.18
Woman with leaven represents God	13.33
Daughter of Zion	21.5
Jerusalem as mother	23.37
Birth pangs of new age	24.8

Women in Direct Narratorial Comments

Genealogy	1.1-17
Israel as Rachel	2.18
Besides women and children	14.21; 15.38
Pilate's wife	27.19

THE FATHER IN THE GOSPEL OF MATTHEW

Julian Sheffield

Introduction

The term πατήρ, father, is used generally in the New Testament to refer to God, to human fathers and ancestors, and to revered elders (spiritual fathers).[1] Matthew's use of πατήρ, however, is carefully shaped both to emphasize the fatherhood of God and to displace the earthly father in favor of the father in heaven. This displacement of the human father in favor of God-as-father serves in turn to relativize patriarchy with respect to the relations of disciples one to another as well as to justify the replacement of the family of origin with a new kinship group.

Matthew's Special Use of 'Father'

Chart 1 demonstrates that Matthew is by far the most concerned of the Synoptists to associate the word 'father' with God.[2] Of Matthew's

---

1. BAGD, pp. 635-36.
2. Ulrich Luz, *Matthew 1-7* (Minneapolis: Augsburg, 1989), p. 65, identifies 45 references in Matthew to God as father, but since his total count of the word πατήρ is the same as mine (p. 63) I suggest the difference is a matter of classification. It is possible that Luz identifies the father in the parable of the obedient and the disobedient son, 21.31, as God. Although I exclude 21.31 from my classification of father-as-God references, I do include 25.34, the parable of the sheep and goats. There seems to me from the outset of this parable to be significant differences between the references to 'father' in the two parables. In 21.28-32, the protagonist is introduced simply as a person who had two sons. The identification of this person with God is tenuous at best, resting on the subsequent commentary by Jesus, 'Truly I tell you, the tax collectors and the prostitutes are going into the kingdom of God ahead of you'. The parable itself is simply a story drawn from observation of typical family relationships.

On the other hand, the parable of the sheep and goats in 25.31-46 is established at the outset as a parable about judgment in the kingdom of God, and the protagonist is identified immediately as 'the Son of Man'. In this context, the references to God as father, 70 per cent are unique to Matthew. Chart 2A shows exclusively Matthean material, Chart 2B shows Matthean expansion of Mark or Q, and Chart 2C shows Matthean redaction, adding πατήρ to material common to Mark and Luke. Chart 2D shows where Matthew parallels other uses of πατήρ for God, with Matthew's redactional emphasis noted.[3]

Chart 1. *Uses of* πατήρ *in the Synoptic Gospels*

Synoptic Gospel	Total uses of πατήρ	πατήρ used for God	% πατήρ = God
Matthew	63	44	70%
Mark	18	4	22%
Luke	56	17	30%
Total Synoptic	137	65	47%

References to God as πατήρ constitute almost half the synoptic uses of πατήρ. Matthew's use of πατήρ for God constitutes more than two-thirds of the synoptic uses (44/65, or 68%). Thirty-one (70%) of Matthew's 44 uses of πατήρ for God are unique to Matthew. This is in contrast to Luke, of whose 17 references to God as πατήρ only 6 (35%) are unique to Luke.

Chart 2A. *Uses of* πατήρ *in Exclusively Matthean Material*

1	5.45	so that you may be sons of your Father who is in heaven
2	6.1	you will have no reward from your Father who is in heaven.
3	6.4	your Father who sees in secret
4	6.6	pray to your Father who is in secret;
5	6.6	and your Father who sees in secret will reward you.
6	6.8	for your Father knows what you need before you ask him.
7	6.18	that your fasting may not be seen by men but by your Father who is in secret;
8	6.18	and your Father who sees in secret will reward you.

king's (i.e. Son of Man's) reference to 'my father' can only refer to God. Hence, I have included 25.34 in my count of father-as-God references. Robert Mowery, 'God, Lord and Father: The Theology of the Gospel of Matthew', *BibRes* 33 (1988), pp. 24-36, has also analyzed the uses of God, Father, and Lord in Matthew. Mowery does not draw any conclusions from the data which he has assembled.

3. Unique: 5.45; 6.1, 4, 6 (×2), 8, 18 (×2), 26; 13.43; 15.13; 16.17; 18.19, 35; 23.9; 25.34; 26.53; 28.19. Expansions: 5.16; 6.15; 18.10, 14; 26.42. Addition: 6.26; 7.21; 10.20, 29, 32, 33; 12.50; 20.23; 26.29. The issue of Matthean expansions of Markan and Q materials is explored by Graham N. Stanton, *A Gospel for a New People: Studies in Matthew* (Edinburgh: T. & T. Clark, 1992), pp. 326-45. Except where noted, English text in all tables is RSV.

9	13.43	Then the righteous will shine like the sun in the kingdom of their Father.
10	15.13	Every plant which my heavenly Father has not planted will be rooted up.
11	16.17	flesh and blood has not revealed this to you, but my Father who is in heaven.
12	18.19	it will be done for them by my Father in heaven.
13	18.35	So also my heavenly Father will do to every one of you
14	23.9	And call no man your father on earth, for you have one Father, who is in heaven.
15	25.34	Come, O blessed of my Father
16	26.53	Do you think that I cannot appeal to my Father,
17	28.19	in the name of the Father and of the Son and of the Holy Spirit,

Chart 2B. πατήρ *Added in Expansion of Parallel Material*

	Matthew (expansion in bold)	Parallels
1	5.15-**16**	Mk 4.21; Lk. 8.16; 11.33
2	6.14-**15**	Mk 11.25*
3, 4	18.10, 12-13, **14***	Lk. 15.3-7
5	26.39-42a, **42b**	Mk 14.36-40; Lk. 22.41-46*; Jn 12.27

*Mt. 18.11, Mk 11.26, and Lk. 22.43-44 are omitted as generally agreed to be suspect.

Chart 2C. πατήρ *Added in Redaction of Parallel Material*

	Matthew	Parallels
1	6.26 your heavenly Father	Lk. 12.24 God
2	7.21 my Father who is in heaven	Lk. 6.46 what I tell you
3	10.20 the Spirit of your Father	Lk. 12.12 the Holy Spirit
4	10.29 without your Father's will	Lk. 12.6 before God
5, 6	10.32-33 my Father who is in heaven (×2)	Lk. 12.8-9 the angels of God
7	12.50 the will of my Father in heaven	Mk 3.35 the will of God Lk. 8.21 the word of God Jn 15.14 what I command you
8	20.23 it has been prepared by my Father	Mk 10.40 it has been prepared
9	26.29 my Father's kingdom	Mk 14.25 the kingdom of God Lk. 22.16, 18 the kingdom of God

Chart 2D. πατήρ Parallels (all phrases use πατήρ for God)

	Matthew (with redaction of phrase)	Parallels
1	5.48 heavenly	Lk. 6.36
2	6.9 Our...who [art] in heaven	Lk. 11.12
3	6.14 the heavenly-one*	Mk 11.25 the [one] in the heavens*
4	6.32 heavenly	Lk. 12.30
5	7.11 your...the [one] in the heavens*	Lk. 11.13 from heaven
6-10	11.27 nor does anyone know the Father*	Lk. 10.22 or who is the Father
11	16.27	Mk 8.38; Lk. 9.26
12	24.36	Mk 13.32
13	26.39 My Father	Mk 14.36 *Abba* Father; Lk. 22.42, Jn 12.27 Father

*My translation to emphasize differences in Greek.

Matthew's shaping of references to God as father has implications that move in two different, but perhaps not disconnected, directions. First, Matthew's use of 'father' rather than 'God' or 'Lord' on Jesus' lips shapes the representation of Jesus' theology. Second, the preferential treatment Matthew gives to the divine father, at the expense of the human father, suggests something about the structure of Matthew's community. The nature of the relationship between a community's theology and its structure is debatable; the existence of some such relationship is not.

Matthew's theology focuses on God as father; the gospel insistently and virtually exclusively locates that father in heaven. God the father is identified as 'heavenly' or 'in heaven' 20 times.[4] The charts clearly indicate that 'heaven' is Matthew's value-added take on the fatherhood of God: only two of these references have parallels (chart 2D): Mt. 6.14//Mk 11.25, and Mt. 7.11//Lk. 11.13. In both of these, Matthew makes subtle but perhaps significant changes.[5] Even in the fourth

---

4. 5.16, 45, 48; 6.1, 9, 14, 26, 32; 7.11, 21; 10.32, 33; 12.50; 15.13; 16.17; 18.10, 14, 19, 35; 23.9.

5. Mt. 6.14 reads 'your heavenly father', ὁ πατὴρ ὑμῶν ὁ οὐράνιος where Mk 11.25 reads 'your father who is in heaven', ὁ πατὴρ ὑμῶν ὁ ἐν τοῖς οὐρανοῖς). The Matthean version indicates a greater intimacy with the father, especially in light of the future indicative of the verb ἀφίημι contrasted with Mark's aorist subjunctive. Mark's context also is less secure in the father's willingness to forgive: 'And when you stand praying, if you have anything against anyone, forgive, so that your

gospel, with 115 references to God as father, *not one* identifies God as 'heavenly father' or 'father in heaven'.[6]

Such interpretation of God as heavenly father firmly situates Matthew's community in the context of Rabbinic prayer language. Mary Rose D'Angelo has argued that the two wars against Rome may have contributed to increasing the importance of 'father' in Jewish prayer; the language suggests the juxtaposition of the two authorities, father/God versus Rome.[7] The father/God in Jewish prayer language relates to given, already existing communities, perhaps in the context of the synagogue. Matthew, however, co-opts the heavenly father as the head of a kinship[8] group which is coming into being through affiliation with the father's son.

The Use of 'Lord' and 'God'

Matthew's Jesus overwhelmingly prefers the use of 'father' when speaking to the disciples, cf. Chart 3. In Matthew, as in Mark, Jesus

father who is in heaven might forgive you your trespasses'. This is a sort of blanket insurance policy, by contrast with Matthew's 'For if you forgive others their trespasses, your heavenly father will also forgive you.' [...you your heavenly father also will forgive.] The bracketed clause is not a good English translation, but it gives a better sense of the emphasis of the Greek, with ὁ πατήρ bracketed by ὑμῖν...ὑμῶν. The Q parallel, Q11.13//7.11, shows a possibly more significant difference. Matthew uses the identical phrase to describe the father as Mk 11.25, ὁ πατήρ ὑμῶν ὁ ἐν τοῖς οὐρανοῖς. Luke, however, describes the father as ὁ πατήρ [ὁ] ἐξ οὐρανοῦ. The bracketed ὁ indicates debate whether it should be included in the text and is a compromise solution, the textual evidence being entirely inconclusive. (Bruce Metzger, *A Textual Commentary on the Greek New Testament* [Stuttgart: United Bible Societies, 1975], pp. 157-58.) If the ὁ is included, ἐξ stands in as an unusual but not unprecedented substitute for ἐν, in the sense where something is both in and coming out of something (BAGD *s.v.* ἐκ 6.a, p. 236). In this case, the only significant redaction Matthew has made is the addition of 'your' to the 'father who is in heaven'. If, however, as half the evidence apparently indicates, the ὁ is not authentic, then there is no 'heavenly father' at all in Luke, and 11.13 reads ὁ πατήρ ἐξ οὐρανοῦ δώσει πνεῦμα ἅγιον, 'the father will give the holy spirit from heaven'.

6. That John's father-God is in heaven can be inferred from 6.32, 12.28 and 17.1 where things derive from heaven or Jesus looks to heaven. These oblique references are all that connect the father with heaven, however.

7. Mary Rose D'Angelo, '*Abba* and "Father": Imperial Theology and the Jesus Traditions', *JBL* 111.4 (1992), pp. 611-30.

8. The absence of the word 'fictive' to modify 'kinship' here reflects my belief that this group, despite the current popularity of the concept, is not a fictive kinship group, but a true kinship group, for reasons which I will discuss in my future work.

refers to God as father only in the presence of disciples.[9] Chart 3 shows the comparative uses of 'father', 'God', and 'Lord', both by Matthew and by Matthew's Jesus, and their contexts.[10]

Chart 3. *Jesus' Names for God in Matthew*

Name	Total in Mt.	Used by Jesus	Used among disciples and crowds*	Used to and among adversaries*	Used in Scripture quotes*
Father	44	44	44	0	0
God	51	33	8* (5.8, 9, 34; 6.24, 30, 33; 19.24, 26)	25* (4.4, 7, 10; 12.4, 28[x2]; 15.3, 4, 6; 16.23; 19.6; 21.31, 43; 22.21[x2], 29, 32[x4], 37; 23.22; 27.46[x2]†)	8* (4.4, 7, 10; 22.32[x3], 37; 27.46[x2]†)
Lord	18	8	2* (5.33; 11.25)	6* (4.7, 10; 21.42; 22.37, 44; 23.39)	7* (4.7, 10; 5.33; 21.42; 22.37, 44; 23.39)

* Context instances may add up to more than the total number, as some uses fall into two context categories.
† 27.46 is the only instance in Matthew where Jesus uses 'God' rather than 'father' to address God.

Matthew's Jesus uses 'Lord' to refer to God only in direct quotes from Scripture,[11] and coupled with 'father' in 11.25. The word 'God' is used by Matthew's Jesus in discourse with antagonists 25 times,[12] in discourse with disciples eight times, and in speaking from the cross, possibly quoting scripture, twice.[13] The eight instances in discourse with disciples occur in three discreet sections, two in the Sermon on

---

9. Lk. 23.34, 46 are in the presence of enemies.
10. Possibly 'Lord of the harvest' in 9.38 also refers to God, although this seems more likely to refer to Jesus himself, in the light of 10.1-42, where Jesus does the sending out.
11. Direct quotes from Scripture: 4.7, 10; 5.33; 21.42; 22.37, 44; 23.39.
12. These include 16.23, Jesus' rebuke to Peter, where Peter is clearly functioning in a role adversarial to the father and to Jesus, and 22.37, in direct quote from Scripture, spoken to the lawyer sent to test Jesus. Both the purpose of the lawyer, to test Jesus, and Matthew's redactional excision of Jesus' commendation (Mk 12.34; Lk. 10.28) indicate that Matthew places this lawyer among Jesus' adversaries.
13. Matthew as writer prefers to call God 'Lord' (7×) and to ascribe to others the use of 'God' (14×).

the Mount, 5.8, 9, 34, and 6.24, 30, 33;[14] and the third immediately following Jesus' rejection by the rich young man, 19.24, 26.

The last instance of Jesus' use of the word 'God', the cry from the cross, deserves attention (27.46). Only here, in this passage clearly taken over from Mark (Mk 15.34), does Matthew allow Jesus to address God directly in any terms other than father. Luke, on the other hand, as Mowery points out without observing the irony in this, never depicts Jesus as addressing God other than as father, even from the cross in the presence of his enemies.[15]

Clearly, Matthew deliberately structures Jesus' mode of address to God in order to associate God-as-father with the believing community. Only the company of disciples, those in communion with Jesus, may witness Jesus' relationship with the father. Matthew's Jesus at no time exposes his or his community's special relationship with God-as-father to the gaze of enemies. Matthew's five unique references to the father 'in secret'[16] further indicate that in Matthew, Jesus' relationship with the heavenly father is one of the 'hidden things' revealed only to 'little ones', disciples.

The Displacement of the Earthly Father

By contrast with Matthew's insistent emphasis on relationship to God as 'father', Matthew almost unilaterally rejects the claims of relationship with earthly fathers. This rejection is implied in the general disruption of the family of origin, and it also appears in several other contexts.

The Pharisees

The only two passages where Matthew uses πατήρ to refer to progenitors, 'ancestors' as the NRSV translates it, address the Pharisees, 3.7-10 (Lk. 3.7-9) and 23.30-32. In the preaching of John the Baptist, the injunction not to presume on Abraham as father has a typically Matthean twist: it specifically addresses adversaries, the Pharisees and Sadducees, for whom, Davies and Allison suggest, 'Abrahamic descent was not only a necessary condition for salvation but a sufficient con-

---

14. The inclusion of τοῦ θεοῦ in 6.33 is questionable (Metzger, *Textual Commentary*, p. 18).

15. Robert L. Mowery, 'The Disappearance of the Father: The References to God the Father in Luke–Acts' (paper given to the SBL meeting, San Francisco, November 1992).

16. 6.4, 6(×2), 18(×2).

dition'.[17] John the Baptist requires repentance for salvation, and in Matthew he rejects the Pharisees and Sadducees because they do not repent. They claim Abraham as πατήρ but according to John they are not 'children of Abraham' but γεννήματα ἐχιδνῶν (3.7), 'offspring of vipers', and God can replace them with true 'children of Abraham'.

In the second passage, 23.30-32, Jesus himself condemns the Pharisees' attempt to disassociate from their ancestral fathers' shedding of the prophets' blood, with Matthew's redactional emphasis 'you are the sons of those who murdered the prophets' (23.31). Continuing this polemic against the Pharisees in 23.33, Jesus repeats John's phrase γεννήματα ἐχιδνῶν, 'offspring of vipers', as an epithet for the Pharisees, and consigns them to Gehenna, the place of eternal fire, echoing John's 'unquenchable fire' (3.12).[18]

These two references to πατήρ as ancestor thus form an *inclusio* for all the references to God as 'your father', all the teaching of Jesus to his disciples. This emphatically places the Pharisees *outside* the community which relates to God as father and to whom God relates as father.

Further, although the Pharisees justify themselves through descent from 'their father Abraham', they abjure relationship with their intervening 'fathers' who murdered the prophets (23.30). And yet they recapitulate that relationship in their own treatment of John and Jesus and so attest to their affinity with those murderous ancestors. Moreover, in 27.25 the Pharisees affiliate their own children with the very sin for which they have disowned their fathers: 'His blood be upon us and upon our children'.[19] This, to say the least, does not model appropriate paternal behavior; hence the Pharisees are condemned not only because they justify themselves by claiming one 'father-ancestor' while disclaiming other 'father-ancestors', but also because they themselves act as criminally irresponsible 'fathers'.

---

17. W.D. Davies and D.C. Allison, Jr, *A Critical and Exegetical Commentary on the Gospel According to St. Matthew*. I. *Introduction and Commentary on Matthew 1–7* (Edinburgh: T. & T. Clark, 1988), p. 309.

18. O. Böcher, 'γέεννα', in H. Balz and G. Schneider (eds.), *Exegetical Dictionary of the New Testament* (3 vols.; Grand Rapids: Eerdmans, 1990), I, pp. 239-40.

19. The persons saying this are the people, not the Pharisees; but 'Matthew connects the λαός [that is hardened] with its representatives—up to and including the cultic-legal didactic self-condemnation of 27.25...', H. Frankenmölle, 'λαός', in Balz and Schneider, *Exegetical Dictionary*, II, pp. 339-44 (342).

The Disciples: James and his Brother John

Several pericopes in Matthew reflect displacement of the earthly father in relationship to disciples. Perhaps the most exhaustive treatment of a disciple-earthly father relationship concerns James and John, the sons of Zebedee. Chart 4 shows some of the texts pertinent here.

Chart 4. *James and John as Brothers or Sons*

The Call

Mt. 4.21-22 — he saw *two other brothers*, James the son of Zebedee and John his brother, in the boat with *Zebedee their father*, mending their nets, and he called them. Immediately they left the boat *and their father*, and followed (ἀκολουθέω) him.

Mk 1.19-20 — he saw James the son of Zebedee and John his brother, who were in their boat mending the nets. And immediately he called them; and they left their father Zebedee in the boat *with the hired servants*, and followed (ἀπέρχομαι) him

The Two Seats

Mt. 20.20-24 — Then the *mother of the sons of Zebedee* came up to him, with her sons, and kneeling before him she asked him for something. And he said to her, 'What do you want?' She said to him, 'Command that these *two sons of mine* may sit, one at your right hand and one at your left, in your kingdom...but it is for those *for whom it has been prepared by my Father*.' And when the ten heard it, they were indignant at *the two brothers*.

Mk 10.35-41 — And *James and John, the sons of Zebedee*, came forward to him, and said to him, 'Teacher, we want you to do for us whatever we ask of you.' And he said to them, 'What do you want me to do for you?' And they said to him, 'Grant us to sit, one at your right hand and one at your left, in your glory...but it is for those *for whom it has been prepared*.' And when the ten heard it, they began to be indignant at *James and John*.

Gethsemane

Mt. 26.37 — And taking with him Peter and the *two sons of Zebedee*...

Mk 14.33 — And he took with him Peter and *James and John*...

The Crucifixion

Mt. 27.56 — Mary the mother of James and Joseph, and the *mother of the sons of Zebedee*.

First, Matthew displays his prejudice toward rejection of the earthly father in his redaction of James and John's initial call (4.21-22//Mk 1.19). Matthew emphasizes the fraternal relationship by adding the phrases 'two other brothers' and 'with Zebedee their father' to the Markan narrative. By omitting mention of the hired servants, Matthew heightens the sense of abandonment of Zebedee the father; by separating the leaving of the boat from the leaving of Zebedee the father, Matthew emphasizes that the brothers left both their way of life and their family of origin. The redaction leaves the earthly father completely alone. The brothers' abandonment of their earthly father for relationship with Jesus makes them eligible for transfer of their sonship to the heavenly father. Matthew emphasizes the nature of this relationship with Jesus by his use of ἀκολουθέω, 'follow *along with*', in place of Mark's ἀπέρχομαι with its more subordinating connotation of 'following *after*'.

Matthew's description of James and John depends on how they are relating to Jesus at any given moment in the narrative. James and John behave either as 'sons of Zebedee' or as brothers. Matthew does identify James as 'of Zebedee (ὁ τοῦ Ζεβεδαίου) *and his brother John*' in his list of apostles (10.2); the reference to Zebedee here functions to distinguish this James from James son of Alphaeus. While Matthew has taken over the list from Mk 3.17, observe that Matthew ignores Mark's nickname for James and John, 'sons of thunder'! At the Matthean Transfiguration, Jesus takes James and John *his brother* with him (17.1). Here Matthew has added the phrase 'and his brother' to both Mk 9.2 and Lk. 9.28.

These three citations emphasize the fraternal significance of the relationship and essentially annul the filial relationship to Zebedee. On all three occasions, James and John behave as true members of the community, 'brothers' of Jesus as well as of each other, in filial relationship to the heavenly father through brotherhood with Jesus.

But there are three other Matthean references to James and John in which the brothers behave in a way which is, if not actively antagonistic to Jesus, certainly inappropriate and unseemly for true 'brothers' of Jesus.

The first of these is the episode of the seats beside the throne of Jesus (20.20-28). Matthew, in an uncharacteristic elaboration on Mk 10.35-45, re-routes James and John's request through their mother, *the mother of the sons of Zebedee*. This mother comes *with her sons* to Jesus to place the request. Luz uses this episode in support of his argument that Matthew enhances the image of the disciples.[20] In fact, Jesus clearly locates responsibility for the request with the brothers by addressing his response to them and not to their mother. I would suggest that a different interpretation pertains here: James and John act as sons of two earthly parents, with no filial relationship whatsoever to the heavenly father. The mother reinforces this in 20.21, 'Command that these two sons *of mine*...' Jesus then rebukes James and John and reminds them of the identity of the true parent in 20.23, where Matthew adds 'by my father' to the Markan explanation that those seats have 'been prepared'. Only after this rebuke and the reassertion of the heavenly father are James and John restored to the status of 'brothers'. The brothers thus have disassociated themselves from their heavenly father by their ambition, and they are subsequently rebuked and then restored to the community as well as to a right relationship with their heavenly father.

James and John revert a second time to being sons of their earthly father in 26.36-46. Jesus takes with him to Gethsemane 'Peter and the two sons of Zebedee' (26.27). Matthew omits even the names James and John (Mk 14.33). In Jesus' hour of distress, the sons of Zebedee fail in their duty to their brother by falling asleep: they are unable to keep watch over Jesus' final hour of privacy. They cannot merit the name of brother. Here, Peter and James and John are false disciples: since they are asleep, and therefore false disciples, they do not qualify to hear Jesus' prayer to the father. Peter at least wakes up long enough to be rebuked. But the sons of Zebedee, forsaking the need of their brother Jesus in the apostasy of sleep, after countless warnings in parables against falling asleep, have surrendered every claim to filial association with Jesus' father. They have reverted to being sons of their earthly father Zebedee, and nameless ones, at that.

The last reference to James and John, 27.56, again identifies them only as 'the sons of Zebedee'. Where 'the mother *of the sons of Zebedee*' witnesses the crucifixion, the sons themselves are conspicuously absent. They have abandoned their brother Jesus and remain disassociated from the heavenly father.

Thus the six appearances of James and John become a case-study in Matthew's use of affiliation (literally) to reflect communal approval or

---

20. Ulrich Luz, 'The Disciples in the Gospel According to Matthew', in Graham Stanton (ed.), *The Interpretation of Matthew* (Issues in Religion and Theology, 3; Philadelphia: Fortress Press, 1983), pp. 98-128.

disapproval. When James and John are behaving as befits true members of the community, i.e., as true sons of Jesus' father, they are identified by fraternal relationship: 'James and his brother John', or 'the two brothers'. When they are behaving in ways that locate them outside the heavenly father's family, they are called 'sons of Zebedee'. Just as one cannot serve two masters, one cannot be the son of two fathers. The heavenly father must displace the earthly in the disciples' allegiance.

The Earthly Father Discredited

Matthew's argument against the earthly father, which culminates in 23.9, 'Call no one your father', begins at the outset of the gospel, with the genealogy: a genealogy not of Jesus, but of Joseph. Nowhere in the gospel, including the genealogy, does Matthew identify an earthly father of Jesus. The infancy narratives refer consistently to Joseph's actions towards the 'child and his mother' (2.13, 20, 21). In Mark the people of Jesus' hometown ask, 'Is not this the carpenter?' (Mk 6.3). The answer to the question asked in Mark is, of course, yes, this is the carpenter; the people see who Jesus is, but they miss the meaning. Matthew emends Mark's question to, 'Is not this the carpenter's *son*?' (13.55), to which the answer, of course, is no. The people cannot even see who Jesus is; their fundamental premise is in error.

Matthew himself obeys the command to 'call no one father' where he changes Luke's 'what *father* among you', (Lk. 11.11), to 'what ἄνθρωπος [man] among you' (7.9). In fact, other than Zebedee, there is only one person identified by Matthew as being *anyone's* earthly father: Herod, Archelaus's father (2.22), whose infamous treatment of Bethlehem's children cannot recommend the role of earthly father. Precisely because the son is likely to reflect the qualities of the father, Joseph turns aside from Archelaus's territory and settles in a different region (2.22-23).

One disciple does request to bury his earthly father before following Jesus (8.21-22). Jesus' response, 'Let the dead bury their dead', shows clearly the displacement of the earthly father. The rejection of filial obligation to the earthly father directly contradicts Rabbinic law: 'duties connected with burying a close relative override the obligations to make the daily prayers at the proper time'.[21] Jesus' unsym-

---

21. Daniel J. Harrington, *The Gospel of Matthew* (Sacra Pagina; Collegeville, MN: Liturgical Press, 1991), p. 119.

pathetic answer can only imply complete non-recognition of the relationship.

The displacement of the earthly father does not, however, release him from the obligation to provide for the child. Matthew describes men seeking the healing of a daughter (9.18-26) and a son (17.14-21). These men, however, Matthew refuses to identify as *father*. This reflects more redactional displacing of the earthly father: Matthew has stripped both Markan and Lukan narratives of all reference to earthly father or family.[22] Matthew's only expression of concern about kinship in these healings focuses on care for children, the little ones.

Matthew assumes that people will provide only good things for their own children (7.9-10), but as the earthly father is displaced, the burden of responsibility for the little ones shifts to become a community burden. Thus Matthew shows the centurion in 8.5-13 seeking healing for a servant, someone even 'littler' and more marginalized than a child, out of (fatherly) concern. Whatever the relationship between the two, the centurion models nurturing care for the servant. Matthew may simply preserve the earlier version of the text, as Fitzmyer suggests.[23] Nevertheless, while the Lukan version contends that the centurion requires multiple justifications (love of the Jews, building of the synagogue) to get Jesus' attention, in Matthew, the centurion's concern for the subordinate by itself commands Jesus' response. Perhaps Matthew has indeed shaped the tale to emphasize the importance of caring for the less powerful in one's community.

Nurture, far more than domination, characterizes the relationship of the heavenly father to the disciples of Jesus, as Matthew describes it. It is true that, in Matthew and Luke, the father's children must do their Father-God's will (7.21//Lk. 6.46) and must be like the father (5.48//Lk. 6.36). But Matthew adds special qualities to the father: the father bestows good on the 'righteous and unrighteous' (5.45), rewards the disciples (6.1, 4, 6, 18), knows what the disciples need before they ask (6.8); values the disciples and feeds them (6.26), reveals the nature of Jesus (16.17), and grants requests made in consensus (18.19). The perfection of the father which disciples emulate clearly must include nurturing concern and provision for the heavenly father's children, the little ones.

---

22. Mk 5.21-43//Lk. 8.40-56; and Mk 9.14-27//Lk. 9.37-43.
23. Joseph Fitzmyer, *The Gospel According to Luke I–X* (AB, 28; New York: Doubleday, 1981), pp. 648-49.

The Reconstitution of the Family

There remain two more clusters of πατήρ references to examine, those concerning the disruption of the human nuclear family and its reconstitution under the heavenly father (10.21-22, 35-37; 12.46-50; 19.29); and those concerning the commandment to honor (earthly) father and mother (15.4-7; 19.16-22). On the face of it, these passages would appear to be mutually contradictory.[24] I suggest, however, that they are far more congruent than they appear. These passages, particularly as they inform each other, confirm that the earthly father's responsibility for his children becomes transformed into the community's responsibility for the little ones under the aegis of the heavenly father.

The language of the disruption of the earthly nuclear family and reconstitution of the heavenly father's family points to a systematic displacement of the earthly father. The family that must be abandoned includes the earthly father (10.21, 35, 37; 19.29); Jesus constructs a new family which does not include an earthly father: 'Whoever does the will of my father in heaven is my *brother and sister and mother*' (12.50).

In light of this displacement of the earthly father, how are we to understand Jesus' discussion of the commandment to 'honor father and mother'? The texts appear in Chart 5.

Chart 5. *Honouring Father and Mother*

Mt. 15.4-9	Mk 7.6b-13
'For God commanded, "**Honor your father and your mother**", and, "He who speaks evil of father or mother, let him surely die". But you say, "If any one tells his father or his mother, What you would have gained from me is given to God, he need not *honor his father*". So, for the sake of your tradition, you have made void the word of God. You hypocrites! Well	'Well did Isaiah prophesy of you hypocrites, as it is written, "This people **honors me** with their lips, but their heart is far from me; in vain do they worship me, teaching as doctrines the precepts of men". You leave the commandment of God, and hold fast the tradition of men'. And he said to them, 'You have a fine way of rejecting the commandment of God,

---

24. Amy-Jill Levine, for example, says of 12.46-50, 'Matthew insists that biological relationships are to be replaced by new mothers, brothers, sisters: the men and women who do the father's will' and, in the same paragraph, that 15.4-7 and 19.19 'assert that one must honor and indeed provide for both father and mother', in 'Matthew', in C.A. Newsom and S.H. Ringe (eds.), *The Women's Bible Commentary* (Philadelphia: Westminster/John Knox Press, 1992), pp. 252-62 (260).

| did Isaiah prophesy of you, when he said: "This people **honors me** with their lips, but their heart is far from me, teaching as doctrines the precepts of men"'. | in order to keep your tradition! For Moses said, "**Honor your father and your mother**"; and, "He who speaks evil of father or mother, let him surely die"; but you say, "If a man tells his father or his mother, What you would have gained from me is Corban" (that is, given to God) — then you no longer permit him to *do anything for his father or mother*, thus making void the word of God through your tradition which you hand on. And many such things you do'. |

The first passage, 15.4-9, is located in a defense against Pharisees and scribes who accuse Jesus of breaking with tradition. Jesus, in turn, accuses the Pharisees and scribes of perverting tradition; he cites their ruling that if individuals give to the Temple the money that would normally be used to support their parents, those people have no more Torah obligation to their parents.

Matthew has taken over this narrative from Mk 7.6b-13 and has redacted it in three small but significant particulars, as the chart demonstrates. First, Matthew drops *the mother* from the passage and changes *do anything* to *honor*. Then Matthew places the Isaiah prophecy, 'This people honors me with their lips...', after the challenge to the Pharisees. Three features of this redaction suggest that God is the father who merits honor, and honor for the earthly father derives from and is subordinate to honor for God: first, the triple use of the word 'honor' tying together the prophecy with the teaching; second, the progression from teaching about natural parent to prophecy about God (*qal vahomer*); third, the omission of 'mother' in 15.5.

The second passage about honoring father and mother, 19.16-22, is included in a list of commandments cited by Jesus in response to the question, 'What good deed must I do, to have eternal life?' The commandments are axiomatic; the potential disciple, whose wealth validates the goodness of his life, seeks some work of supererogation, some act which will provide credit for the spiritual balance sheet. Jesus' reply, besides undermining the disciple's self-image, puts an unexpected spin on the command to honor father and mother: 'Sell what you possess and give to the poor, and come, follow me'.

The moral dilemma, for the disciple, arises: how, if he sells everything and follows Jesus, will he be able to continue to keep the Law, which demands supporting father and mother? How can the demands of Torah righteousness be in conflict with Jesus' call to discipleship? Is there, in fact, any real difference between what Jesus says to the disciple, and what the Pharisee says to the potential donor, 'give to the Temple, and forget your parents' old age'? The net result is the same: in the end, the disciple has no resources with which to provide for the parents. By obeying the command of Jesus, the disciple becomes unable to keep the Law.

To argue that this is not a general teaching but a specific command to one potential disciple does not lessen the implication for the Law. The Law binds everyone; the Law excuses no one from its obligations in this respect, as Jesus himself has emphasized in 15.6. So how can this call to discipleship, this call to leave family, be reconciled with the command to honor father and mother?

The construction of a new family in relationship to Jesus and the heavenly father provides a new context in which the command to honor father and mother will be obeyed. By leaving the family of origin and becoming a brother or sister of Jesus, the disciple honors the heavenly father. As a member of the heavenly father's family, the disciple has new mothers to honor, as well as new sisters and brothers to care for. In the best of all possible worlds, the biological mother and father may become brother and sister and mother in the new family, and the responsibilities in 'honoring' the new kin exceed the honor of mother and father required by the Torah.

Questions Raised by Matthew's Reconstitution of the Family

Matthew's new kinship group excludes the earthly father but retains the mother. The exclusion of the earthly father raises one substantial question: where does the authority lie in this community? One immediately obvious answer to this question arises from Mt. 18: the community (ἐκκλησία) exercises authority collectively. The retention of the mother points to a corollary question: do women exercise authority in Matthew's community? Are women fully enfranchised with the ability to share in the collective exercise of authority?

Source material alone cannot account for Matthew's retention of the mother; far too often the gospel includes mothers by Matthew's hand. The one episode in which Jesus does appear to reject his mother has the force of double attestation in Mk 3.31-35 and Lk. 8.19-21; such a strong tradition required inclusion. The liberal addition of mothers to Matthew's Gospel offsets, and may even interpret this saying, as I shall show below.

Many have tried to explain the anomalous inclusion of women in Matthew's genealogy.[25] No interpretation that I have encountered focuses on the status of these women as mothers. Yet motherhood is the one thing that all four women (five, if Mary be included) indisputably share. Further, all four women, Tamar, Rahab, Ruth, and the wife of Uriah the Hittite (Bathsheba), take strong and effective initiatives to secure their motherhood; or, looked at from a different perspective, to ensure the succession through their offspring.[26] Mary, by contrast, is singularly passive. She is, however, the sole human actor in the generation of Jesus; the other women in the genealogy required and secured male cooperation for the generative act! Mary does require the acceptance and protection of Joseph (1.20-25; 2.13-15, 19-23), but Matthew demonstrates her importance by naming her and not mentioning Joseph at the visit of the μάγοι, 'magi' (2.10-12).

Although the sons of Zebedee failed in their duties in 20.20-24 and 27.55-56 discussed above, these episodes provide another occasion for Matthew to emphasize the role of the mother. Mark makes no mention of their mother in describing the power play (Mk. 10.35-36). Further, having introduced the mother into this story, Matthew attaches no blame to her; the plural form of the verbs and the content of Jesus' rejoinder (20.22-23) make it clear that Jesus addresses the two sons. Again Matthew presents a mother acting on behalf of her children, attempting to secure their succession. At the crucifixion, Matthew names the mother of the sons of Zebedee as present, showing two mothers present with Mary Magdalene by comparison with Mark's one mother and Salome (15.40-41).

Matthew's narrative enhances the strong character of another woman who is mother by implication if not by name, the Canaanite woman (15.21-28; Mk. 7.24-30). In Mark, the woman prevails after only one rejection; in Matthew, the woman persists through three rejections and receives the affirmative 'great is your faith' (μεγάλη σου ἡ πίστις), a clear contrast to the 'little faith folk' (ὀλιγόπιστοι) of Matthew's community.

25. E.g., the sinful woman theory (G.W. Kittel, *TWNT*, θαηάρ,ʹΡαχβ,ʹΡούθ, ἡ τοῦ Οὐρίου', III, pp. 1-3), the theory that marital irregularities provide the setting for God's intervention (K. Stendahl, 'Quis et Unde?, An Analysis of Mt. 1–2', in W. Eltester [ed.], *Judentum – Urchristentum – Kirche*, BZNW 26.2 [1964], pp. 19-105); the intrusion of the Gentile theory (E. Schweizer, *The Good News According to Matthew* [Atlanta: John Knox Press, 1975], p. 9).

26. Tamar: Gen. 38.6-30; Rahab: Josh. 2.1-21; 6.25; Ruth 3.1-14; Bathsheba: 1 Kgs 1.11-31.

Matthew inherits another mother from Mark: Herodias (14.3-11; Mk. 6.17-28). Here again a mother acts decisively and effectively. Herodias, however, does not put herself at risk to secure the welfare of her child. On the contrary, Herodias, a mother outside and inimical to the new family defined by relationship to Jesus and the father, abuses her role as mother and turns her child into an agent for Herodias's own security.

The mothers in Matthew act; they act independently, decisively and effectively. Even the apparent censure of Jesus' biological mother (12.46-50) serves to emphasize that, however scandalous their actions appear to be, the mothers in the new family act to accomplish the will of the father in heaven.

While there is little direct evidence to support any determination about the enfranchisement of women in the exercise of community authority, the actions of the mothers in Matthew, most clearly in the case of the Canaanite women, might be described as being authoritative. Further, the allocation of roles in the new family—brother, sister, mother—itself suggests that women may function more actively than is immediately apparent. They fill, after all, two of the three available family roles.

Matthew's Use of 'Father': Some Conclusions

From the above, we can see that the word πατήρ has special meaning for Matthew; it is virtually exclusively applied to the heavenly father. Matthew's community is defined by relationship to the heavenly father. Earthly fathers are completely displaced in favor of the heavenly father, but there remains a place for the mother in the new community. Care for the little ones of the community remains a compelling concern of the heavenly father, and becomes the filial duty of all related to the father through Jesus. The heavenly father's care and nurturing of little ones is of a maternal nature.

By virtue of the relationship with the heavenly father received through discipleship to Jesus, a new kinship group replaces the family of origin in Matthew's community, allowing for incorporation of those who are not related through common ancestors, i.e., Gentiles. Matthew thus redefines qualification for membership in the community of the faithful.

DISCHARGING RESPONSIBILITY: MATTHEAN JESUS,
BIBLICAL LAW, AND HEMORRHAGING WOMAN*

Amy-Jill Levine

Introduction

Scholarship on the Gospel of Matthew is presently in flux: debates rage over the social setting of Matthew's community (Galilee, Antioch, the Decapolis), its relation to the synagogue (*intra vs. extra muros*), and its connection to 'Judaism' (a deviant group, the new Israel, the true Israel, the 'new people of God', a *corpus mixtum*, a predominantly Gentile association). Nevertheless, at least two constructs have attained the status of consensus. First, Matthew reserves a central role for the Scriptures—the Prophets, the Psalms, and, especially, Mosaic Law. Second, Matthew offers new life for all who follow Jesus. The invitation extends to fishermen like Peter and John and to a rich, politically connected figure like Joseph of Arimathea. It goes as well to all those considered by modern scholarship to be marginal to or disenfranchised from the 'Jewish system': tax collectors, prostitutes, sinners, lepers, the diseased, the possessed, and, especially, women. Problems arise, however, when the two constructs are related, since the Gospel is explicit neither on how the Law is (to be) practiced nor on how the Matthean community views women. Consequently, not the evangelist but modern scholarship provides us the details of the Matthean practical Torah; not the evangelist but modern scholarship provides us the Matthean tractate on women.

The two issues—of the Law as practiced in Matthew's social world and of women's representation and role in Matthew's Gospel—come together inexorably in the scholarship on Mt. 9.18-26. The majority of commentators argue that this conjoined story of a bleeding woman

* Originally published in David R. Bauer and Mark Allan Powell (eds.), *Treasures New and Old: Recent Contributions to Matthean Studies* (Atlanta: Scholars Press, 1996), pp. 379-97. Reprinted by permission.

and a dead girl depicts two individuals marginalized in Jewish society because of both gender and purity regulations. Each character is first identified as marginal because she is female; further, the woman is categorized as 'unclean' because of what is assumed to be chronic uterine bleeding, and the girl is 'unclean' because she is dead (i.e., a corpse). In turn Jesus is depicted as overcoming the barriers Jewish society and Law erect between men and women, clean and unclean. By healing both women, he affirms what his Jewish social context denies: their humanity and worth; by touching them, he ignores and thereby dismisses purity codes. And, once the barriers between clean and unclean are abrogated, the way is open for the establishment of an egalitarian community.

This particular conjunction of women and purity relies on two major premises: that women were marginalized in Matthew's Jewish environment because of its interpretation of biblical Law, and that Jesus overcomes or even transgresses such legal concerns. As Marcus Borg puts it, Jesus substitutes a system of purity with a system of compassion.[1]

I think both premises are wrong. Indeed, I think they are dangerously wrong, and for several reasons: they rely on an interpretation of Matthew's Gospel that is not supported by the text itself, and thus they are bad exegeses; they rely on a construction of both early Judaism and of the Matthean community that cannot be well supported from either internal or external evidence, and thus they are bad history. They proclaim a supersessionist rather than a reformist perspective, and thus they are bad theology. Finally, by concentrating on ritual practices and a monolithic view of gender categories based on an artificial good/bad dichotomy, the premises and the readings they generate are in bad faith. Their narrow foci cause interpreters to underemphasize or even to miss major points of the pericope: that all involved in the action are Jews, and that no one 'violates' Jewish practice; that Jesus' 'following' the dead girl's father has implications for Matthew's view of discipleship; and that the bodies of women serve as figurations for Jesus' own body as it hangs on the cross and rises from the tomb.

---

1. Marcus Borg, *Jesus in Contemporary Scholarship* (Valley Forge, PA: Trinity Press International, 1994), p. 26 and elsewhere. Reconstructions of Jesus' own attitude toward the Law translate in the scholarship to Matthew's view. See the discussion of purity legislation in the works of Borg, N.T. Wright, and J.D. Crossan by Paula Fredriksen, 'Did Jesus Oppose the Purity Laws?', *BR* (1995), pp. 18-25, 42-47.

Bad Exegesis

Students of Christian origins are obsessed with Levitical purity legislation: it may well be that scholars worry more about such matters, particularly as they concern women, than did many Jewish women in the first century. In the same way that biblical commentators usually assert that Luke's 'Woman who was a sinner' must have been a prostitute (as if women could commit no sin other than one involving the body in general, and sexuality in particular), so too do they usually insist that if a woman has a medical problem, the problem must have something to do with 'female troubles'. And in all cases, Levitical concerns provide these diagnoses a cause.

Symptomatic of this approach is Elaine Wainwright's observation that Peter's mother-in-law, described as lying in bed and sick with a fever (Mt. 8.2-3, 5-7) 'is a possible pollutant especially if this sickness is connected to her time of ritual uncleanness'.[2] Thus general sickness bleeds over into menstrual issues. Wainwright continues: by touching the woman Jesus breaks open the boundaries defining 'clean' and 'unclean'. Her analysis of Mt. 9.20, where she describes Jesus as being 'touched by a menstruating woman',[3] makes similar claims. Donald Hagner observes that not only did the woman face 'the inconvenience [!] and physical danger of such regular loss of blood but also suffered the stigma of ritual uncleanness in that culture and consequent ostracism'.[4] Commenting on Mt. 8.2–9.35, David Garland asserts that Jesus 'discounts the demarcation of society along purity lines. He does not shun the impure and unholy. He touches a leper, a menstruant, and a corpse...the Kingdom of Heaven does not respect the boundaries of purity that the Pharisees and others use to categorize persons and places and to isolate them'.[5] Janice Capel Anderson invokes Lev. 15.25-33 in observing: 'The woman with the hemorrhage is ritually unclean'.[6] And, alas, in my own contribution to the *Women's Bible*

---

2. Elaine Wainwright, *Towards a Feminist Critical Reading of the Gospel According to Matthew* (BZNW, 60; Berlin: W. de Gruyter, 1991), p. 84, repeated in her 'The Gospel of Matthew', in E. Schüssler Fiorenza (ed.), *Searching the Scriptures. II. A Feminist Commentary* (New York: Crossroad, 1994), pp. 635-77 (648).
3. Wainwright, 'Gospel of Matthew', p. 637.
4. Donald Hagner, *Matthew 1–13* (WBC, 33a; Dallas, TX: Word Books, 1993), p. 248.
5. David Garland, *Reading Matthew: A Literary and Theological Commentary on the First Gospel* (New York: Crossroad, 1993), p. 107. Garland's association of 'impure' with 'unholy' is not uncommon.
6. Janice Capel Anderson, 'Matthew: Gender and Reading', *Semeia* 28 (1983), pp. 3-27 (11). [Article reprinted in this volume.]

Commentary, I followed Anderson.[7] Wainwright goes farther. Narrowing the intertext of Mt. 9.18-26 to Lev. 15.25-27, she proclaims:

> It is clear that this [hemorrhaging] debars the woman not only from participation in the religious community but from normal human social relations and especially from sexual relations with her husband. Her unavailability for sexual intercourse or fertility could well have produced a divorce and would certainly have prevented her from remarrying.[8]

Such New Testament scholarship almost invariably reinforces the claim that menstruants were ostracized within Jewish society by citing, in their discussion of Mt. 9.18-26, select Jewish (usually rabbinic) materials. The detailed New International Critical Commentary on Matthew by Davies and Allison, for example, notes 'other Jewish texts which involve restriction of and repugnance for menstruous women include Ezek. 36.17; CD 4.12-5.17; 11QTemple 48.15-17; Josephus, *Bell.* 5.227; *C. Ap.* 2.103-104; *m. Niddah*, passim, and *m. Zabim* 4.1'.[9] Wainwright evokes the Mishnaic tractate *Niddah* as operative at the time of Matthew and likely within Matthew's Jewish community.[10] Garland adds that the term *Niddah* means 'banished'.[11] And Davies and Allison even include such charming rabbinic suggestions for curing female discharges as fetching barley grain from the dung of a white mule and holding it for three days, or smearing oneself with 60 pieces of sealing clay.[12] Wainwright concludes that the '*inhuman* restrictions and suffering placed upon her by the Law [are] over and above the suffering due to her illness itself'.[13] Thus the Law and those who practice it are

---

7. Amy-Jill Levine, 'Matthew', in C.A. Newsom and S.H. Ringe (eds.), *The Women's Bible Commentary* (London: SPCK; Louisville, KY: Westminster/John Knox Press, 1992), pp. 256-57.

8. Wainwright, *Feminist Critical Reading*, p. 199, n. 52.

9. W.D. Davies and Dale C. Allison, Jr, *A Critical and Exegetical Commentary on the Gospel According to Matthew*. II. *VIII–XVIII* (ICC; Edinburgh: T. & T. Clark, 1991), p. 128.

10. Wainwright, *Feminist Critical Reading*, p. 199 n. 53.

11. Garland, *Reading Matthew*, p. 106. Garland is technically correct, but etymological origin and actual use are not necessarily equivalent. Thus Jacob Milgrom, *Leviticus I–XVI* (AB, 3; New York: Doubleday, 1991), pp. 744-45, claims that the scriptural use of *Niddah* is capable of three meanings: 'menstrual impurity'; 'impurity in general' or 'abomination'; and 'lustration'. Following etymological observations, he concludes that 'in the case of the menstruant, the word originally referred to the *discharge* or *elimination* of menstrual blood, which came to denote menstrual impurity and impurity in general'; emphasis original. Only later does it come to connect the menstruating woman with certain restrictions.

12. Davies and Allison, *Critical and Exegetical Commentary*, p. 128, citing *b. Šab.* 110a-b.

13. Wainwright, *Feminist Critical Reading*, p. 200; emphasis mine. Analyses of

74   *A Feminist Companion to Matthew*

not human; they are bestial or demonic. No wonder these poor women needed liberation: Leviticus is worse than death, and those who enforce it must be children of the devil.

Opposed to all this are Jesus and the Matthean church. For Davies and Allison, Mt. 9.18-26 'seems to offer a contrast. The woman with an issue is presented in a wholly positive light. The subject of her uncleanness is not mentioned or alluded to. Her touch does not effect indignation. Onlookers do not whisper that Jesus has come into contact with an unclean woman. All of this is surprising'.[14]

What is surprising is that such interpretations accompanied by such details attach to a pericope in which, as Davies and Allison observe, uncleanness is never mentioned. The commentators transform an absence of reference into a telling silence, and it is upon this silence that their arguments are based. Ironically, had they wished to draw a negative contrast between the church's view of women and that of its Jewish roots, they had the right story but the wrong part. The *Acts of Pilate* 7 records the following interchange at Jesus' trial: 'And a woman called Bernice crying out from a distance said, "I had an issue of blood and I touched the hem of his garment, and the issue of blood, which had lasted twelve years, ceased." The Jews said, "We have a law not to permit a woman to give testimony."'[15]

Surprising also are the pronouncements about the bleeding that the

the parallel pericopes of Mark and Luke are similar. Most recent, and expressed with his typically arresting phrasing, is J.D. Crossan's comment on Mk 5.22-43, 'Think about the theological implications of that intercalation, of a purity code in which menstruation is impure so that, from Mark's viewpoint, women start to die at twelve and are walking dead thereafter', in *Who Killed Jesus? Exposing the Roots of Anti-Semitism in the Gospel Story of the Death of Jesus* (San Francisco: HarperSanFrancisco, 1995), p. 101. See also Marla J. Selvidge, *Woman, Cult and Miracle Recital: A Redactional Critical Investigation of Mark 5:24-34* (Lewisburg, PA: Bucknell University Press, 1990), p. 83, which claims that the woman with the hemorrhage 'stands as a symbol for all Hebrew women [whose] biological differences prevented her...experiencing initiation rites, from serving in the sanctuary, and even from participating in the feasts'; and *idem*, 'Mark 5:24-34 and Leviticus 15:19-20: A Reaction to Restrictive Purity Regulations', *JBL* 103 (1984), pp. 619-23. Mary Rose D'Angelo, 'Gender and Power in the Gospel of Mark: The Daughter of Jairus and the Hemorrhaging Woman', a version of which was delivered in the Woman in the Biblical World section of the annual meetings of the AAR/SBL (November, 1994), corrects Selvidge's 'inappropriate generalization, extravagant rhetoric and naive or specious use of language' (p. 3). I thank Professor D'Angelo for permission to cite from her manuscript.

14. Davies and Allison, *Critical and Exegetical Commentary*, p. 128.
15. Citation from Ron Cameron, *The Other Gospels: Non-Canonical Gospel Texts* (Philadelphia: Westminster Press, 1982), p. 171.

secondary sources make. For example, Jesus is not touched by a menstruant *per se*, so already the scholarship has muddied analytical categories.[16] Nor is it clear that the woman's bleeding is vaginal, since Matthew says nothing about the location of the hemorrhage.[17] Matthew's expression, a participle derived from the compound verb αἱμορροέω, is otherwise unattested in the gospels. It is not the same term used in Mark's parallel pericope; there the expression is οὖσα ἐν ῥύσει αἵματος; Mk 5.25, cf. LXX to Lev. 15.19, 25; 20.18). Nor is it clear that Mark had Levitical legislation in mind. The Matthean term does appear in the LXX to Lev. 15.33, where it apparently translates דוה which means 'sickness' or 'infirmity' in the expression הדוה בנדתה: 'the infirmity of her menstrual impurity'. There are other types of infirmity, which is why Leviticus modifies the expression with בנדתה, 'of her menstrual flow'. Thus neither the Hebrew nor the Greek provides firm or even necessary indication that the flow is uterine or vaginal. If the woman had a sore on her leg, her breast, her nose, etc. — and all these places are possible given the semantic range of 'hemorrhage' — then while she would still be ill, she would not be impure.

What then comes first in Matthean scholarship: does one begin with the potentially anti-Jewish supposition that Jesus overcomes exceptionally restrictive Levitical purity legislation and therefore conclude that the bleeding is vaginal? Or does one begin with the potentially sexist presupposition that women's bodies are necessarily represented as sexual bodies and so that the bleeding must be vaginal — granting that there is Markan support for this — and therefore conclude that Jesus must be abrogating Levitical Law?

To this connection between impurity and sexuality, perhaps the intercalated story of the ruler's daughter can shed some light. The hemorrhaging woman may not have been bleeding vaginally, but it is

---

16. The connection of any sort of discharge to menstruation is not uncommon; it already appears in the Talmud, cf. *b. Nid.* 66a, and the comments in S.J.D. Cohen, 'Menstruants and the Sacred in Judaism and Christianity', in Sarah B. Pomeroy (ed.), *Women's History and Ancient History* (Chapel Hill: University of North Carolina Press, 1991), pp. 277-78. This innovative homologizing dates to the third century CE.

17. Davies and Allison, *Critical and Exegetical Commentary*, p. 128, are quite sanguine: 'A uterine hemorrhage is undoubtedly meant.' Ben Witherington III, *Women in the Ministry of Jesus: A Study of Jesus' Attitudes to Women and their Roles as Reflected in his Earthly Life* (SNTSMS, 51; Cambridge: Cambridge University Press, 1984), p. 175 n. 104, has 'probably a uterine hemorrhage, making the woman religiously unclean for the whole period'; cf. Hagner, *Matthew 1-13*, p. 248, on the hemorrhage as 'probably (though not necessarily) from the womb'.

certain that the ruler's daughter is dead. Matthew's ἄρτι ἐτελεύτησεν is much starker than Mark's 'close to death'. Wainwright represents the consensus on the intercalation: 'Both are female, both can be considered dead (one socially and religiously, the other physically), and both therefore have the capacity to contaminate life and hence need to be carefully controlled.'[18] The girl's father, who states, 'My daughter has just died; but come and lay your hand on her, and she will live' (9.18), consequently asks that Jesus place himself in a state of impurity.

The text, of course, says nothing about corpse uncleanness. To invoke Leviticus here would be as much of an overreading as to invoke it in an analysis of Mt. 8.21-22 (cf. Mk 4.35; Lk. 9.57-60). To the disciple who asked 'Lord, first let me go and bury my father', Jesus responds, 'Follow me, and let the dead bury their own dead' (Mt. 8.21-22). This is not an attempt to preserve the man from corpse contamination. Nor is touching a corpse 'wrong' or 'unholy' (although there are certain restrictions placed upon priests) as the book of Tobit in particular demonstrates; to bury a dead body is a commendable and important form of practical piety.

Some scholars even suggest that the father's request is anomalous in Jewish society not simply because it involves corpse uncleanness, but also because it is concerned with a mere daughter. Once again, Wainwright: 'The request is even more extraordinary when one realizes that the child is not a son, an heir needed for the continuation of the patriarchal family line, but rather a daughter, a young unmarried girl as the latter part of the story indicates (v. 25, *korasion*)'.[19]

The suggestion that the Jewish father would not care about his daughter is at best uncharitable. By analogy, one might similarly cite Mt. 10.35-36 and conclude that Jesus is against parent-child relationships since his message establishes enmity between son and father, daughter and mother, 'members of one's own household'. But as with the above reference to Mt. 8.21-22, such a citation in such a context would be inappropriate and inaccurate. Rather, Matthew directly suggests that the audience of the Gospel would expect parents to care for their children, of both genders. Otherwise, the comment in 10.37b, 'Whoever loves son or *daughter* more than me is not worthy of me', would have no impact.

18. Wainwright, *Feminist Critical Reading*, p. 199, citing Num. 19.11-13 on corpse uncleanness and Lev. 15.31, which she claims in n. 53 'links uncleanness to death'. The text actually states: 'Thus you shall keep the people of Israel separate from their uncleanness, so that they do not die in their uncleanness by defiling my tabernacle that is in their midst.'

19. Wainwright, *Feminist Critical Reading*, p. 87.

The various contextualizations of Mt. 9.18-26 in terms of purity and patriarchy are possible, but they are by no means necessary. They are supported by no internal textual clues; they are premised on overdrawn stereotypes of Judaism and women. They also fail to engage Matthew's own apparent preservation of the Law from which 'not one jot or tittle' will pass away (5.18). Matthew does not abrogate the laws of physical purity any more than the dietary regulations. The woman is healed of her sickness; the girl is raised from the dead. The point is that those who were sick and dead are now alive and healthy, not that Jewish practices have been transgressed or overcome.

Actually, the best intertexts for the raising of the dead girl are other cases where corpses are resuscitated. For example, the raising of the girl evokes the actions of Elijah (1 Kgs 17.17-24) and Elisha (2 Kgs 4.32-37), and so continues Matthew's interest in appropriating scriptural models. Thus the pericope locates Jesus within Jewish tradition without undermining the Law in any way or, indeed, even here evoking it. More, the raising fulfills the response to John's disciples, 'the dead are raised' (11.5), and thus it points to Jesus' messianic identity.

Bad History

Even if the hemorrhage were uterine, the readings of social ostracism occasioned by Levitical legislation and cultural codes are themselves overstated. Leviticus 15.19-33 states:

> When a woman has a discharge, her discharge being blood from her body, she remains in her menstrual impurity seven days; every one who touches her shall be [ritually] unclean until the evening... If a man lies with her, her menstrual impurity will be on him, and he shall be [ritually] unclean seven days, and any bed on which he lies shall be [ritually] unclean. If a woman has a discharge of blood for many days, not at the time of her menstrual impurity, or if she has a discharge beyond the time of her menstrual impurity, all the days of the discharge she shall be [ritually] unclean; as in the days of her menstrual impurity, she shall be [ritually] unclean. Any bed on which she lies during all the days of her discharge shall be for her as the bed of her menstrual impurity, and anything on which she sits shall be [ritually] unclean, as in the [ritual] uncleanness of her menstrual impurity. And anyone who touches them shall be [ritually] unclean and shall wash his clothes, and bathe in water, and be [ritually] unclean until the evening...

There is nothing here to prevent this woman from participating in 'normal human social relations'. She is not inhumanly restricted or socially ostracized. There is no prohibition against her touching anyone. Indeed, the concern in the Law for her bedding and anything on which she sits 'can only mean that in fact her hands do not transmit impurity... The consequence is that she is not banished but remains at home. Neither is she isolated from her family'.[20] Even the Talmud states that a menstruating woman may attend to all of her family's needs, with the exceptions of filling her husband's cup of wine, making his bed, and washing him (*b. Ket.* 61a).[21] Neither is it clear that she is unavailable for sexual intercourse, as the phrase 'If any man lies with her' indicates, although Lev. 18.19 and 20.18 do suggest that there is divine punishment for both partners if they have intercourse while the woman is in a state of impurity. Here one might cite, albeit tentatively, *b. B. Meṣ.* 83b-85a, especially on Rabbi Eliazar's giving permission for marital intercourse to 60 women who have had a flux that may or may not be menstrual.[22]

Uncleanness is not a disease, and it implies no moral censure; it is a ritual state in which both men and women likely found themselves most of the time.[23] There are no laws obliging those who come into contact with a *Niddah*, or a corpse, etc., to appear before a court. Indeed, like the man who has a genital discharge, the woman is responsible for her own activities. As Jacob Milgrom observes, 'The absence of the priest from the diagnosis and his confinement to the sanctuary to officiate at the sacrifices (vv 13-15, 28-30) confirm the fact that the diagnosis of genital discharges is left entirely to the skill and honesty of the affected person'.[24]

The consequence of such cultic uncleanness primarily involves restriction from the Temple precincts. But there was little if any reason for most people to go to the Temple. Moreover, Matthew—like

---

20. Milgrom, *Leviticus I-XVI*, p. 936. The principal text on which such a conclusion concerning complete isolation could be connected is Num. 5.1-14, in which the leper, the זבה or זב (one experiencing a discharge from, respectively, vagina or penis), and anyone who has come in contact with a corpse are to be removed from the camp. Nevertheless, as Cohen observes, 'If this law were enforced, the number of Israelites outside the camp would rival the number of those within'. See his 'Menstruants and the Sacred', p. 276.

21. For discussion, cf. Milgrom, *Leviticus I-XVI*, p. 949.

22. See discussion, and well-taken warnings concerning rabbinic control over female sexuality, in Daniel Boyarin, *Carnal Israel: Reading Sex in Talmudic Culture* (Berkeley: University of California Press, 1993), pp. 204-205.

23. Paula Fredriksen, *From Jesus to Christ* (New Haven: Yale University Press, 1988), p. 106 n. 14. See also E.P. Sanders, *Jesus and Judaism* (Philadelphia: Fortress Press, 1985), pp. 182-83.

24. Milgrom, *Leviticus I-XVI*, pp. 905-906. Then again, self-policing can also be a form of social oppression, here fully internalized. This observation applies also to the *bet hatum'ot* discussed below, n. 27.

Mark—locates the woman not in Jerusalem but in Galilee. The immediate geographical reference is 9.1: 'He crossed the sea and came to his own town'. Any concern for the purity required by the Temple's holiness is therefore mitigated.[25] Finally, Matthew is apparently writing after the Temple's destruction.

More difficult to evaluate is the practice of such ritual concerns among the Jews in Matthew's own community. The Pharisees may well have been engaged in directing the practices of Temple purity to the home, such that the household table mirrors the Temple altar, and those at the Table eat with the same status as the priests serving in Jerusalem. Thus the Pharisees would be particularly concerned that their food be properly tithed, and that they not be in states of ritual impurity. Particularly in the land of Israel, after the destruction of the Temple, there may well have been increasing attention paid to matters of cultic impurity as they related to daily life. Yet even for Matthew, the Pharisees do not concern themselves with the woman's so-called impurity (as Davies and Allison note). Nor would Pharisaic men always be in ritually pure states. Leviticus 15.10 states that 'If a man lies with a woman and he has an emission of semen, both of them shall bathe in water, and be unclean until the evening' (Lev. 15.18). Yet 'Be fruitful and multiply'—a command also in the Pharisaic purview—requires precisely that a man lie with a woman and have an emission of semen. Pharisaic men, like all men, were subject to their genital discharges, and these would have put them in a state of impurity.

Although the majority of the biblical laws concerning the exclusion of women because of menstruation and vaginal discharges are directly related to the Temple and the system of purity which surrounds it, one—Lev. 18.19 and 20.18, the prohibition against 'drawing near' to a menstruant for sexual intercourse—does not. Therefore, 'Even when the purity system would lapse after the destruction of the second temple in 70 CE, the prohibition of union with a menstruant would

---

25. See also D'Angelo, 'Gender and Power', p. 11. S.J.D. Cohen observes that from the mid-second century BCE until the destruction of the Second Temple, various Jewish groups extended the sanctity of the Temple to their daily lives. However, he also avers that this practice 'had only a minimal impact on the Jews at large, who continued to regard the Temple as the single locus of sanctity and the sole place that demanded ritual purity of its entrants'. See his 'Purity and Piety: The Separation of Menstruants from the Sancta', in S. Groomsman and R. Haute (eds.), *Daughters of the King/Woman and the Synagogue: A Survey of History and Contemporary Realities* (Philadelphia: Jewish Publication Society, 1992), pp. 103-115 (106).

remain'.²⁶ Consequently, these laws might be seen as relevant to the interpretation of Matthew's hemorrhaging woman, if she is seen as having a vaginal discharge in the first place.

Yet even here we cannot conclude that the social implications of the laws concerning such a woman were enforced. There is no unambiguous evidence from the Mishnah, Josephus, the Gospels, etc. that Jewish groups in Hellenistic and Early Roman times removed the menstruant or one suffering from abnormal vaginal or uterine bleeding from social contact.²⁷ Such a person was not even barred from religious activities, according to the early Rabbinic view. While the Mishnah prohibits an ejaculant from reciting aloud various benedictions, no parallel restrictions accrue to the lepers, those who have touched a corpse, a menstruant, or even men and women with abnormal discharges. The Tosefta, *Ber.* 2.12, reads: 'Men who have an abnormal sexual discharge (זבים), women who have an abnormal sexual discharge (זבות), menstruants, and parturients are permitted to read the Torah, and to study Mishnah, Midrash, laws, and homilies. But the ejaculant is prohibited from all these'.²⁸ Boyarin remarks on *b. Ber.* 22a, which reads, 'Gonnorheics and lepers and *those who have had*

---

26. See Cohen, 'Menstruants and the Sacred', p. 276.
27. Cohen, 'Menstruants and the Sacred', p. 278. Cohen observes (pp. 278-79) that 'Possible evidence for the social isolation of the menstruant in the real world comes from a stray phrase in the Mishna [*bet hatum'ot* or *bet hateme'ot* in *Niddah* 7.4] and from the later practices of the Samaritans and the black Jews of Ethiopia, but this evidence is ambiguous and uncertain'. Citing the same Mishnaic passage, Milgrom, *Leviticus I–XVI*, p. 949, is unhesitant in asserting that the menstruant in the land of Israel was 'quarantined in a special house'. Cohen appears to be correct: it is unclear whether the Mishnah concerns actual quarantine or simply a place menstruating women frequent. Even if the women are not quarantined, they might choose to use such a place so as not to render their usual furniture unclean by sitting on it. The Babylonian Gemara says nothing about the passage. Yerushalmi covers only the first four chapters of *m. Nid.* See also Milgrom's discussion of Josephus, *Ant.* 3.261 and several Qumran scrolls on the possible isolation within the community (rather than banishment) of menstruants. Milgrom nevertheless concludes that the 'lenient' rulings in the Babylonian Talmud are those consistent with Levitical legislation (p. 949).
28. Cited in Cohen, 'Purity and Piety', p. 107. Cohen adds that while the Jerusalem Talmud follows the Tosefta, *b. Ber.* 22a has been adapted to conform to the later view that menstruants are not permitted to read Torah. The *Bavli* also omits *zabot* and parturients, and substitutes 'men who have intercourse with menstruants', for 'menstruants'. See Cohen, 'Purity and Piety', p. 114 n. 8, as well as Cohen's 'Menstruants and the Sacred', pp. 283-84, where he concludes (p. 284) that 'neither Talmud raises any obstacle before a menstruant who wishes to pray, study Torah, or recite benedictions'.

intercourse with menstruants are permitted to study Torah, but men who have had a seminal emission may not'.[29] And thus, as Shaye Cohen concludes, the 'Gospel story about the woman with a twelve-year discharge, clearly a case of זבה, does not give any indication that the woman was impure or suffered any degree of isolation as a result of her affliction (Mt. 9.18-26; Mk 5.21-43; Lk. 8.40-56)'.[30]

Finally, before we leave the Mishnah, we need to diagnose one other stain on the surface of the secondary sources. Davies and Allison also appeal to *m. Zab.* 5.1, 6 to indicate, correctly, that for the Tannaim the impurity of a menstruant can be transmitted through touch.[31] Whether Matthew followed Mishnaic rather than biblical rulings is an inevitable question; the Gospel itself provides no help concerning this specific pronouncement. What Davies and Allison do not mention, however, is that almost the entire Mishnaic tractate is dedicated to male discharges. These, too, are not mentioned explicitly in the Gospel of Matthew, yet surprisingly enough scholars have not attempted to read these into Jesus' contacts with men in various states of despair. If Peter's mother-in-law was in her 'state of monthly uncleanness', then it seems likely that there would have been זבים — men in states of Levitical impurity because of discharges — among all those who were sick and afflicted with various diseases and pains (4.24) whom Jesus healed. Oddly enough, this possibility has not been raised.[32]

To be sure, the rabbinic sources do contain much that is oppressive concerning female sexuality and women's bodies in general, as well as vaginal bleeding and menstruation in particular. Nevertheless, the majority of Gospel commentators neither present a balanced treatment of these sources nor engage in detail the problems of their dating and their relevance for Matthew or Jesus. A late Talmudic gloss is given as much historical weight as an earlier Mishnaic pronouncement, and both are retrojected back to the first century.[33] The rabbinic sources

---

29. Boyarin, *Carnal Israel*, p. 180 and discussion, pp. 180-81; emphasis his.

30. Cohen, 'Purity and Piety', p. 279, although as noted above, I question whether the Matthean woman is even a זבה.

31. Davies and Allison, *Critical and Exegetical Commentary*, p. 128.

32. Cohen, 'Menstruants and the Sacred', p. 276, observes that 'the biblical record as a whole shows much greater concern over the potential desecration of the sacred by an ejaculant than by a menstruant'.

33. Dating is often flagged as a problem, and then the Mishnah is cited anyway. Nor do the secondary sources do much in terms of distinguishing general concerns from specific laws. Cf. Wainwright, *Feminist Critical Reading*, p. 199 n. 53 on *m. Ohol.*, concerning corpse uncleanness and *m. Ned.* on menstruants, 'both of which belong to the Order of Purities of which Neusner claims that "the

then are seen as reflecting the practices of Matthew's Jewish social world (regardless of the setting of the Gospel, its Greek concerns, its particular form of 'Judaism', etc.).

Moreover, the citation of Jewish sources that postdate the time of Jesus should be balanced by some discussion of contemporaneous Christian and pagan viewpoints. The gap in citation leads to the conclusion that Jews were the primary if not the only people in antiquity concerned with female discharges. As D'Angelo observes, 'It is frequently assumed among interpreters of the NT, both scholarly and popular, that Purity is a Jewish concern of no real interest to either the Greeks or Romans'.[34] Missing in most scholarship on the Gospels and menstruation are citations from, for example, Isidore of Seville, who records in his *Etimologias* 11.1.141 that menstrual blood causes fruits not to germinate, wine to sour, plants to parch, trees to lose their fruit, iron to be corroded, bronze to turn black, and dogs to become rabid if they eat anything that has come into contact with it.[35] Omitted are the restrictions placed upon menstruants by ecclesiastics such as Hippolytus and Dionysius of Alexandria.[36]

Bad Theology

There is no indication in Matthew's account of the hemorrhaging woman and the dead girl that Jesus transgresses any sort of purity legislation and therefore that he breaks with Jewish tradition. To the contrary, both the placement and the content of the pericope reinforce

---

principal and generative ideas of the system as a whole are to be located at its very beginning, some time before the turn of the first century"' (*Method and Meaning*, p. 121 n. 22).

34. D'Angelo, 'Gender and Power', p. 4, citing as an example L. William Countryman, *Dirt Greed and Sex: Sexual Ethics in the New Testament and Their Implications for Today* (Philadelphia: Fortress Press, 1988), who treats purity as, in her words, a 'Jewish preoccupation'. D'Angelo provides the details of ancient Greek and Roman purity regulations, which are quite similar to those of Leviticus in their concern for the holiness of sanctuaries and for appropriate sexual intercourse. Ironically, as n. 35 below indicates, the church Fathers on occasion followed classical sources on the question of vaginal bleeding.

35. Isodore is apparently following Pliny's *Natural History* 7.15.64.

36. Hippolytus's *Apostolic Tradition* bars a catechumen from baptism should she be menstruating; Dionysius says the menstruant 'would not dare in such a condition either to approach the holy table or touch the body and blood of Christ. For even the woman who had the twelve-year discharge and was eager for a cure touched not him but only his fringe'. Citations from Cohen, 'Menstruants and the Sacred', p. 288. See also his discussion (p. 289) of the *Didascalia*.

the Matthean Jesus' conformity to the Law. Mt. 9.18-26 appears in the narrative portion of the Gospel that extends from 8.1 to 9.38. This section of the Gospel begins with an insistence on the Law: Jesus heals a leper and commands him: 'see that you say nothing to anyone, but go, show yourself to the priest, and offer the gift that Moses commanded, as a testimony to them' (Mt. 8.4).

Interest in practicing the Law reappears in the details of the pericope under discussion. In the account of the woman with the hemorrhage, Jesus does not touch the woman. Rather, she comes up from behind and touches him. Specifically, she touches τοῦ κρασπέδου τοῦ ἱματίου (Mt. 9.20; cf. Lk. 8.44), his ציצית or fringes, those fringes Jewish men wore in compliance with Num. 15.38-41, and Deut. 22.12. Matthew brings together the ציצית and healing again in 14.34-36, 'When they had crossed over, they came to the land of Gennesaret. After the people of that place recognized him, they sent word throughout the region and brought all who were sick to him, and begged him that they might touch even the fringe of his cloak; all who touched it were healed' (cf. Mk 6.56). These fringes might then be related to those of the Pharisees and Scribes (cf. Mt. 23.5), where the term is used in connection with ostentatious practices.

What tale then do these tassels tell? For Wainwright, the ציצית do not have a relation to 'ritual requirement connected to Mitzvot as is found in the Torah but rather is used in a worship context (Zech. 8.20-22) and it is the Gentiles...who take hold of the robe of a Jew...'[37] The Hebrew in Zechariah is כנף not ציצית, although the LXX does read κρασπέδου. She goes on, 'Well may the original storyteller have used this same phrase for the action of the woman whose illness rendered her an outsider...'[38] Yet there is no fulfilment citation to Zechariah here, and there is no indication that the woman is a Gentile or an 'outsider' because of her illness. In addition, given that Mt. 23.5 explicitly uses the term κράσπεδα in relation to ritual requirements, and given that Matthew does insist that the Law will not pass away, we can at the very least see both the legal and the prophetic interpretations as woven into Jesus' clothing.[39]

---

37. Wainwright, *Feminist Critical Reading*, p. 201. J.T. Cummings, 'The Tassel of His Cloak: Mark, Luke, Matthew—and Zechariah', in E.A. Livingston (ed.), *Studia Biblica 1978*. II. *Papers on the Gospels* (JSNTSup, 2; Sheffield: JSOT Press, 1980), pp. 41-61 (51-52), also proposes a connection to Zech. 8.23.

38. Wainwright, *Feminist Critical Reading*, p. 201.

39. Geza Vermes, *The Religion of Jesus the Jew* (Minneapolis: Fortress Press, 1993), p. 16 n. 6, recounts the following anecdote: 'The children requesting the charismatic miracle-worker Hanan, grandson of Honi the circle-drawer, to end a

Matthew's intercalated story does not present Jesus as abrogating the Law or as coming into contact with individuals marginalized because of gender or ritual impurity. This pericope rather emphasizes Jesus' conformity to the Law and his concern for healing those who seek his power.

Healthy Readings

To concentrate on Levitical impurity, a point not mentioned by the text, detracts from what is mentioned. First, only here does Jesus 'follow' (ἀκολουθεῖν) another person;[40] in the rest of the Gospel, individuals and crowds follow Jesus. Since the term has connotations of discipleship for Matthew,[41] the pericope opens to the concerns of appropriate action. Second, the conjoined stories speak of bleeding and death followed by healing and resurrection; these motifs offer proleptic indicators of Jesus' own fate.

That Jesus 'follows' is clear, but the implications of the term are not. It may well lack any technical indication in Mt. 9.19. Kingsbury correctly argues that ἀκολουθεῖν can simply 'signify accompaniment in the literal sense of the word', and he points to Mt. 9.19 as the best example of this nontechnical use: 'Now if Matthew had regarded *Akolouthein* exclusively as a *terminus technicus* connoting discipleship, obviously he could not have written these words, for he would thereby have made Jesus the disciple of the ruler.'[42]

Nevertheless, the technical use of the term elsewhere encourages speculation about its import when ascribed to Jesus. At least two possible readings of 'to follow' in 9.19 conform to themes located elsewhere in the Gospel: the reversal of status indicators and the proper

---

drought, seized the fringe of his mantle *(shippule gemileh)* and cried, "Abba, Abba, give us rain!" *(b. Ta'an.* 23b). A rabbinic anecdote preserved in the Tannaitic midrash *Sifre* on Numbers ... and in the Talmud *(b. Men.* 44a), recounts how a young Jew, getting ready to go to bed with a beautiful high-class prostitute, was prevented from sinning by the miraculous intervention of the tassels on his garment'. In neither case is Zechariah relevant, but each case individually matches the Matthean story: the first anecdote suggests the connection between imploring and the tassels; the second suggests that the culture attributed magical power to the tassels.

40. As pointed out by Matthew Collins, whose insights into this section of the pericope contributed substantially to the following discussion.

41. Jack Dean Kingsbury, 'The Verb *Akolouthein* ("To Follow") as an Index of Matthew's View of his Community', *JBL* 97 (1978), pp. 56-73.

42. Kingsbury, '*Akolouthein*', p. 58.

use of authority, and Jesus as a model of discipleship. Particularly when read in the context of the other individuals with authority found described in Matthew's Gospel, the ruler of Mt. 9 emerges as an exemplar of discipleship as well as of church leadership. He would therefore be an appropriate person for members of Matthew's church to follow. Jesus already provides the model for the disciples in terms of healing, teaching, and suffering; he may here provide the model for following, which is something 'leaders' in the Matthean community must also do.

The ruler of ch. 9 finds a helpful comparison in the centurion of ch. 8. In both cases, Matthew presents a person in a position of authority who in turn places himself under the authority of Jesus. The centurion appeals to Jesus and expresses his humility by stating 'I am not worthy to have you come under my roof' (8.9). The ruler 'kneels' (προσκυνέω, with connotations of worshiping) before Jesus and expresses faith in his ability not simply to heal but to raise from the dead. Both men, identified not by names but only by titles that convey power,[43] are powerless to accomplish what they most want. Both implore Jesus to heal a younger and weaker person who cannot make a personal supplication. Both are rewarded. The two accounts thus present the proper use of authority: a ruler or leader must be humble, must recognize the limitations of earthly authority, must make the effort to seek the sacred, must appeal on behalf of others.

Contrasted to the ruler and the centurion are other people in positions of authority. The Gentile centurion finds his opposite in the Gentile Pilate and his soldiers, who use their authority to harm rather than to help. More striking, the Jewish 'ruler' — and he is Jewish, since Matthew makes clear when characters are Gentile both through specific identification and through Jesus' hesitation to enter their homes or perform cures on their behalf[44] — may be compared to the other two 'Jewish' rulers of the Gospel: Herod the Great and his son, Herod Antipas.

Herod the Great does not seek the life of a child; he seeks the death of the 'child who has been born king of the Jews' (2.2). In his search, he causes the deaths of others. This Jewish ruler leaves only Rachel,

43. Contrast the parallels in both Mark and Luke, where the girl's father is named Jairus, and where he is identified as a 'synagogue' ruler.

44. Reading 8.7 as a question; comparing Mt. 15.21-28 to the parallel in Mk 7.31-37; noting 10.5b-6 and 15.24, etc. See Amy-Jill Levine, *The Social and Ethnic Dimensions of Matthean Salvation History: "Go Nowhere Among the Gentiles..." (Matt. 10:5b)* (Studies in the Bible and Early Christianity, 14; Lewiston, NY: Edwin Mellen Press, 1988).

'weeping for her children...because they are no more' (2.18). Complacent, entrenched in Jerusalem with his courtiers, removed from Jesus, he is a direct contrast to the 'ruler' of ch. 9: active, in Galilee, unaccompanied, appearing at Jesus' feet.[45]

More closely related to the ἄρχων of Mt. 9 is the depiction of Herod Antipas. Once again, a Jewish ruler is presented in relation to a child, and here the parallels are more extensive: both Mt. 9.18-26 and Mt. 14.1-12 depict rulers who cannot exercise their power (the ruler of Mt. 9 cannot raise his daughter; Herod Antipas cannot retract his oaths or disappoint his guests); a young girl associated with death (κοράσιον: 9.24-25; 14.11); a concern for resurrection (9.25; 14.2); a woman who interrupts the story (the woman with the hemorrhage, Herodias); music (from the flute players of ch. 9 to the dance in ch. 14); and a story that becomes well known. Yet the ἄρχων's story ends with life restored while Herod Antipas's account ends with the beheading of John and the burying of his corpse.

These contrasts do much more than show Matthew's literary artistry. They indicate that the good and the bad, the saved and the damned, are not categorized according to social status, gender, or ethnic group. Leaders as well as followers may find themselves in the ἐκκλησία of disciples, provided those leaders appropriately perform their duty to serve others. Jews as well as Gentiles are welcome in the Matthean church, as are men and women. The issue is not who one is; the point for Matthew is what one does.

The ruler of Mt. 9 acts appropriately. It is therefore entirely fitting that Jesus, as a model for disciples as well as rulers, should follow such a leader. With some generosity, one can even locate the ruler's

---

45. Almost all commentators note that the children killed in Bethlehem were boys. This view is based on the parallels in the Matthean infancy account to Exod. 1-2 and the notion that Herod would not fear a female rival or expect a female messiah. However, the terms used for the children who are slaughtered are παῖδας in 2.16 and τέκνα in 2.18. Both might include girls. Such a general reading (cf. the English 'children') has much to commend it: it heightens the crime of which Herod and his soldiers are guilty, it fits in terms of verisimilitude the outrages of military brutality (i.e. if the soldiers will not take the time to distinguish between a newborn and a two-year old, why would they take the time to distinguish girls from boys?), it conforms to Matthew's interest in women in general from the genealogy to the tomb as well as in particular to daughters, and it helps to explain both the shift from the LXX (Jer. 38.15, cf. MT Jer. 31.15), which reads τοῖς υἱοῖς αὐτῆς, 'for her sons' and Matthew's addition of πολύς, 'much' in 2.18. If the dead children are to be seen as including daughters, then the connection of Herod the Great to the ruler of Mt. 9 is increased. My thanks to Alicia Erickson for suggesting the inclusive interpretation for the murdered children.

request as mirroring the technical aspects of the term ἀκολούθειν. According to Kingsbury, 'following' has the connotations of discipleship when it involves personal commitment (one follows if one is summoned directly by Jesus) and cost (there is some personal sacrifice involved).[46] The pericope in question actually has both concerns: here Jesus is summoned by the ἄρχων, and to comply with the ruler's demands, he must interrupt his missionary preaching.

Jesus therefore serves several functions in this pericope: he is both the miracle worker who recognizes the faith of those in need, and he is the exemplar who shows both by his healing and by his willingness to follow how other disciples are to behave. He is a ruler who can command the flute players and mourners to depart; he is a servant who can follow and acquiesce to a request when appropriate. More, Jesus shares much in common with both the woman and the child: his physicality is reflected in the depictions of their bodies. The woman suffers, she bleeds, she acts in humility by coming up behind Jesus, she retains her faith but she does not speak. Jesus too will suffer, will bleed, will act in humility, will remain silent and yet retain his faith. Like the ruler's daughter, Jesus is a ruler's son. At the time of his death, he will be surrounded by a commotion, by people who laugh at or mock him. Like the girl, he will die. And, like the girl, he also will be raised from the dead. And the report of this resurrection too will 'spread throughout that district'.

Women's bodies thus provide a model for the body of the Christ; women's suffering provides the model for the suffering of the Christ, and women's healing provides the model for the resurrection of the Christ. Matthew makes a christological point not through negative contrast or devaluation of the Law, not through anti-Jewish pronouncements nor through appeals to marginalization or 'female problems'. The pericope depicts the healing of bodies from ailments that could affect anyone—bleeding and death—ailments that affect even the Christ. These are women's issues, yes, as are the diseases of sexism and anti-Semitism. But even more, they are human issues. Would that all such issues be discharged, and that the report of this healing be spread throughout the land.[47]

---

46. Kingsbury, 'Akolouthein', p. 58.
47. My gratitude to Mary Rose D'Angelo and Shaye J.D. Cohen for providing copies of their articles, and to Matthew Collins, Kathleen Corley, Jay Geller, Nicole Kirk, and Adele Reinhartz for suggestions and criticisms.

JESUS AS WISDOM:
A FEMINIST READING OF MATTHEW'S WISDOM CHRISTOLOGY

Celia Deutsch

Introduction

In recent years, scholars have begun to explore New Testament Wisdom Christology as well as the early biblical and Jewish development of the metaphor of Lady Wisdom in light of feminist issues and questions of gender.[1] Some would attribute Wisdom speculation a positive valence in relation to women's experience, status, and roles.[2] Others believe that use of the metaphor may actually have had deleterious results for women.[3]

---

1. E.g. S. Cady, M. Ronan and H. Taussig, *Sophia: The Future of Feminist Spirituality* (San Francisco: Harper & Row, 1986), pp. 16-75; eadem, *Wisdom's Feast: Sophia in Study and Celebration* (San Francisco, CA: Harper & Row, 1989); C. Camp, *Wisdom and the Feminine in the Book of Proverbs* (Bible and Literature, 11; Sheffield: Almond Press, 1985); eadem, 'The Female Sage in Ancient Israel and in the Biblical Wisdom Literature', in J.G. Gammie and Leo G. Perdue (eds.), *The Sage in Israel and the Ancient Near East* (Winona Lake, IN: Eisenbrauns, 1990), pp. 185-203; J.C. Engelsman, *The Feminine Dimension of the Divine* (Philadelphia: Westminster Press, 1979), pp. 74-120; T. Frymer-Kensky, *In the Wake of the Goddesses: Women, Culture and the Biblical Transformation of Pagan Myth* (New York: Free Press, 1992), pp. 179-83; A.-J. Levine, 'Who's Catering the Q Affair? Feminist Observations on Q Paraenesis', *Semeia* 50 (1990), pp. 145-61; C. Mulack, *In Anfang war die Weisheit: feministische Kritik des männlichen Gottesbildes* (Stuttgart: Kreuz Verlag, 1988); B. Newman, 'The Pilgrimage of Christ-Sophia', *Vox Benedictina* 9 (1992), pp. 9-18; C. Newsom, 'Woman and the Discourse of Patriarchal Wisdom: A Study of Proverbs 1-9', in P. Day (ed.), *Gender and Difference in Ancient Israel* (Minneapolis: Fortress Press, 1989), pp. 142-60; E. Schüssler Fiorenza, *In Memory of Her: A Feminist Theological Reconstruction of Christian Origins* (New York: Crossroad, 1985), pp. 130-40; eadem, *Jesus: Miriam's Child, Sophia's Prophet: Critical Issues in Feminist Christology* (New York: Continuum, 1994).

2. E.g. Camp, *Wisdom and the Feminine*; Fiorenza, *In Memory of Her*, pp. 130-40; idem, *Jesus*, pp. 131-62; Engelsman, *Feminine Dimension*, pp. 74-120; E. Wainwright, *Shall We Look For Another? A Feminist Rereading of the Matthean Jesus* (Maryknoll, NY: Orbis Books, 1998), pp. 66-83.

3. E.g. Frymer-Kensky, *In the Wake*, pp. 179-83; Levine, 'Who's Catering',

While much of this discussion has been of a general nature, there has also been more extended analysis of specific texts.[4] I would like to join the conversation by addressing the issue of *Matthew's* use of the metaphor of Lady Wisdom in the context of gender and social structure.[5] I will demonstrate the ways in which Matthew heightens the identification, found in his sources, of a female metaphor with an historical, if exalted, male figure. And I will suggest that Matthew's use of that metaphor does not necessarily reflect women's religious experience or enhance their roles within the community; rather, his use of the Wisdom metaphor occurs within the context of a male scribal group and legitimates the status of those participating in that group.[6]

Metaphor and Lady Wisdom

I believe that the most helpful way of studying Matthew's use of Lady Wisdom is to consider the latter as a metaphor.[7] Understanding the metaphorical process, particularly in reference to social context, will allow us to understand why and how Matthew came to identify Wisdom with Jesus.

Metaphor is a function of speech in which two terms that are usually separate are brought together. That process is *interactive*.[8] That is, both

---

p. 155. Wainwright acknowledges the possibility of such negative effects; see *Shall We Look*, p. 68.

4. E.g. Camp, *Wisdom and the Feminine*; Levine, 'Who's Catering'; Newsom, 'Woman and the Discourse'.

5. A minority would argue that Matthew does not present Jesus as Wisdom, e.g. F.T. Gench, *Wisdom in the Christology of Matthew* (Lanham, MD: University Press of America, 1997); M.D. Johnson, 'Reflections on a Wisdom Approach to Matthew's Christology', *CBQ* 36 (1974), pp. 44-64; D. Orton, *The Understanding Scribe: Matthew and the Apocalyptic Ideal* (JSNTSup, 25; Sheffield: JSOT Press, 1989), pp. 154, 235 n. 42. For the majority view, see M.J. Suggs, *Wisdom, Christology and Law in Matthew's Gospel* (Cambridge, MA: Harvard University Press, 1970); and my own *Hidden Wisdom and the Easy Yoke: Wisdom, Torah and Discipleship in Mt 11.25-30* (JSNTSup, 18; Sheffield: Sheffield Academic Press, 1987); *eadem*, 'Wisdom in Matthew: Transformation of a Symbol', *NovT* 32 (1990), pp. 13-47.

6. I discuss these questions at greater length in *Lady Wisdom, Jesus, and the Sages: Metaphor and Social Context in Matthew's Gospel* (Valley Forge, PA: Trinity Press International, 1996). Elaine Wainwright examines Mt. 11.2-30 in light of questions of gender and social context in *Shall We Look*, pp. 67-83.

7. On personified Wisdom as metaphor, see Camp, *Wisdom and the Feminine*, pp. 70-77; on metaphor and Matthew's use of personified Wisdom, see my *Lady Wisdom*; Wainwright, *Shall We Look*, pp. 26-28.

8. M. Black, *Models and Metaphors* (Ithaca, NY: Cornell University Press, 1962),

terms of the metaphor—tenor (the content, the less familiar) and vehicle (the more familiar)—acquire new meaning. And metaphor allows one to 'say what cannot be said of literal meanings alone',[9] as tenor and vehicle acquire new significance.[10] Moreover, not only the individual words, but whole ranges of meaning and feeling come together and mutually inform each other. In our case, the bringing together of 'Lady' (or Woman) and 'Wisdom' creates a semantic context in which both terms acquire new meanings. With this linguistic move, 'Lady' tells us something about the nature of wisdom and 'Wisdom' tells us something about the nature of lady.

'Lady Wisdom' is a personification, a kind of metaphor which gives 'the attributes of a human being to an animal, an object, or a concept'.[11] Sometimes, in mythopoeic thought, the metaphorical process of personification extends to the point where the metaphor acquires the quality of personal entity: it becomes a quasi-independent being. In that instance we speak of 'hypostasis', which is a concretization of a divinity's attributes.[12] In our case, God's wisdom becomes a concrete entity, a personal entity even though subordinate to God.

In the concretization of a deity's attributes, the hypostasis itself sometimes becomes a divinity, with attendant cult. This is widely exemplified in the cult of virtues in Greek and Roman religion from the classical period and throughout late antiquity. These deified virtues were usually feminine, e.g., Eirene, Themis, Nike, Tyche in the Greek world, and Fortuna, Salus, Concordia, Victoria in the Roman world.[13] Sometimes deified virtues were identified with the emperor

---

pp. 38-45; P. Henle, 'Metaphor', in *idem* (ed.), *Language, Thought, and Culture* (Binghamton, NY: Vail-Ballou, 1958), pp. 173-95; P. Ricoeur, *The Rule of Metaphor* (trans. R. Czerny; Toronto: University of Toronto Press, 1977). Some understand this process as a *substitution* of one thing for another; cf. L. Perrine, *Sound and Sense: An Introduction to Poetry* (San Diego: Harcourt, Brace, Jovanovich, 6th edn, 1982), pp. 56-57; N. Frye, *The Great Code: The Bible and Literature* (San Diego: Harcourt, Brace, Jovanovich, 1982), p. 15.

9. Henle, 'Metaphor', p. 186

10. J.D. Sapir, 'The Anatomy of Metaphor', in *idem* and J.C. Crocker (eds.), *The Social Use of Metaphor: Essays on the Anthropology of Rhetoric* (Philadelphia: University of Pennsylvania Press, 1977), pp. 3-32 (3).

11. Perrine, *Sound and Sense*, p. 60

12. Cf. H. Ringgren, *Word and Wisdom* (Lund: Haken Ohlssons, 1947), pp. 190-91. Cf. M. Hengel, *Judaism and Hellenism: Studies in Their Encounter in Palestine during the Early Hellenistic Period* (2 vols.; trans. J. Bowden; Philadelphia: Fortress Press, 1974), I, pp. 153-54.

13. *Honos* is an important instance in which the virtue is personified as a man; cf. M. Bieber, '*Honos* and *Virtus*', *AJA* 49 (1945), pp. 25-34 (30).

or other charismatic leader.[14] For example, Cicero identifies Marius as Hope.[15] Occasionally deified virtues could be identified with a woman: Pietas and Salus were identified with Livia.[16]

Matthew uses a metaphor—Lady Wisdom—which was familiar to him from biblical and Jewish sources. Thus, it will be helpful to study its use in earlier materials in order to ascertain its significance in Matthew's own text. Certain writers in the Restoration, Second Temple, and Tannaitic periods spoke of divine Wisdom metaphorically as a woman.[17] 'Woman', for whom 'Lady' is the honorific, is the vehicle of the metaphor. Although in some passages the woman's portrait is attenuated[18]—in Matthew the female all but disappears—in other texts it is clearly drawn. In the latter, Lady Wisdom appears as householder, street preacher, and prophet of repentance, as well as hymnist, teacher, mother, mistress and wife, patroness of rulers, queen, and God's daughter.[19] She sends prophets and makes of them friends and children of God.[20] She is companion and counselor to kings. Lady Wisdom performs not only the domestic roles associated with women (e.g. wife, mistress, mother), but public roles as well (e.g. teacher, prophet).[21]

---

14. E.g. J.R. Fears, 'The Cult of Virtues and Roman Imperial Ideology', *ANRW*, II.17.2 (1981), pp. 827-948.

15. *Sest.* 38; quoted in Fears, 'Cult of Virtues', p. 861.

16. Fears, 'Cult of Virtues', p. 891.

17. E.g. Prov. 1.20-33; 3.13-18; 8.1-31; 9.1-6, 10-12; Job 28.1-28; Sir. 1.1-10; 4.11-28; 6.18-31; 14.20–15.10; 24.1-34; 51.13-30; Bar. 3.9–4.4; Wis. 6.12–11.1; Philo, *passim*; *1 En.* 42; 84.3; *4 Ezra* 5.9-12; 4Q185; 11QPsa 21.11-17; 22. 1; *b. Sanh.* 101a (*baraita*); ARNa 31. The dating of Tannaitic sources is notoriously problematic. I include selected references as part of a broader framework for the late first century CE in which Matthew wrote his Gospel. For specification and analysis of relevant texts, see my 'Wisdom in Matthew', pp. 17-31, and *Lady Wisdom*, pp. 10-22.

18. Job 28; Bar. 3.9–4.4; *1 En.* 42.

19. Lady Wisdom appears as householder in Prov. 9.1-6; Sir. 14.24-25; 24.19-22; 11QPsa 18.8; street preacher and prophet in Prov. 1.22, 28; 8.1-8; Wis. 8.8; hymnist in 1QPsa 18.12; teacher in Prov. 1.20-21; 8.2-3, 32-36; 9.3; Sir. 4.11, 17; 6.20-31; 15.5; 51.27; mother and nurse in Prov. 16.16 (LXX); Sir. 1.15; 15.2-3; Philo, *Det. Pot. Ins.* 115-116; *Fug.* 109; *Conf. Ling.* 49; bride, wife, and mistress in Prov. 4.6-9; Sir. 14.20-15.8; 51.13-30; Wis. 7.8-9, 11; 8.2; patroness and counselor to rulers in Prov. 8.14-16; Wis. 8.9-14; queen in Wis. 8.1-2; God's daughter in Prov. 8.23-24, 27; *b. Sanh.* 101a (*baraita*).

20. Wis. 7.27; 11.1

21. On the categories 'domestic' and 'public' see M. Zimbalist Rosaldo, 'Woman, Culture and Society: A Theoretical Overview', in M.Z. Rosaldo and L. Lamphere (eds.), *Woman, Culture and Society* (Stanford, CA: Stanford University Press, 1974), pp. 17-42.

In Philo's writings, the imagery is dual in gender, for Wisdom is occasionally male. For instance, Philo tells us that Wisdom impregnates the σοφός (γονας ἀρετῆς, 'impregnation of Virtue' *Congr.* 9).[22] At the same time, he distinguishes gender and function: 'Let us not, then, be concerned with the discrepancy in the gender of the words, and say that the daughter of God, even Wisdom, is masculine and father (ἄρρηνά τε καὶ πατέρα), sowing and begetting in souls aptness to learn, discipline, knowledge, insight, good and laudable actions' (*Fug.* 62).[23] The fluidity in the gender of Philo's imagery will help us to understand Matthew's referral of a female metaphor to a male figure.

The vehicle of the metaphor, then, is a woman with multiple roles. However, the vehicle occasionally has a dual gender, a fact which will allow us to understand how Matthew has used the metaphor to interpret the significance of Jesus. What is the context, the tenor of this metaphor? The tenor is divine wisdom, pre-existent,[24] both immanent[25] and transcendent.[26] Wisdom is the blue-print of creation,[27] the principle of order within it and in human governance.[28] One learns the order of creation and human governance pre-eminently by studying Torah and so, beginning with Sir. 24, Wisdom and Torah are often identified.[29]

Repeated use of the metaphor Lady Wisdom resulted in the emergence of certain 'stories'; there seem to be implicit narratives behind

22. Ἀρετή and σοφία are used synonymously in this passage.

23. My translation: Philo associates the female with sense perception and passivity, and the male with the rational and active; cf. R.A. Baer, *Philo's Use of the Categories of Male and Female* (Leiden: E.J. Brill, 1970), pp. 48-49, 57-62; W. Meeks, 'The Image of the Androgyne: Some Uses of a Symbol in Earliest Christianity', *HR* 13 (1974), pp. 165-208 (176); D. Sly, *Philo's Perception of Women* (BJS, 209; Atlanta: Scholars Press, 1990), p. 56; J.R. Wegner, 'Philo's Portrayal of Women—Hebraic or Hellenic?', in A.-J. Levine (ed.), *'Women Like This': New Perspectives on Jewish Women in the Greco-Roman World* (Atlanta: Scholars Press, 1991), pp. 47-50.

24. E.g. Prov. 8.27, 30a; Job 28.27; Sir. 1.4; Wis. 7.22; 8.6; Philo, *Det. Pot. Ins.* 225-26.

25. E.g. Lady Wisdom is immanent in the order of creation; see Prov. 8.22-30; Sir. 1.10; 24.3, 6; Philo, *Ebr.* 30-31.

26. Wisdom's transcendence is implied in descriptions of Wisdom's divine origins and dwelling; e.g. Sir. 1.1; Wis. 8.3; 9.10.

27. E.g. Prov. 8.30; *Gen. R.* 1.1 (*proem*).

28. E.g. Prov. 8.15-16; Wis. 6–9.

29. E.g. Sir. 24; Bar. 4.1-4; *b. Sanh.* 101a; *ARNa* 31; *Sifre Deut.* 48; *Lev. R.* 20.10. Deut. 4.6 associates wisdom and Torah; however, wisdom is not a metaphor in that text.

the use of the metaphor in certain texts, and one could speak of a composite 'myth'.[30] Lady Wisdom is transcendent yet, according to some of these 'stories' she is found in the order of creation, in the sage's instruction, and in Torah.[31] Other traditions describe Lady Wisdom as seeking out humankind, being rejected, and therefore withdrawing.[32]

Why the metaphor? Why a myth? The nature of metaphor allowed the user to say something about the tenor wisdom and to do so with greater impact than through discursive speech.[33] The metaphor suggests in imaginative terms that wisdom is beautiful, life-giving and nurturing, a sustainer of order and well-being. It suggests in affective terms that the quest for wisdom requires passion, the engagement of the sage on affective as well as cognitive and moral levels.

Moreover, the implied narratives allowed people of the Second Temple and Tannaitic periods to ask the questions of cosmogony and theodicy: How did the world come to be? How does a person know God and the divine will? Why does evil happen to Israel? How does God save Israel?[34]

But why is it *wisdom* that is so personified through such an elaborately defined metaphor? Why is *wisdom* given such attention, and why it is personified as a *woman*? For our purposes, I think it beneficial to look at the social nature of metaphor itself. Myth, symbol, and metaphor belong to the realm of 'concerned knowledge'.[35] Sacred symbols, of which the metaphor Lady Wisdom is one, 'formulate the basic congruence between a particular style of life and a specific (if most often, implicit) metaphysic, and in so doing sustain each other

30. Cf. R. Bultmann, 'Der religionsgeschichtliche Hintergrund des Prologs zum Johannes-Evangelium', in H. Schmidt (ed.), *Eucharisterion: Studien zur Religion und Literatur des Alten und Neuen Testaments* (Göttingen: Vandenhoeck & Ruprecht, 1923), pp. 1-11; H. Conzelmann, 'The Mother of Wisdom', C.E. Carlston and R.P. Scharlemann (trans.), in J.M. Robinson (ed.), *The Future of our Religious Past* (London: SCM Press, 1971), pp. 230-43; B. Mack, 'Wisdom Myth and Mythology', *Int* 24 (1970), pp. 46-60.

31. E.g. Prov. 2.1-19; 8.22-31; Sir. 24.1-34; 51.13-30; Wis. 6.1–9.18. I use 'sage', 'teacher', and 'scribe' interchangeably in this essay to signify learned professional groups who functioned in a variety of social contexts and who were concerned with the transmission of the tradition. Cf. A.J. Saldarini, *Matthew's Christian-Jewish Community* (Chicago Studies in the History of Judaism; Chicago: University of Chicago Press, 1994), pp. 101-102.

32. E.g. Prov. 1.20-33; *1 En.* 42; 84.3; *4 Ezra* 5.9-12.

33. See my 'The Sirach 51 Acrostic: Confession and Exhortation', *ZAW* 94 (1982), p. 406; Frymer-Kensky, *In the Wake*, pp. 181-82.

34. Cf. B. Mack, 'Wisdom Myth'.

35. Frye, *Great Code*, p. 47. Frye actually uses this phrase only of myth.

with the borrowed authority of the other'.[36] Religious symbols, then, serve to maintain socially constructed reality.[37] They emerge from the social structures of the collective and legitimate them.[38]

The association, even identification, of wisdom with the teacher's instruction[39] suggests that the metaphor *Lady* Wisdom, as it occurs in our texts, may have originated in the school, or the instructional setting, a social context which was usually exclusively male.[40] The school varied in form: e.g. the family educational context reflected in some strata of the book of Proverbs (a context in which at its earliest Restoration point, the mother held correspondibility with the father as source of instruction[41]); those gathered around Ben Sira;[42] those addressed by the apocalyptic seers, whether the entire community (e.g. *1 Enoch*) or select groups (*4 Ezra*); the sectarian community at Qumran, the Tannaitic sages.

The literature describes the sages in various ways which parallel descriptions of Lady Wisdom and which give a context for understanding better Matthew's use of metaphor. Learning is relational, and teachers are often called 'father'.[43] Indeed, the author of the *Hodayot* calls himself both 'father' and 'mother'.[44] Teachers are hymnists who

---

36. C. Geertz, *The Interpretation of Cultures: Selected Essays by Clifford Geertz* (New York: Basic Books, 1973), pp. 89-90.

37. P. Berger, *The Sacred Canopy: Elements of a Sociological Theory of Religion* (Garden City, NY: Doubleday, 1969), p. 42.

38. Berger, *The Sacred Canopy*, p. 34.

39. E.g. Prov. 1.2-19; 2.1-8; 4.1-9; 8.32-33; Sir. 24.30-34; 51.23, 25; 4Q185 1.13-14.

40. Regarding the instructional setting as place of origin for the metaphor of Lady Wisdom, see R.N. Whybray, *Wisdom in Proverbs: The Concept of Wisdom in Proverbs 1–9* (SBT; Naperville, IL: Alec R. Allenson, 1965), pp. 74-77; W. McKane, *Proverbs: A New Approach* (Philadelphia: Westminster Press, 1970), pp. 7-10.

41. E.g. Prov. 1.8; 4.3; 6.20; 15.20; 23.22, 25; 31.1-9; cf. Camp, *Wisdom and the Feminine*, pp. 82, 188, 199.

42. On the exclusion of women from the school in Ben Sira's work, see C. Camp, 'The Female Sage in Ancient Israel and in the Biblical Wisdom Literature', in J.G. Gammie and L.G. Perdue (eds.), *The Sage in Israel and the Ancient Near East* (Winona Lake, IN: Eisenbrauns, 1990), pp. 196-97.

43. E.g. Prov. 1.8; 4.1; Sir. 3.1-11; *Sifre Deut.* 34, 305, 335; *Mek. Vayassa* 1.130-31; cf. *b. 'Erub.* 73a. On the use of the title 'father' in wisdom literature, see P. Nel, 'The Concept "Father" in the Wisdom Literature of the Ancient Near East', *JNSL* 5 (1977), pp. 53-66. On the use of the title in the Tannaitic literature, see K. Kohler, '"Abba", Father: Title of Spiritual Leader and Saint', in H.Z. Dimitrovsky (ed.), *Exploring the Talmud. I. Education* (New York: Ktav, 1976), pp. 150-63.

44. 1QH 7.20-22; cf. CD 13.9-10.

sing God's praises and join angelic choirs.[45] Teachers are described in prophetic terms as teaching and interpreting Torah under the inspiration of God's spirit[46] and sometimes as using prophetic forms such as the woe.[47]

Teachers are described as visionaries and/or ecstatics. They interpret the apocalyptic mysteries (closely related to wisdom) as well as Torah under the impulse of visionary experience.[48] The relationship between wisdom and vision appears explicitly in places like *1 En.* 37.2, where the Book of Similitudes is called 'the words of wisdom'. Philo, speaking in ecstatic terms, tells us that he is often god-possessed (θεοληπτεῖσθαι, *Cher.* 27.2), and that he often interprets the text of Moses 'irradiated by the light of wisdom' (φωτὶ τῷ σοφίας ἐναυγάζομαι, *Spec. Leg.* 3.6).[49]

The literature frequently describes these sages in *anawim* language; they are 'poor', 'meek', 'lowly'.[50] Lady Wisdom herself is not described in such terms, but she frequently appears in contexts where the sages are so designated, and this will be important for our understanding of Matthew. Such terms of self-description may indeed reflect a liminal state characterized by status reversal in which those who understand themselves to be of high status reverse the language in which they express their self-identification to emphasize humility and lowliness.[51] At the very least, the vocabulary reflects the 'piety and poverty' widespread in late antiquity.[52]

45. E.g. Sir. 39.12-43.33; Wis. 9.1-18; *1 En.* 39.11-14; *Apoc. Abr.* 17.8-21; 1QS 9.20-11.22.

46. Cf. Sir. 24.33; 39.6; *t. Soṭ.* 13.3, 4; *y. Soṭ.* 1.4 (16d, 45ff.); 9.17 (24c, 29ff.); *t. Pes.* 1.27; *y. Šeb.* 9.1 (38d, 37ff.); *Lev. R.* 21.8.

47. E.g. *1 En.* 94.6-11; 98.9-16; 99.1-2, 11-16; 100.7-9; G.W.E. Nickelsburg, 'The Apocalyptic Message of 1 Enoch 92–105', *CBQ* 39 (1977), pp. 309-28.

48. E.g. *1 En.* 72–82 regarding the calendar.

49. Similarly, the Tannaitic sources speak of the mystical ascent to the heavens and clearly relate it to the observance of Torah; e.g., *t. Ḥag.* 2.2; *y. Ḥag.* 2.1; *b. Ḥag.* 14b. It is not clear, however, that the sages there actually interpret Torah out of that experience.

50. E.g. CD 6.16, 21; 1QM 14.7; 1QSb 5.22; 1QH 5.16, 18; 1QS 10.26; 1QH 1.35-36, 4.2-6. In the Qumran materials, this terminology refers usually to the entire community. Cf. also *Mek. ba-Hodesh* 9.99-116; *Sifre Deut.* 48; *t. Soṭ.* 13.3; *Lev. R.* 1.5.

51. V. Turner, *The Ritual Process: Structure and Anti-Structure* (Ithaca, NY: Cornell University Press, 1969), pp. 189, 195-96. C.W. Bynum indicates the limitations of Turner's categories of liminality when analyzing women's stories and symbols; 'Women's Stories: Women's Symbols. A Critique of Victor's Theory of Liminality', in R.L. Moore and F.E. Reynolds (eds.), *Anthropology and the Study of Religion* (Chicago, IL: Center for the Scientific Study of Religion, 1984), pp. 104-25.

52. Cf. G. Theissen, 'The Sociological Interpretation of Religious Traditions: Its

96   *A Feminist Companion to Matthew*

As we have noted, many texts suggest that Israelite and Jewish sages were male in the overwhelming majority of cases. There are exceptions, of course: the women sages behind the early strata of Prov. 1-9,[53] the Therapeutae,[54] and Beruriah the wife of Rabbi Meir.[55] And certain of the pseudepigraphical texts suggest that there were women who had received the sort of training required for apocalyptic visions.[56] 1QSa 1.4-11, which refers to the instruction of women, suggests the possibility of women teachers at Qumran. Thus, the personification of Wisdom as a *woman* presents certain parallels to *some* women's lives and roles, public as well as private.

But the texts do not necessarily suggest women's experience and use of that metaphor.[57] For it is male social contexts—scribal and other scholarly groups—which provide the background for the texts that preserve the metaphor. And the texts available to us reflect that metaphor as it was used by males. The metaphor, occurring as it does in frequently erotic terms, conveys to a male audience the nature of the quest for wisdom as intimate, engaging the depths of human affectivity. And it implies that intimacy with Wisdom will also bring the person into intimacy with God.[58] Finally, the use of a *female* personification

---

Methodological Problems as Exemplified in Early Christianity', in N.K. Gottwald (ed.), *The Bible and Liberation: Political and Social Hermeneutics* (Maryknoll, NY: Orbis Books, 1983), pp. 38-48 (48).

53. Cf. Camp, 'The Female Sage', pp. 190-94 n. 30 (above).

54. *Cont.* 12, 32-33, 68-69, 83-88.

55. *T. B. Qam.* 1.6; 4.17; *Sifre Deut.* 307; *b. Ber.* 10a; *b. 'Erub.* 53b-54a; *b. Pes.* 62b; *b. 'Abod. Zar.* 18a-b; *Lam. R.* 3.6. Cf. D. Goodblatt, 'The Beruriah Traditions', *JJS* 26 (1975), pp. 68-85. As Goodblatt notes, the traditions which give her name as 'Beruriah' and describe her as possessing an advanced education are all later, dating from the fourth or fifth centuries. In the earlier materials she is simply the wife of R. Meir.

56. E.g. *Jos. Asen.* 14-17; *T. Job* 46-53; *Jub.* 25.14; 35.6; *LAB* 30.2; 31.1; 33.1; cf. R.D. Chesnutt, 'Revelatory Experiences Attributed to Biblical Women in Early Jewish Literature', in Levine (ed.), *'Women Like This'*, pp. 107-25.

57. Claudia Camp's words regarding Ben Sira's treatment of women are helpful in this larger context. 'Men's writing and thinking about women—particularly though hardly exclusively in a society as "gendered" as the Mediterranean—may be seen as part of the system of signs through which they encode and create the world. To understand better how this has been done may or may not tell much about women's actual lives. It may, however, tell a great deal about the dynamics of the symbolic world men create for women to live in' ('Understanding a Patriarchy: Women in Second Century Jerusalem Through the Eyes of Ben Sira', in Levine [ed.], *'Women Like This'*, pp. 1-39 [pp. 1-2 n. 2]).

58. Cf. R.A. Horsley, 'Spiritual Marriage with Sophia', *VC* 33 (1979), pp. 30-54.

allows the sages, members of a patriarchal social structure and an overwhelmingly, usually exclusively, male teaching class, to bring the female into themselves and to appropriate it.[59] That process means that it is primarily male scribes who mediate female Lady Wisdom for the community.

The interactive nature of metaphor means that each member of the metaphor—'Woman' and 'Wisdom'—tells us about the other. And yet, the texts which use the metaphor say nothing of the ways in which the metaphor of Woman Wisdom may have impacted on actual women. Many of these texts, such as Proverbs, Sirach, the Qumran literature, of course, were originally addressed to circles which were primarily, usually exclusively, male. Through the canonization process, however, some of the texts acquired a broader audience. Thus, the metaphor would have been familiar to some women, especially to learned women. Would the metaphor have allowed women to articulate their experience of the divine in female terms? Would it have enhanced women's understanding of their roles as wives, mothers, counselors, prophets, and teachers? Both are indeed possible.

But it is equally possible that the metaphor served, in its insistence on the sage as the one who unites with Lady Wisdom, further to exclude women from access to scholarly learning and to other forms of public service and leadership.[60] Examination of the relevant materials leads me to conclude that these questions must remain open. Indeed, the metaphor of Lady Wisdom could have functioned in all of these ways, depending on the social context and the religious and intellectual ambiance. While the portrayal of Lady Wisdom certainly reflects some of the many roles women exercised in late Israelite and early Jewish society—including, occasionally, public roles—it says nothing of the significance of the metaphor for *women's* religious experience or of *women's* understanding of their roles.

---

59. Regarding such appropriation in other contexts, see Elliot R. Wolfson, 'Woman—The Feminine as Other in Theosophic Kabbalah: Some Philosophical Observations on the Divine Androgyne', in L. Silberstein and R. Cohn (eds.), *The Other in Jewish Thought and History* (New York: New York University Press, 1994), pp. 166-204; idem, 'Female Imaging of the Torah: From Literary Metaphor to Religious Symbol', in J. Neusner *et al.* (eds.), *From Ancient Israel to Modern Judaism: Intellect in Quest of Understanding* (BJS, 173; 4 vols.; Atlanta: Scholars Press, 1989), II, pp. 271-307. I am very grateful to Professors Wolfson (New York University) and Angela Zito (New York University) for their insights on the symbolization of the feminine.

60. Cf. Frymer-Kensky, *In the Wake*, p. 183.

Matthew and Jesus-Wisdom

It has frequently been observed that Matthew heightens the wisdom motif already present in his sources, Q and M.[61] The evangelist describes Jesus as Wisdom in several places: 8.19-22; 11.19, 25-30; 23.34-36 and 37-39.[62] Matthew 8.19-22 (Lk. 9.57-60) specifies Jesus as Son of Man and as homeless teacher:

> A scribe then approached and said, 'Teacher, I will follow you wherever you go'. And Jesus said to him, 'Foxes have holes, and birds of the air have nests; but the Son of Man has nowhere to lay his head'. Another of his disciples said to him, 'Lord, first let me go and bury my father'. But Jesus said to him, 'Follow me, and let the dead bury their own dead'.[63]

The pericope recalls the association of Wisdom with the Son of Man present in 1 Enoch[64] as well as within Matthew's own text at 11.16-19, Wisdom's role as teacher who calls and instructs disciples, and the motif of Wisdom's homelessness present in some of the sources available to Matthew.[65]

The evangelist's redaction of 8.19-22 and its context (chs. 8–9, 10) emphasizes the portrayal of Jesus-Wisdom as teacher by inserting titles like γραμματεύς (Mt. 8.19) and διδάσκαλη (8.19; 9.11), by adding the reference to Jesus' 'teaching in their synagogues' to the summary statement in 9.35, and by assembling material on the nature of discipleship (9.9, 14-17, 37; ch. 10). And Matthew's redaction, with its note of opposition, echoes the motifs of Wisdom rejected and homeless suggested in that earlier material.[66] The parallels with traditions about Lady Wisdom suggest that Matthew is portraying Jesus as Wisdom in

---

61. Cf. Lk. 7.35; 10.21-22; 11.49-51; 13.34-35; Mt. 11.28-30.
62. For a more detailed analysis and bibliography, see my 'Wisdom in Matthew', pp. 31-47; *Lady Wisdom*, pp. 42-65.
63. Unless otherwise indicated, all biblical citations are from the NRSV.
64. E.g. *1 En.* 48–49.
65. On Wisdom as teacher who calls disciples, see, e.g., Prov. 1.20-21; 8.2-3, 32-36; 9.3; Sir. 24.19-22. On the rejection and homelessness of Lady Wisdom, see Prov. 1.20-33; Sir. 24.7; *1 En.* 42; 94.5; *2 Bar.* 48.36.
66. E.g. the Pharisees' opposition in 9.11 and 34, and the reference to 'their synagogue' in 9.35. See M. Hengel, 'Jesus als messianischer Lehrer der Weisheit und die Anfänge der Christologie', in *Sagesse et Religion: Colloque de Strasbourg, 1976* (Paris: Presses Universitaires de France, 1979), pp. 147-90 (165); J. Gnilka, *Das Matthäusevangelium* (2 vols.; Freiburg: Herder, 1988), I, p. 311; R. Hamerton-Kelly, *Pre-Existence, Wisdom and the Son of Man: A Study of the Idea of Pre-Existence in the New Testament* (SNTMS, 21; Cambridge: Cambridge University Press, 1973), p. 29.

8.19-22. However, in doing so, Matthew erases the feminine quality of the metaphor.

In 11.19, Matthew changes the Q saying, 'Yet Wisdom is vindicated by all her children' (Lk. 7.35) to read, 'Yet Wisdom is vindicated by her deeds'. The saying concludes a rather large block of Q material (Lk. 7.18-35 // Mt. 11.2-19). The replacement of 'children' with 'deeds' forms an inclusion with 'deeds' (ἔργα) in 11.2 and suggests that Matthew is presenting Jesus, not as Wisdom's envoy with John the Baptist, but as Wisdom's own self.[67]

But why would Matthew have done this? In 11.2 the redactor introduces the Q section with the question about the deeds of Christ. In 11.4-6 Jesus recounts the list of his 'deeds'. Among them is preaching. The parable of 11.16-19 implies that Wisdom's teaching meets with success at least among tax collectors and sinners. Moreover, in 11.20-24, immediately following the saying about Wisdom's deeds, Jesus speaks prophetically to the Galilean cities which reject him. And, in 12.38-42 Jesus is compared to the prophet Jonah as well as to the wise Solomon and declared greater than both.[68] Matthew thus identifies Jesus as Wisdom because Jesus, like Wisdom, is prophet of repentance and sage. And, like Wisdom, he is both accepted and rejected.[69] In 11.19, the evangelist retains the noun σοφία—'she' does not disappear completely. However, the female is subsumed into the male figure through Matthew's identifying her with Jesus.

In 11.25-30, Matthew takes over vv. 25-27 from Q (Lk. 10.21-22), where there is already an implicit Wisdom Christology.[70] The saying attributes to Jesus the same characteristics of hiddenness and transcendence, revelation and mediation of knowledge, that earlier sources attribute to Lady Wisdom.

The identification of Jesus with Wisdom becomes explicit with the addition of vv. 28-30, an M saying.[71] The invitation, the image of the

---

67. It makes more sense to interpret Matthew as having made the change to form the *inclusio* and thus edited the material in a more polished manner than to suggest that Luke has changed the term and thereby done away with the *inclusio*.

68. Gnilka, *Das Matthaüsevangelium*, I, p. 467.

69. Acceptance and rejection are major themes in 11.2–13.54; cf. my 'Wisdom in Matthew', p. 32; *Hidden Wisdom*, p. 21.

70. J.M. Robinson, 'Jesus as Sophos and Sophia', in R.L. Wilken (ed.), *Aspects of Wisdom in Judaism and Early Christianity* (CSJCA, 1; Notre Dame: University of Notre Dame, 1975), pp. 8-10; J. Kloppenborg, ' Wisdom Christology in Q', *LTP* 34 (1978), pp. 139-47; Deutsch, 'Wisdom in Matthew', p. 37.

71. There are redactional traces in 11.28-30 (πάντες, πραΰς). However, its independent occurrence in *Gos. Thom.* 90 suggests that it is more likely that the saying is traditional than that it is a redactional construct; see my *Lady Wisdom*, p. 57.

yoke and promise of rest, recall passages referring to Lady Wisdom particularly in Sirach (24.19-22; esp. 6.25; 51.26).[72] Moreover, the nature of the invitation, echoing that of the sage in Sir. 51.26 as well as that of Lady Wisdom in Sir. 24.19-22, suggests that Mt. 11.25-30 represents a convergence of sage and personified Wisdom in Matthew's portrait of Jesus. Wisdom, we recall, is a teacher. In Matthew, however, the gender of the metaphor is transformed, and Wisdom the teacher is male.

Matthew 11.25-30 occurs in the longer unit 11.2–13.58, where one finds 11.19 with its retention of σοφία and traces of female imaging. It is possible that some, particularly learned women, might have inferred that Jesus, Sophia and Teacher, was associated with female as well as male wisdom and learning.

Jesus is shown throughout 11.20–13.58 as a teacher of apocalyptic mysteries—this is particularly evident in ch. 13, with its parables about the mysteries of the Kingdom (cf. v. 13.11). Moreover, he is authoritative interpreter of Torah, as is clear in the two Sabbath pericopae which follow immediately 11.25-30. The passage in its immediate context suggests that teaching, whether of apocalyptic mysteries or *halakha*, occurs in discipleship to the sage who is identified with Wisdom. And that discipleship is a matter of affective engagement. Thus, Matthew legitimates Jesus' teaching over against that of opposing teachers, the ubiquitous Matthean scribes and Pharisees (cf. 12.1-8, 9-14).[73]

And, finally, Matthew describes Jesus as personified Wisdom in 23.34-36 and 37-39. For our purposes, the significant alterations in Matthew's redaction of the first saying occur in 23.34. The Q verse reads: 'Therefore also the Wisdom of God said, "I will send them prophets and apostles, some of whom they will kill and persecute"' (Lk. 11.49). Matthew has: 'Therefore, I send you prophets, sages, and scribes, some of whom you will kill and crucify, and some you will flog in your synagogues and persecute from town to town' (23.34). Matthew thus places Wisdom's words on Jesus' lips and assigns to him the function of sending envoys, a function proper to Wisdom in the Wisdom of Solomon and Q.[74] Wisdom is now identified with the

---

72. D. Hill believes that the view 'that Jesus is speaking *in persona sapientiae* goes too far' (*The Gospel of Matthew* [NCB; Grand Rapids: Eerdmans, 1972], p. 208).

73. On the scribes and Pharisees as Jesus' usual opponents in the Gospel of Matthew, see my *Hidden Wisdom*, p. 30. On these groups in the broader context of opposition by Israel's leaders, see Saldarini, *Matthew's Christian-Jewish Community*, pp. 44-67.

74. E.g. Wis. 7.27; 10.1–11.14.

male Jesus. And the fact that Matthew recasts the saying by using the present tense makes the oracle contemporaneous with the prophets, sages, and scribes in his community.[75] As we will see, it is likely that these are male.

The immediate context of this oracle is the woes against the scribes and Pharisees, whom Matthew's Jesus accuses of hypocrisy[76] and whose manner of leadership comes under stern condemnation. In 23.1-12 Jesus contrasts the scribes and Pharisees' leadership with that to be exercised by his disciples. Jesus' manner of interpreting *halakha* and that of his disciples recalls 11.28-30 — they stand in lowliness and solidarity with the community — unlike the scribes and Pharisees. And those prophets, sages, and scribes sent out by Jesus stand over against the scribes and Pharisees' envoys. Thus Matthew identifies Jesus as Wisdom because Jesus, like Wisdom, sends forth envoys. That identification, moreover, legitimates Jesus' teaching, his interpretation of *halakha*, over against that of his opponents. And it legitimates the teaching of the prophets, sages, and scribes of Matthew's community — Wisdom's envoys — over against *their* opponents.[77]

In 23.37-39, Matthew has with the oracle of vv. 34-36 a lament which occurs in another context in Q (Lk. 13.34-35)[78] and which describes Jesus' wish to gather the inhabitants of Jerusalem 'as a hen gathers her brood under her wings' (v. 37). It is not at all clear that 23.37-39 was originally a lament of *Wisdom*.[79] But it is clear that oracle and lament stand together in the Matthean context without any transitional phrase, thus suggesting that *Matthew* thought the lament to be a Wisdom saying, possibly because it describes Jesus in maternal terms. Wisdom is, after all, a mother, and the Septuagint implicitly compares

75. Cf. Gnilka, *Das Matthaüsevangelium*, II, pp. 298-300.
76. Note Matthew's frequent use of ὑποκριτής in ch. 23 and his expansion of Q in that material (vv. 13, 15, 23, 25, 27, 29). The adjective, as well as the noun ὑπόκρισις (23.28), is redactional in all instances in ch. 23.
77. On the social and rhetorical functions of the woes, see J.A. Overman, *Matthew's Gospel and Formative Judaism: The Social World of the Matthean Community* (Minneapolis, MN: Fortress Press, 1990), pp. 142-43; A.J. Saldarini, 'Delegitimation of Leaders in Matthew 23', *CBQ* 43 (1992), pp. 659-80.
78. It is actually debatable whether the Matthean or Lukan version represents the original context or whether both have displaced the lament. Cf. J.S. Kloppenborg, *The Formation of Q: Trajectories in Ancient Wisdom Collections* (Studies in Antiquity and Christianity; Philadelphia: Fortress Press, 1987), p. 227.
79. Cf. P. Hoffmann, *Studien zur Theologie der Logienquelle* (NTAbh, 8; Münster: Aschendorff, 1972), p. 172. Contra R. Bultmann, *History of the Synoptic Tradition* (trans. J. Marsh; New York: Harper & Row, 1963), p. 115; Suggs, *Wisdom, Christology*, pp. 64-66; Kloppenborg, *Formation of Q*, p. 228.

102   A Feminist Companion to Matthew

her to a mother bird.[80] From a perspective of gendered language, the maternal image used in this passage for Jesus contrasts with and balances the exclusive 'one Father, who is in heaven' in 23.9.[81]

Wisdom the Teacher enters the Temple in 21.23 and leaves in 24.1, immediately after the lament which tells us that the Temple is forsaken; this suggests in the context of vv. 34-36 that Wisdom has left the Temple because he has been rejected.[82] Once again, Matthew has described Jesus as Wisdom because that which applies to Wisdom—in this case maternity, rejection, and withdrawal—applies pre-eminently to Jesus.

Matthew thus transforms the metaphor Lady Wisdom to present us with Jesus-Wisdom. As a result, Jesus the vehicle tells us something about Wisdom the content of the metaphor; if we would know what Wisdom is, Matthew implies, we are to look at the teaching and life of Jesus. Jesus' story is Wisdom's story. Wisdom is one of the ways in which Matthew identifies Jesus; if we wish to know who Jesus is, we should look to the metaphor of Wisdom. Jesus-Wisdom originates with God and is a principle of intelligibility for Matthew and his community: How do we know God? Through the life and teaching of Jesus-Wisdom. How is God present to the community? Through Jesus the Wisdom and immanence of God. How do we know God's will and respond? Through the interpretation of Torah and apocalyptic disclosure of mysteries given by Jesus who is Wisdom. Why does evil befall Israel? Because Israel rejects Jesus who is Wisdom.[83] How does God regard the community, even when it turns away from the divine? As a mother who wants to shelter her children.

(A word of caution is in order when speaking of Israel's 'rejection' of Jesus. Matthew's Gospel, as well as other New Testament documents, has been used in subsequent periods to legitimate Christian anti-Semitism. Matthew writes in a context in which two groups, his community and their opponents, are trying to define themselves.[84] They do so using the rhetorical conventions of late antiquity.[85] Thus,

    80. Prov. 16.16 (LXX); Sir. 1.15.
    81. On the community's relationship with God as Father, see Saldarini, *Matthew's Jewish-Christian Community*, pp. 93-94.
    82. Cf. Gnilka, *Das Matthaüsevangelium*, II, pp. 302-303.
    83. See my 'Wisdom in Matthew', p. 47; *Lady Wisdom*, pp. 75-76.
    84. On the function of conflict in the process of self-definition, see L. Coser, *The Functions of Social Conflict* (Glencoe, IL: Free Press, 1956).
    85. Cf. L.T. Johnson, 'The New Testament's Anti-Jewish Slander and the Conventions of Ancient Polemic', *JBL* 108 (1989), pp. 419-41.

Matthew's Gospel should not be understood as presenting an objective view of first-century Judaism or of the Pharisees.)

As Wisdom, Jesus is hidden and revealed. He is the prophet who calls to repentance, the revealer who discloses the mysteries of God's reign. Jesus-Wisdom is a sage and authoritative interpreter of Torah whose call to discipleship is accompanied by the paradox of an easy burden and the promise of rest. And Jesus-Wisdom sends forth prophets, sages, and scribes. Matthew's identification of Jesus as Wisdom legitimates Jesus' interpretation of Torah, his announcement of judgment and prophetic call to repentance, and the teaching authority of his envoys. Thus, Matthew's transformation of the metaphor tells us something about his understanding of Jesus' identity and role.[86]

That transformation presents us with a figure of Jesus, a historical if exalted male, as identified with Wisdom's self. Why has Matthew done this? To be sure, the redactor has found that identification present at least implicitly in Q as well as M, but he has heightened it, emphasized it. In that process Matthew has also erased the female from Wisdom's portrait. Earlier, we discovered the relationship of the metaphor to educational settings in ancient Israel and Second-Temple Judaism. The texts in which we find the metaphor emerged there. In those contexts the metaphor Lady Wisdom served to legitimate the sages' authority. They spoke of themselves as true purveyors of wisdom precisely insofar as they possessed Lady Wisdom, and were possessed by her.

If we look at the immediate context of Matthew's Wisdom sayings we see that the disciples are described in school language.[87] They are infants (νήπιοι), recalling the disciples of the Teacher in the *Hodayot* who calls himself a wet nurse (יוֹנֵק) to a suckling child (עוֹלֵל, 1QH 7.21-22), and the very youngest students in Tannaitic sources (e.g. *Sifre Deut.* 46).[88] Indeed, all Israel is compared to a suckling child when studying words of Torah (*Sifre Deut.* 321). Matthew's disciples are to be meek, humble (5.3-10; 11.25-30; 23.8-12), traits associated with learning, wisdom, and revelation in Second Temple and Taanaitic sources.[89]

---

86. Cf. my 'Wisdom in Matthew', pp. 46-47.

87. Cf. A.C. Wire, 'Gender Roles in a Scribal Community', in D.L. Balch (ed.), *Social History of the Matthean Community: Cross-Disciplinary Approaches* (Minneapolis: Fortress Press, 1991), pp. 87-121.

88. In Amoraic sources, see *Lev. R.* 30.2; *Esth. R.* on Esth. 3.9; *b. Šab.* 119b.

89. E.g. *4 Ezra* 8.47-49; 11.41-42; CD 6.16, 21; 1QM 14.7; 1QH 5.21-22; 1QSb 5.22; 4Q171 2.8-11; *Sifre Deut.* 48, 95; ARNa 25, 35. Despite the use of such language, as well as the presence of the master-disciple relationship in Matthew's

Matthew uses language familiar from earlier sources, including the descriptions of Lady Wisdom, to tell us of leadership roles in his community. There are the scribes trained for the Kingdom. The context of 13.52 suggests that their role has to do with understanding and transmitting the mysteries of the Kingdom disclosed by Jesus[90] as well as interpreting the tradition received from Judaism.[91]

In Matthew's narrative, Jesus-Wisdom sends forth disciples as prophets, sages, and scribes.[92] While the specific nature of those roles is not explicit here, one ascertains from the context that they are to proclaim the message of the Kingdom and to decide *halakhic* matters in solidarity with their community, in contrast to the opposing teachers, namely, the scribes and Pharisees. Ultimately, Matthew's prophets, sages, and scribes are legitimate teachers because they are *Wisdom's* envoys, unlike those of scribes and Pharisees. Nonetheless, they like Wisdom will be rejected, killed, crucified, scourged (23.34-36).[93]

Beyond the immediate context of the Wisdom texts, Matthew further describes the disciples' scribal functions in ways which recall teaching roles in the earlier material where Lady Wisdom surfaces. The tone of the pertinent texts is apocalyptic, concerned with revelation and with the interpretation of the tradition. In Mt. 16.17-19, Jesus acknowledges the revelation granted to Peter and gives him authority to bind and loose, to make *halakhic* decisions concerning what is permitted and what is forbidden[94] as well as to admit to and exclude from the community.[95]

Gospel, it is not clear that the author worked out of a 'formal school of the Greek or Jewish type' (Saldarini, *Matthew's Christian-Jewish Community*, p. 97).

90. Cf. O.L. Cope, *Matthew: A Scribe Trained for the Kingdom of Heaven* (CBQMS, 5; Washington, DC: Catholic Biblical Association of America, 1976), pp. 13-27.

91. Cf. Gnilka, *Das Matthaüsevangelium*, I, p. 511; Orton, *The Understanding Scribe*, pp. 166-68; J. Zeller, 'Zu einer jüdischen Vorlage von Mt 13, 52', *BZ* 20 (1976), pp. 224-25; W. Trilling, *Das wahre Israel: Studien zur Theologie des Matthäus-Evangeliums* (SANT, 10; Munich: Kösel, 3rd edn, 1964), p. 204.

92. On the nature of these roles, see Saldarini, *Matthew's Christian-Jewish Community*, pp. 102-107; Overman, *Matthew's Gospel*, pp. 115-19.

93. Cf. 16.21-22; 17.22; 20.19.

94. Cf. Gnilka, *Das Matthaüsevangelium*, II, p. 65; Orton, *Understanding Scribe*, p. 237; W. Trilling, 'Amt und Amtverständnis bei Matthäus', in A. Descamps and R.D.A. de Halleux (eds.), *Mélanges bibliques en hommage au R.P. Béda Rigaux* (Gembloux: Duculot, 1970), p. 43; M. Wilcox, 'Peter and the Rock: A Fresh Look at Matthew 16.17-19', *NTS* 22 (1975-76), p. 82.

95. Cf. G.W.E. Nickelsburg, 'Enoch, Levi, and Peter: Recipients of Revelation in Upper Galilee', *JBL* 100 (1981), pp. 575-600 (594).

In ch. 17 Matthew edits the transfiguration narrative in such a way as to suggest that the disciples are apocalyptic seers. His description of their reaction to the vision—fear, prostration—accords with that of apocalyptic seers in Second Temple literature (17.6).[96] And the same is true of the reassurance and the command to rise (17.7).[97]

Finally, in the closing words of the Gospel, the risen Jesus bids his disciples to make disciples of all nations, 'teaching them to obey everything that I have commanded you...' (28.20), presumably referring to the teaching contained in the gospel and continued by the scribes of Matthew's community.[98]

Those scribes, as far as I can tell, are male.[99] Nowhere does the evangelist offer female teachers as models of learned leadership. The fact that Wisdom is now identified with Jesus, an earthly if exalted male figure, may be understood as legitimating a male teaching class in Matthew's community: the prophets, sages, and scribes.

Moreover, the polemical context of the Wisdom passages, already present in Q and emphasized by Matthew, suggests that Matthew's teachers perceive themselves to be facing fierce competition.[100] Thus, the identification of Jesus with Wisdom not only legitimates the various groups in Matthew's community, but does so in face of the opposition.[101]

Matthew, then, describes the disciples in school language. In several places it is clear he refers to functionaries in his own community: sages, prophets, scribes, seers. The particularly 'scribal' nature of the

---

96. Cf. Dan. 8.17-18; 10.9-12; *1 En.* 14.14-15; *4 Ezra* 7.1; also Ezek. 1.28; Rev. 1.17. See my 'The Transfiguration: Vision and Social Setting in Matthew's Gospel (Matthew 17.1-9)', in V. Wiles *et al.* (eds.), *Putting Body and Soul Together: Essays in Honor of Robin Scroggs* (Valley Forge, PA: Trinity Press International, 1997), pp. 124-37.

97. Cf. Gnilka, *Das Matthaüsevangelium*, II, p. 93; Nickelsburg, 'Enoch, Levi', pp. 590-600. Morton Smith believes an ascent tradition lies behind the original transfiguration story; 'Ascent to the Heavens and the Beginnings of Christianity', *Eranosjahrbuch* 50 (1981), pp. 403-24; *Clement of Alexandria and the Secret Gospel of Mark* (Cambridge, MA: Harvard University Press, 1973), pp. 237-49; 'The Origin and History of the Transfiguration Story', *USQR* 36 (1980), pp. 39-44.

98. G. Barth, 'Matthew's Understanding of the Law', in G. Bornkamm *et al.* (eds.), *Tradition and Interpretation in Matthew* (trans. P. Scott; London: SCM Press, 1982), pp. 58-164 (134). J. Zumstein, 'Matthieu 28.16-20', *RTP* 22 (1972), pp. 14-33 (28).

99. Cf. Wire, 'Gender Roles', pp. 98-108.

100. Cf. Saldarini, 'Delegitimation'.

101. On the context of Mt. 23 in the broader Greco-Roman world, see Johnson, 'New Testament's Anti-Jewish Slander', pp. 433-34.

gospel suggests that the evangelist is himself most likely a member of that group.[102] That is, the evangelist is a learned person with a technical knowledge of the Jewish tradition, as well as the Jesus traditions, who is engaged in transmitting those traditions. Thus, it is natural that Matthew would enhance the Wisdom motif, familiar to the school setting as it is, and transform it.

Matthew's identification of Jesus with Wisdom indeed serves a theological purpose for the evangelist and his community. But it does more; it legitimates Jesus life, teaching, and authorization of disciples. Moreover, it legitimates the authority of the teachers in Matthew's own community; these understand themselves to have been commissioned by Jesus-Wisdom. Matthew's use of the Wisdom metaphor can thus be interpreted as reflecting a social structure—the teaching class—insofar as we can say that it both occurs in an identifiable social class and serves to legitimate that same class.

We have, then, some notion of why Matthew uses the Wisdom metaphor to describe Jesus. But how does he take a highly developed female metaphor and so transform it that he can then identify it with a male historical figure? I believe that Matthew is able to make that identification precisely because of the nature of metaphor. Metaphor is tensive, as we have noted. It extends to incorporate and express new meanings. In the process, one or another aspect of the metaphor may be re-imagined or abandoned altogether. Matthew has abandoned consideration of Wisdom's role in creation, as well as conflation of σοφία and λόγος. Earlier we observed the fluidity of gender in some of Philo's writing. Similarly, in describing Jesus as Wisdom, Matthew has abandoned the female aspect of the metaphor Lady Wisdom.[103] Jesus is Wisdom, not because she has become male or because Jesus has become female. Rather, Jesus is Wisdom because he *does* the things Wisdom does, *functions* as does Wisdom.

There is another way in which to understand *how* Matthew can identify Wisdom with Jesus. Earlier we noted that Wisdom, as it occurs in late biblical and early Jewish sources, can usually be understood as an hypostasis. She is something like the deified virtues— usually female—of Greek and Roman religions which were sometimes identified with the emperor or other charismatic leaders.

I do not mean to imply that Matthew has any intention of comparing Jesus with Caesar in relation to the issue I am exploring. But

---

102. Cf. Cope, *Matthew: A Scribe*, pp. 121-30.

103. There is precedent for this in Philo's occasionally bisexual imagery for personified Wisdom, as we observed earlier in this essay; see, e.g., *Congr.* 9; *Fug.* 52.

Matthew was a person of late antiquity. He lived in a world in which people considered that they had access to deified virtues through charismatic figures, particularly the emperor, with whom those virtues and powers were identified. Moreover, in Matthew's thought-world, human self-consciousness could be replaced by a spirit, either evil or good. He—and his predecessors—may have believed that Jesus was thus 'possessed' by hypostatized Wisdom.[104] In the male Jesus they believed Wisdom received its earthly manifestation.

Wisdom and Gender in the Matthean Community

But what does Matthew's use of the Wisdom metaphor tell us of women's experience in his community? What would it have meant to them to know that they had access to Lady Wisdom in the man Jesus? Conversely, what would it have meant to them to hear Jesus identified with her? What does that identification tell us about women's roles in the Matthean community? Did Matthew identify Jesus with Lady Wisdom because he saw women in the roles of mother, prophet, teacher? Did the identification of Jesus with Lady Wisdom enable or encourage women in the Matthean community to assume public roles more freely, as did their sisters in other first-century Christian communities?[105]

Unfortunately, Matthew's description of Jesus as Wisdom tells us nothing directly of women's experience. Indeed, from the perspective of the questions raised above, I believe that Matthew's use of the metaphor Lady Wisdom betrays ambivalence. On the one hand, Matthew's use of the metaphor suggests admiration for Lady Wisdom in her roles as prophet, teacher, mother, and householder. One would be tempted to say that Matthew's use of Lady Wisdom empowered women to assume such roles and encouraged the community to acknowledge their leadership. On the other hand, in using the metaphor to articulate certain aspects of his understanding of Jesus, Matthew has erased the female in his use of the traditional material.[106] Once the female

---

104. J.M. Robinson thus interprets the Wisdom Christology of Q; 'Very Goddess and Very Man: Jesus' Better Self', in K. King (ed.), *Images of the Feminine in Gnosticism* (Philadelphia, PA: Fortress Press, 1988), pp. 115-23.

105. See Levine's comments on Q and Sophia Christology, 'Who's Catering', pp. 155-57.

106. I am grateful to Professor A.-J. Levine for her insight on this aspect of Matthew's use of the metaphor Lady Wisdom. See also Bernard J. Lee, *Jesus and the Metaphors of God: The Christs of the New Testament* (New York: Paulist Press, 1993), pp. 136, 142.

character of the metaphor had disappeared, only the literate among the community—male and female—with access to extracanonical as well as canonical sources, would have understood the allusions.

I believe that the gender-related ambivalence present in Matthew's use of the metaphor Lady Wisdom appears elsewhere in his Gospel. Women are minors as is the case in patriarchal societies. Thus, in the redactional additions in 14.21 and 15.38, they are placed with the children, in distinction from the men, as part of the crowds which Jesus feeds miraculously.[107] To be sure, Matthew treats women cordially and ascribes to them a wide variety of roles: wife, mother, servant, mother-in-law, prostitute, etc. But these are precisely the roles which we would expect in a text emerging from a patriarchal community. Even Pilate's wife, high-born though she be, is *wife* (27.19).[108]

Women do all the things one would expect. They intervene on their children's behalf (15.21-28; 20.20-28).[109] They serve guests (8.14-15). In the parables, they give birth (24.19),[110] make bread (13.33),[111] go to weddings (25.1-13). Women make their needs known, sometimes with an audacity which is itself praised (15.21-28). They are sometimes in need of help, for themselves or for someone dependent on them. They ask for it and thus give evidence of their faith.[112] Their example itself becomes a challenge to Matthew's audience to learn faith from those, he implies, whose status would seem to preclude such privilege.[113]

However, the genealogy in 1.1-17 includes women who puzzle us: Tamar, Rahab, Ruth, the wife of Uriah (Bathsheba), and Mary the mother of Jesus, all of whom produce male heirs in irregular, anomalous ways.[114] Rahab is a prostitute, Tamar must pretend to be a prosti-

107. See Mk 6.44; 8.9.
108. The appearance of Pilate's wife is a Matthean redactional insertion; cf. Mk 15.6-14; Lk. 23.17-23; Jn 18.39-40.
109. See Mk 7.24-30; 10.35-45.
110. See Mk 13.17; Lk. 21.23.
111. See Lk. 13.20-21.
112. E.g. Mt. 9.20-22; Mk 5.25-34; Mt. 15.21-28; Mk 7.24-30. In the first text, Matthew's redaction emphasizes the word πίστις (faith), found in Mark, by deleting what he considers to be extraneous material; in the second text, Matthew changes the Markan version in order specifically to praise the woman's faith; on Matthew's redaction of the miracle stories to underline faith and discipleship, see H.J. Held, 'Matthew as Interpreter of Miracle Stories', in Bornkamm, Barth and Held (eds.), *Tradition and Interpretation*, pp. 165-299.
113. Wire, 'Gender Roles', p. 106.
114. J. Capel Anderson, 'Matthew: Gender and Reading', *Semeia* 28 (1983), pp. 3-28 (9) (pp. 25-51 above); Raymond Brown summarizes various interpretations of this aspect of the genealogy in *The Birth of the Messiah: A Commentary on the Infancy*

tute in order to receive her due, and Bathsheba is an adulteress. Ruth is a foreigner who places Boaz in a compromising situation, and Mary is said to have given birth to her son, not by conceiving him by a human father, but 'by the holy spirit' (1.18, 20). These women, liminal characters whose domestic arrangements are anomalous, are part of Jesus' 'family tree'. Their presence suggests that their descendent will cross boundaries of gender, ethnicity, culture, and social status.

Furthermore, the presence of these women in the genealogy, in the opening verses of Matthew's Gospel, alerts us to the fact that not only will women be present in his Gospel in conventional roles, but they also will be present in startling ways, for example as foreigners (15.21-28) and prostitutes (21.31-32), praised for repentance and faith as are their male counterparts (8.5-14; 21.31-32; cf. 9.10; 11.19).

Earlier we observed that Matthew's transformation of the metaphor Lady Wisdom not only describes Jesus but also reflects the role of teachers, specifically scholarly teachers, in his community, and legitimates that role. Is there any indication that some of these teachers were women? It would *seem* not. 'Disciple' (μαθητής) does not refer to women, but to the men who follow Jesus. They are Jesus' 'brothers' (12.48-49). And the great commissioning of 28.16-20 concludes the Gospel with official leadership, teaching office, left to 11 men.

But closer examination of Matthew's text suggests a more complex situation, for the household of the ἐκκλησία includes all who do the Father's will as 'my brothers and sisters and mother' (12.50). Women, as well as men, have faith and believe (9.22; 15.28).

In 12.38-42, Matthew edits the Q passage (Lk. 11.29-32) to parallel more closely Nineveh's response to Jonah's preaching of repentance and the journey made by the Queen of the South to hear Solomon's wisdom.[115] Her search echoes the sages' quest for wisdom in the earlier materials.[116] It suggests the possibility of women sages in Matthew's community.

Furthermore, Matthew's redaction of Mark's description of the women witnesses of the crucifixion emphasizes ἀκολουθέω ('follow') and διακονέω ('serve') taken from the Markan source by placing the verbs early in the pericope (27.55; Mk 15.41). The first indicates discipleship, and the second suggests service in the community.[117] These

Narratives in the Gospels of Matthew and Luke (Garden City, NY: Doubleday, 1993), pp. 71-74.

115. Cf. my *Lady Wisdom*, pp. 60-63.

116. E.g. Prov. 8.17; Wis. 8.2; Sir. 14.22; 51.13-14. I overlooked the significance of this aspect of the text in my earlier work.

117. *Lady Wisdom*, pp. 212-13. Regarding these two verbs, Claudia Setzer asks,

women who followed and served, who remain at the scene of the crucifixion, contrast favorably to the male disciples who had fled when Jesus was arrested (26.56). Their courage highlights the male disciples' cowardice.

Ἀκολουθέω and διακονέω do not specify a precise role such as teaching. But following the master was the disciple's proper way of life,[118] both literally and metaphorically; in using διακονέω of women, Matthew suggests that they indeed are disciples of the one who had come 'not to be served but to serve' (οὐκ ἦλθεν διακονηθῆναι ἀλλὰ διακονῆσαι, 20.28). If διακονέω refers literally to service at table, these women could be seen as disciples of Wisdom who hosts a banquet.[119] Nonetheless, the indication of public service to the community present in the second verb, and its possible allusion to the metaphor of Lady Wisdom, open the possibility that one of the ways in which women served was in teaching.

Furthermore, Matthew's redaction of Mark's resurrection narrative in 28.1-10 emphasizes the apocalyptic nature of the passage, present already in Mk 16.1-8. In 28.2, Matthew has an earthquake accompany the angel's descent. Where Mark has a young man dressed in a white robe (16.5), Matthew has an angel whose 'appearance was like lightning, and his clothing white as snow' (28.3). The guards fall prostrate (28.4). Matthew changes Mark's version of the angel's words 'Do not be alarmed' (μὴ ἐκθαμβεῖσθε, 16.6) to the apocalyptic 'Do not fear' (μὴ φοβεῖσθε ὑμεῖς, 28.5). Matthew follows Mark and has the angel commission the women to tell the disciples the news of the resurrection (28.7).[120] However, he abbreviates Mark's description of the women's emotion in response to the angel's commission and tells us that they 'ran to tell his disciples' (28.8).

In a redactional insertion, Matthew describes the women as meeting the risen Jesus on their way to tell his disciples the news of the resurrection (vv. 9-10). Jesus tells the women to tell 'my brothers' (ἀδελφοῖς μου) to go to Galilee where he would appear to them. In Matthew's

---

'Were male names or the names of the Twelve substituted here, would anyone doubt for a moment that they were disciples?' ('Excellent Women: Female Witness to the Resurrection', *JBL* 116 [1997], pp. 259-72 [263]). Cf. also E. Wainwright, *Towards a Feminist Critical Reading of the Gospel According to Matthew* (BZNW, 60; Berlin: W. de Gruyter, 1991), pp. 296-97; eadem, *Shall We Look*, pp. 109-10.

118. E.g. Mt. 4.18-22; 9.9.
119. Prov. 9.1-6; Sir. 24.19-22.
120. On the commission, see Wainwright, *Towards a Feminist Critical Reading*, pp. 306-13; eadem, *Shall We Look*, pp. 112-18.

Gospel, then, the women receive their mission not only from the angel (v. 2)[121] but from the risen Christ himself.

The women, in Matthew's version of the resurrection narrative, experience an apocalyptic vision which recalls the transfiguration narrative (17.1-9).[122] Like the seers in apocalyptic texts, they are commissioned in the context of a vision. This characterization may place them in the framework of a group of learned teachers and/or preachers.

Women, then, described as apocalyptic visionaries, deliver the news of the resurrection to the disciples; this suggests the possibility that there were women teachers in the Matthean community. Evidence from Jewish and other Greco-Roman sources indicates the possibility of learned women in Matthew's community.[123] Yet it is the male disciples who receive the closing commission to 'make disciples of all the nations...teaching them to obey everything that I have commanded you' (28.19-20). Inclusion of both commissions suggests possible tensions over gender roles and teaching in the Matthean community.[124] However, Matthew's final word inscribes the dominance of male leadership, at least regarding teaching in the public sphere.

Would women in Matthew's community have perceived his Wisdom Christology as reflecting and legitimating their roles as wives, mothers, hostesses, teachers? We have no evidence. It is certainly possible that women sufficiently learned to interpret correctly the significance of Matthew's use of the metaphor Lady Wisdom could have done so. And such women might have experienced use of the metaphor as empowering their scholarly activity within the context of their households, and possibly beyond.

But what of Matthew's intention? We have already seen that Matthew uses the identification of Jesus with Wisdom to legitimate not

---

121. Cf. Mk 16.6-7.

122. While the vocabulary is not identical, the transfiguration narrative also heightens the references to Jesus' face and garments, describes the disciples' fear and prostration, and has Jesus say 'Do not fear'. See my 'Transfiguration', pp. 127-30.

123. Regarding Jewish women, see nn. 42-45 and text above. Regarding literary activity and women in the Greco-Roman world, see M.R. Lefkowitz and M.B. Fant, *Women's Life in Greece and Rome: A Source Book in Translation* (Baltimore, MD: The Johns Hopkins University Press, 2nd edn, 1992), pp. 166-70; W.V. Harris, *Ancient Literacy* (Cambridge, MA: Harvard University Press, 1989), pp. 132-33, 239-40, 309-10; S.B. Pomeroy, *Women in Hellenistic Egypt from Alexander to Cleopatra* (New York: Schocken Books, 1984), pp. 59-72; idem, *Goddesses, Whores, Wives and Slaves: Women in Classical Antiquity* (New York: Schocken Books, 1975), pp. 131-37, 170-76.

124. Cf. Deutsch, *Lady Wisdom*, p. 141.

only Jesus' teaching, but the authority of the scribal or teaching class in his own community. In light of our comments on the ways in which women are portrayed in Matthew's Gospel, we might say that Matthew uses the identification and legitimation to assert right order through set social roles.[125] In other words, he confirms women in their traditional roles.

Matthew, like Q, identifies Jesus with Wisdom by using the tropes of Jewish tradition. He has used a highly developed female metaphor to describe who Jesus is and what he does. But does this mean that Matthew exhibits thereby an appreciation for the divine as feminine? I would have to give a negative response to that question. One can, I think, apply to Matthew's usage Levine's words regarding the connection between Jesus and Wisdom in Q:

> The connection of Jesus and Sophia may indicate less an appreciation for the role of women in the Q community than a slight discomfort with feminine images. That is, since Sophia is a conventional motif in Wisdom literature, her direct association with Jesus may be less a 'feminizing' of the teacher than a 'masculininzing' of the mythical source of that teaching.[126]

For Matthew, with the partial exception of 11.19—along with earlier sources—has subsumed the female metaphor into the male personage, both singly (the portrayal of Jesus as Wisdom) and collectively (the legitimization of his own scribal class). It would seem to me that this process not only subordinates the female to the male but actually excludes the female from egalitarian participation.[127]

Is this Matthew's intention? I rather think not. I believe that Matthew uses the metaphor Wisdom to portray Jesus because he is using Jewish tradition to understand Jesus' life and teaching. Conversely, he reinterprets his tradition through that same life and teaching. And Lady Wisdom is part of that tradition. Moreover, Matthew is engaged in a struggle with teachers of the opposition and is trying to legitimate

---

125. Deutsch, *Lady Wisdom*, p. 141.
126. Levine, 'Who's Catering', p. 155; cf. R.S. Kraemer, *Her Share of the Blessings: Women's Religions among Pagans, Jews, and Christians in the Greco-Roman World* (New York: Oxford University Press, 1992), pp. 140-41.
127. Cf. Wolfson, 'Woman—The Feminine'; also in another context, see Luce Irigaray, 'Questions to Emmanuel Levinas on the Divinity of Love', M. Whitford (trans.), in R. Bernasconi and S. Critchley (eds.), *Re-Reading Levinas* (Bloomington: Indiana University Press, 1991), pp. 109-11. For another interpretation of male appropriation of female metaphors, see Tori Moi's discussion of Julia Kristeva in T. Moi, *Sexual/Textual Politics: Feminist Literary Theory* (London: Routledge, 1991 [1985]), pp. 166-67.

the authority of his own teaching class. The metaphor of Wisdom becomes an instrument in that struggle.

Matthew's use of the metaphor of Lady Wisdom parallels that of his sources. A sage, he uses the metaphor to legitimate the authority of the scholars' class which leads his community. The tensive nature of metaphor allows Matthew to transform a female metaphor in such a manner that it refers to a male historical figure. Although Matthew is cordial in his description of women, his use of the metaphor does not appear to reflect women's religious experience or to enhance their status. Rather, like his predecessors, Matthew uses the metaphor to legitimate the authority of a male scholars' class.

Whatever Matthew's conscious primary intention may have been, however, I think that one must explore the possibility that his use of the metaphor of Lady Wisdom may have functioned to maintain women in subordinate roles in a community led by a male teaching class.

SURPRISED BY FAITH:
JESUS AND THE CANAANITE WOMAN[*]

Gail R. O'Day

Introduction

On first reading, Mt. 15.21-28 is a text that may gall us because of the portrait of Jesus it presents: Jesus is petitioned for help by a nameless Gentile woman and turns his back on her and her need. It is a text that challenges our preconceptions about Jesus because he does not want to help the woman. His disciples even actively seek the woman's dismissal. The Jesus in this story seems greatly removed from our conventional images of him as the gracious, all-giving healer. Moreover, in the story the Gentile woman gets the better of Jesus in an argument and he changes his mind: he heals where he had at first refused healing. This portrait of Jesus' intransigence and the impingement of the Gentile woman has been a stumbling block to many interpreters. There is a hesitancy to recognize either the mutability of Jesus or the powerful presence of the woman.[1] Both, however, are central to the text.

The story of Jesus and the Canaanite woman is a richly layered and densely textured text. This text cannot simply be read for what it seems to be saying because its substance cannot be plotted on a single line. The text must also be read to see how it is constructed as well as how it communicates. What this story says is inseparable from how it says it.[2] In this essay I will demonstrate the theological and pastoral benefits that can be gained from a close reading of this text. We may

---

[*] Originally published in *Listening/Journal of Religion and Culture* 24 (1989), pp. 290-301. Reprinted by permission.

1. Robert Gundry (*Matthew: A Commentary on His Literary and Theological Art* [Grand Rapids: Eerdmans, 1982]) is an excellent example of this. In his treatment of Mt. 15.21-28 (pp. 309-17), Gundry is at great pains to emphasize Jesus' dominion, no matter how his reading distorts the details of the text.

2. For a discussion of the relationship between the 'how' and 'what' of the text, see Gail R. O'Day, *Revelation in the Fourth Gospel* (Philadelphia: Fortress Press, 1986), pp. 33-48.

find ourselves surprised by Mt. 15.21-28, just as Jesus was surprised by the Canaanite woman.

Matthew 15.21-28 is preceded by two pericopes that focus on keeping the law, and in particular, the purity laws. In Mt. 15.1-9, Jesus, the Pharisees, and the scribes debate the nature of defilement, and in Mt. 15.10-20 Jesus provides his disciples with additional teachings on the same subject. Both the debate and the teachings center on the relation between word and deed, pure and impure, and internal and external sources of defilement. Immediately after these discussions, Jesus turns away from the emissaries from Jerusalem, leaves Judea, and withdraws to Tyre and Sidon (15.21).

The geography of this sequence is more than happenstance. Jesus' rebuke of the Pharisees and scribes is intensified by his movements since he leaves the land and the people who are 'clean', to enter a land that is 'unclean'. The question of what is the source of defilement is thus put to the test by Jesus' very actions. Jesus' move from Jewish to Gentile territory seems to have been part of the tradition, since it also occurs in the Markan parallel (Mk 7.24-30). In Mark, however, Jesus journeys to Tyre (v. 24) and Sidon (v. 31) separately,[3] whereas in Matthew's version, the geographical move into unclean territory is highlighted by the joint reference to Tyre and Sidon. In the prophetic literature of the Old Testament, Tyre and Sidon are more than place names; they were Israel's dangerous and threatening enemies (e.g. Isa. 23; Ezek. 26-28; Joel 3.4).[4] The significance of the names Tyre and Sidon would not be lost on either Matthew or his readers.

Just as Matthew identifies Jesus' destination in Old Testament terms, so, too, does he identify in Old Testament terms the woman who comes out to meet him (15.22). In Mark, the woman is identified as Syro-Phoenician, a designation reflective of the nations of Jesus' own day. In Matthew, however, the woman is identified as Canaanite, the traditional biblical identification of Israel's enemy.[5] The word 'Canaanite' occurs only here in the New Testament, and the only other uses of 'Canaan' in the New Testament occur in retrospectives of Israel's

---

3. There is a minority reading of Mk 7.24 in later manuscripts that includes both Tyre and Sidon.

4. For a discussion of the symbolic value of Tyre in the Old Testament prophets, see Carol Newsom, 'A Maker of Metaphors—Ezekiel's Oracle Against Tyre', *Int* 38 (1984), pp. 151-64.

5. On the Israelite treatment of the Canaanites, see Jon Levenson, 'Is There a Counterpart in the Hebrew Bible to New Testament Antisemitism?', *JES* 22 (1985), pp. 243-60.

history (Acts 7.11; 13.19). We may thus safely judge Matthew's anachronistic use of 'Canaanite' to be an intentional narrative strategy to accentuate the distinctions between Jesus and the woman who approaches him. She is the enemy, not of his kind.

The juxtaposition of the geographic details in the opening verses of our text with the preceding narratives about defilement raises many questions about what is to follow. Will Jesus' actions in 15.21-28 match his words in 15.1-19? How will questions of clean and unclean be resolved when Tyre, Sidon, and Canaan clamor for attention? Will the Canaanite woman be welcomed as an occasion for Gentile mission (cf. Mt. 8.5-13), or rebuffed as an outsider, an enemy? The narrative context and introductory details move us forward into the text itself.

2. Identifying the Form

The form of Mt. 15.21-28 has proved problematic for form critics. At first glance, Mt. 15.21-28 seems to be a story about a healing: it opens with a request for healing and ends with the granting of the request. Yet this pericope is almost uniformly rejected by form critics as a miracle story proper.[6] There is almost no narrative material in this pericope, as the bulk of the text is dialogue, and neither the daughter's illness nor her healing are depicted for the reader. Instead of being the focus of the story, the illness/healing seems to function only as a narrative foil to precipitate the dialogue between Jesus and the Canaanite woman. It is a story in which a healing is reported, but it is not a miracle story *per se* because the miracle is subordinated to other interests.

The story is therefore most frequently classified as a 'saying of Jesus',[7] but Mt. 15.21-28 refuses to be contained by this form-critical category as well. In a 'saying of Jesus' story, or 'apophthegm', the focus is 'entirely confined to the saying of Jesus', and the material is not 'tied up to a particular place or time, or at most only accidentally so'.[8] According to both of these criteria, therefore, Mt. 15.21-28 falls outside

---

6. So Rudolf Bultmann, *History of the Synoptic Tradition* (trans. J. Marsh; New York: Harper & Row, 1963), p. 209, and Heinz Joachim Held, 'The Retelling of Miracle Stories by Matthew', in G. Bornkamm, G. Barth and H.J. Held (eds.), *Tradition and Interpretation in Matthew* (Philadelphia: Westminster Press, 1963), pp. 165-211 (197).

7. Bultmann, *History*, p. 209; Martin Dibelius, *From Tradition to Gospel* (New York: Charles Scribner's Sons, 1965), p. 261.

8. Bultmann, *History*, pp. 62-64.

the conventions of form-critically identified genres. First, the focus is not confined to the saying of Jesus. A final, climactic teaching of Jesus is not the point of this story because the 'point' of the story rests in the change undergone by Jesus. The focus is not as much on what Jesus says as on what is said to him. Second, as already noted, the geography of this story is more than accidental.[9] It is essential to what transpires that the story is set in Gentile territory, and that Jesus' interlocutor is a Canaanite woman. This text, then, refuses classification as either a miracle story or a saying of Jesus.

That this story defies conventional genre categorizations is, like its geography, more than happenstance. Traditional form critical categories work from the assumption that Jesus is the protagonist of each story being studied, and seeks to establish a taxonomy of Jesus' various functions. In our story, however, Jesus is not the protagonist; the Canaanite woman is. Traditional form critical investigation will therefore always come up empty, because it asks inappropriate questions of this text. Matthew 15.21-28 is neither miracle story nor apophthegm by design. It tells an unconventional story with an unconventional protagonist. The story, like the Canaanite woman herself, will not be pigeonholed.

The structure of Mt. 15.21-28 illuminates the relative positions of Jesus and the woman in this story. The pericope breaks down into three units:

> vv. 22-23a   The Canaanite woman and Jesus
> vv. 23b-24   The disciples and Jesus
> vv. 25-28   The Canaanite woman and Jesus

In the first unit (vv. 22-23a), the Canaanite woman approaches Jesus and speaks directly to him, but he does 'not answer a word to her' (v. 23a). She has attempted conversation but her attempt is thwarted. In the second unit (vv. 23b-24), the disciples speak directly to Jesus about the woman, asking that she be sent away. This time Jesus responds, but he addresses himself to the disciples, not the woman. In the third unit (vv. 25-28), the woman approaches Jesus again and this time succeeds in engaging him in conversation.

As the outline makes clear, the story's development hinges on the Canaanite woman. In the first and third units, she initiates contact and 'conversation' with Jesus; in the middle unit she is the goad that prompts the disciples to speak to Jesus. She is indeed the protagonist.

---

9. Bultmann, *History*, p. 64, considers precise indications of place to be secondary additions to the tradition.

The opening words of each unit of the text also focus attention on the woman. Each unit begins with an imperative: have mercy on me, send her away, help me. The Canaanite woman's petitions are ostensibly for herself ('have mercy on *me*', 'help *me*'), although *her* real goal is the restoration of her daughter's health. The ostensible object of the disciples' petition is also the woman ('send *her* away'), although their real aim is their own relief. The disciples are the woman's unwitting allies, because their words about her dismissal actually function to keep her in view. The woman impinges on Jesus from all sides and does not hesitate to make her presence felt and demand known.

Jesus, by contrast, initiates nothing in this story. In fact, in the first and second units, his role is strictly that of refusal. Of the three petitions made of Jesus, the first two are not sanctioned by him.[10] To the first petition, Jesus turns a deaf ear. To the second petition, Jesus responds with a rebuttal concerning his mission's purpose, but does not grant the disciples' request. It is only the third petition, the woman's restatement of her need, that is finally sanctioned. After an involved dialogue in which the woman continues to press her case, the woman's imperative of petition is matched by an imperative of response, 'let it be done to you as you wish' (v. 28). Jesus concedes and grants the woman's wish.

Matthew 15.21-28 is from beginning to end the story of the Canaanite woman. She initiates the movement of the story with her first petition, refuses to be silenced or ignored, and in the end goes away victorious, having been answered and heard by Jesus. She is insistent, demanding, and unafraid to state her claims. She is the lifeblood of this story. Any attempt to classify this text by placing Jesus at its center will ultimately be inadequate. We must instead look to the Canaanite woman's daring insistence as the key to the distinctive shape and form of this text.

3. *Matthew 15.21-28 and the Lament Psalm*

When we listen carefully to the woman's daring words, we hear echoes of words that have been spoken from the beginning of Israel's life of

---

10. The notion of 'sanctioning' a need is a key element of the narrative schema formulated by Greimas (A.J. Greimas and J. Cortes, *Semantics and Language* [Bloomington: Indiana University Press, 1982]). Hendrikus Boers (*Neither on This Mountain nor in Jerusalem* [Atlanta: Scholars Press, 1988]) analyzes the story of the Samaritan woman in Jn 4 from the perspective of the semiotic schema of sanctioning. A thorough semiotic analysis of Mt. 15.21-28 according to the sanctioning of needs would contribute to our understanding of this text.

faith. Commentators on Mt. 15.21-28 frequently note the resemblance between the woman's words of petition and the cries for salvation and deliverance in Israel's lament psalms.[11] In the woman's cry for pity (mercy) (v. 22) one can hear echoes of Ps. 86.16, 'Turn to me and take pity on me'. In her cry for help (v. 25), one can hear echoes of Ps. 109.26, 'Help me, O Lord my God'. The connection between Mt. 15.21-28 and Israel's lament psalms goes deeper than verbal echoes in the woman's petitions, however, and has not been adequately probed by interpreters. The very boldness of the woman's stance before Jesus has its roots in Israel's bold stance before God in the laments. The form which helps readers understand Mt. 15.21-28 is neither miracle story nor apophthegm, but the psalm of lament. Matthew 15.21-28 is a *narrative embodiment of a lament psalm*. To demonstrate this thesis, I will first review the characteristics of the lament psalm and then assess the Matthean text in the light of those characteristics.

The majority of the prayers and songs in the Psalter are laments—individual and communal prayers of desperate longing, heart wrenching brokenness, pained injustice.[12] The laments confront God with startling candor, placing full-bodied pleas and petitions for help and deliverance boldly before God. Israel was not afraid to make its needs known to God and to assert that those needs and injustices, those complaints and fears, were God's business. These candid psalms of lament had a regular home in Israel's liturgy.[13] Israel knew that its worship, as with all its life with God, had to allow for the honest articulation of pain, fear, and need; these human experiences had to be handed over to God in disciplined, liberated speech in order for transformation to become a reality.

The lament psalms are characterized by a clearly recognizable form. They contain two major sections: an opening section of *plea* that gives

---

11. E.g. Eduard Schweizer, *The Good News According to Matthew* (trans. D.E. Green; Atlanta: John Knox Press, 1975), p. 330, and Gundry, *Matthew*, p. 314.

12. For studies of lament psalms that address both their form and theology, see Claus Westermann, *Praise and Lament in the Psalms* (Atlanta: John Knox Press, 1981), and Walter Brueggemann, *The Message of the Psalms* (Minneapolis: Augsburg, 1984).

13. The candid laments of Israel found their place in the liturgy because of Israel's powerful memory of God's salvation and deliverance. See Rainer Albertz, *Persönliche Frömmigkeit und offizielle Religion: religionsinterner Pluralismus in Israel u. Babylon* (CTM, 9; Stuttgart: Calver Verlag, 1978), Gerhard Gerstenberger, *Der bittende Mensch* (Neukirchen–Vluyn: Neukirchener Verlag, 1980), and W. Brueggemann, *Israel's Praise: Doxology Against Idolatry and Ideology* (Philadelphia: Fortress Press, 1988).

way to words of *praise*.[14] The lament psalms thus not only contain words of lament, petition, and complaint, but also words that reflect change and transformation.

Within the first section of the lament, the words of *plea*, the following constituent elements may be found:[15]

(1) Address
(2) Complaint
(3) Petition
(4) Motivations
(5) Imprecations

The petitioner addresses God directly. The complaint is not spoken at random, but to a particular, named addressee. In the complaint the petitioner tells God how bad and desperate the situation has become. The petitioner then asks that God act decisively to rectify the situation of complaint. The address, complaint, and petition form the heart of the plea. To strengthen the petitioner's claim, he or she may add motivations and/or imprecations. In the motivations, the petitioner provides God with reasons why God should act. In the imprecations, the petitioner expresses the rage and hostility (in the form of curses) the desperate situation has provoked.

Words of *praise* follow the words of plea. Scholars have long noted the 'abrupt change in mood' in the lament psalms.[16] The constituent elements of the praise section include:

(1) Assurance of being heard
(2) Payment of vows
(3) Doxology and praise

Psalm 13 is a succinct example of the basic lament form.[17] In vv. 1 and 2 we have the address ('O Lord') and complaint ('How long...?'). In v. 3 we have the petition ('Consider and answer me'), and in v. 4 we have a double motivation ('lest...lest...'). The psalmist knows himself to be in constant pain and sorrow, threatened by enemies, absented from God's presence, standing on the verge of death. At v. 5, however, the mood of the psalm changes, and the petitioner now

14. Westermann's study of this movement from plea to praise (*Praise and Lament*) has had decisive influence on the study of psalms of lament.
15. Hermann Gunkel (*Einleitung in die Psalmen* [Göttingen: Vandenhoeck & Ruprecht, 1933]), and Westermann (*Praise and Lament*) have done the determinative studies of the lament form.
16. This phrase comes from Gunkel, *Einleitung*, p. 243.
17. Brueggemann, *Message of the Psalms*, pp. 58-60, provides an analysis of Ps. 13.

speaks words of praise. Verses 5 and 6 contain the assurance that God has heard and responded ('God has dealt bountifully with me'), and the words of doxology ('I will sing').

By the end of Ps. 13, God's bountiful, gracious acts are as real to the psalmist as God's silence and seeming abandonment were at its beginning. What can account for the move to praise? The most widely accepted hypothesis for this move is that within the context of Israel's liturgy, the answer to the petitioner's plea has been given.[18] At the moment in the liturgy when the complaint and the plea have been placed before God, the priest, the leader of the liturgy, addresses the petitioner with words of assurance. This 'salvation oracle', as the words of assurance are called, tells the petitioner that his or her plea has been heard by God, and that God's presence and help are sure. In the midst of the pain, fear, and need of the petitioner, a word of God enters to transform brokenness and to open the petitioner to new, courageous possibilities for life.

What is most astonishing about Israel's lament psalms is that the candid speaking of pain in the liturgy actually worked: the transformation of pain and the meeting of need did indeed take place. Reality does seem to change for the petitioner from the beginning of the psalm to the end. Israel boldly, often brazenly, placed its claims before God, and God listened and responded.

4. *The Lament Psalm as an Act of Faith*

We are now ready to look at Mt. 15.21-28, and in particular the Canaanite woman's words, against the backdrop of Israel's psalms of lament. The woman's words can be isolated from the larger narrative and written as follows:

> Have mercy on me,
> O Lord, Son of David,
> My daughter is severely possessed by a demon (v. 22)
> Lord, help me (v. 25)
> Yes, Lord,
> For even the dogs eat the crumbs that fall from their
> masters' table (v. 27)

---

18. The hypothesis of the place of the answering salvation oracle in the liturgy of the psalms was most fully developed by Joachim Begrich, 'Das priesterliche Heilsorakel', *ZAW* 52 (1934), pp. 81-92. This study is now reprinted in Walter Zimmerli (ed.), *Gesammelte Studien zum Alten Testament* (Munich: Chr. Kaiser Verlag, 1964), pp. 217-31. There have been some who have contested Begrich's hypothesis, most notably Edgar Conrad ('Second Isaiah and the Priestly Oracle of

It is now possible to outline the Canaanite woman's words according to the basic constitutive elements of the lament form:

>   Petition: Have mercy on me
>   Address: O Lord, Son of David
>   Complaint: My daughter is severely possessed...
>   Address: Lord
>   Petition: Help me[19]
>   Motivation: For even the dogs eat the crumbs...

What we discover is that the woman's words are, in essence, a short lament psalm. Matthew has shaped her words to reflect the traditional, candid speech of Jews before their God.

The woman's words of address, petition, and complaint need no additional commentary. Verse 27, which I have labeled the motivation, deserves special attention, however. After the woman renews her address and petition in v. 25, Jesus finally turns to answer her. His answer, however, is not to grant her request, but to provide a rationale for not granting it. In v. 23, he had told his disciples that his mission was only to Israel, and in v. 26 he reasserts that notion, this time in a more colloquial, proverbial idiom. Jews commonly used 'dogs' as an epithet for Gentiles, and Jesus may be quoting a maxim here.[20] Whatever the origin of Jesus' words, his intent is clear: he will not grant the woman's request because she is not of his people.

The Canaanite woman, however, will not be silenced by this rebuff. Her answer to Jesus is rich with irony.[21] With a masterful use of overstatement (ναί, i.e., yes),[22] she begins by granting the truth of Jesus' maxim, but goes on to show that its truth is nonetheless irrelevant to her claim and request. Even the outsider deserves minimal attention. The motivation element of the lament psalm aids our interpretation of the Canaanite woman's words here. In the motivation, the petitioner

---

Salvation [Reply to J. Begrich]', *ZAW* 93 [1981], pp. 234-46, and *Fear Not Warrior: A Study of 'al tira' Pericopes in the Hebrew Scriptures* [Chico, CA: Scholars Press, 1985]).

19. The repetition of individual elements (as with the repetition of the petition and address here) is standard in lament psalms. See, for example, the repetition of complaint (vv. 1-2, 6-8, 12-18), motivation (vv. 3-5, 9-10), and petition (vv. 11, 19-21) in Ps. 22.

20. On this verse as a maxim, see J.D.M. Derrett, 'Law in the New Testament: The Syrophoenician Woman and the Centurion of Capernaum', *NovT* 15 (1973), pp. 162-73.

21. For a discussion of irony and biblical narrative, see O'Day, *Revelation in the Fourth Gospel*.

22. The Greek particle ναί is used for emphatic repetition (BDF §441). The emphatic is a possible signal to ironic overstatement.

attempts to provide God with reasons to act. The motivations given may range from threat of the petitioner's death to an appeal to God's own power and reputation. The motivation is in many respects a form of bargaining, or even intimidating, as the petitioner works to force God's hand (e.g. Ps. 88.11).[23] That is precisely the function of the Canaanite woman's words in v. 27. The woman contends that even if Jesus' words in v. 26 are true, acts of dignity and charity are still by no means excluded. Even dogs eat crumbs from the table, so who are you to deny me?, she asserts. Is Jesus not gracious enough to provide crumbs? She provides Jesus with a motivation to act that appeals to his sense of vocation.

The woman's motivation holds sway, as the motivation also does in the lament psalms, and Jesus responds. Jesus' words in v. 28 function as a salvation oracle, and complete the embodiment of the lament psalm in this story. Verse 28 contains the words that turn the situation from despair to hope, from plea to praise. In response to the woman's unrelenting insistence, Jesus says, 'O woman, great is your faith! Be it done for you as you desire'. Jesus' words give voice to what the woman's words have already demonstrated: her faith. Israel's placing of needs and hurts before God was an act of faith in God's presence and ability to respond. The Canaanite woman's act of placing her need before Jesus was also an act of faith. Even when circumstances seemed to indicate the opposite, when Jesus and his disciples seemed resolutely determined not to listen, the woman persevered in her faith that she would be heard.

In Mt. 15.21-28, then, we see the narrative enactment of a lament psalm. The woman's words provide the words of plea, Jesus' final response provides the move from plea to praise, and in the aftermath of the story, the daughter's healing, we find the occasion for praise itself. This text is neither miracle story nor a saying of Jesus, but a story about robust faith that will not die, despite all odds against it. The vehicle Matthew uses to tell this story of faith is Israel's lament psalm, the quintessential form of robust faith found in Scripture.

5. *Surprised by Faith*

In Israel's lament psalms, Israel demands that God should be as God has promised to be. God has made promises of life, not death; hope, not despair; wholeness, not brokenness. Israel will not let God forget

---

23. For a discussion of the function of motivations in the lament psalms, see Brueggemann, *Message of the Psalms*, p. 55.

these promises. When the circumstances of life seem to void them, Israel does not run away from God, defeated, but instead confronts God directly. Israel will not let go of God's promises, or let God 'off the hook', because its insistent faith in God's promises is the key to new life. The experience of life may seem to indicate the end of the promises, but Israel will not settle for that. Rather, Israel will remind God in bold petitions about a fresh and hopeful future.

The Canaanite woman in Mt. 15.21-28 is infused with this same spirit of defiant resistance to despair, and bold faith in God's promises. The odds are incontrovertibly against her: she is an outsider, her daughter is demon-possessed; no one will listen to her. Yet, she perseveres, holding Jesus to whom he is, and to what he has promised: God's saving presence.

What a rich irony this text presents, then, in this woman whom Matthew has identified as a Canaanite! This woman, who shows herself to be full heiress of Israel's tradition of lament, is not Jewish at all, but Canaanite. She is not of the chosen people, yet she clings resolutely to their promise. This Canaanite woman is more faithful, indeed, more authentically Jewish, than many of the Jews whom Jesus encounters. She is a fuller embodiment of Jewish traditions than Jesus' own disciples, who want to dismiss her because she is a foreigner and an irritant. The Canaanite woman stands fully in the tradition of Abraham and Moses who were not afraid to bargain with God (Gen. 18.22-33; Num. 11.11-15); she is profoundly linked with all the broken and needy petitioners who sang Israel's songs of lament, with all those in Israel who cling to the faithfulness of the promise. She is not a Jew; she is, nevertheless, fully Jewish.

Matthew's use of the form of the lament psalm to shape this text ensures that the pointedness of the irony of the Canaanite woman's story will not be missed by his readers. Her expression of faith places her within the promise. Matthew holds up as model of faith not simply a woman and Gentile, but a despised Canaanite. And the faith she embodies is not a faith of submission,[24] but of robust boldness and

24. There seems to be a resistance in scholarship on this text to credit the Canaanite woman with much more than submission to Jesus. For example, Held, 'The Retelling of Miracle Stories', p. 200, quotes admiringly A. Schlatter's description of the woman's 'complete submission' to Jesus. Similarly, Gundry, *Matthew*, emphasizes the woman's acquiescence to what Jesus says. Such a view of the Canaanite woman, however, is more determined by preconceptions about the relative positions of Jesus and the woman than by the details of the text itself. This woman does not quietly submit to Jesus, but takes him on directly. Her faith moves beyond stereotypes of female passivity.

vigor. As a model of faith, Matthew has chosen someone from the margin: a Canaanite woman who lives at the boundaries (ἀπὸ τῶν ὁρίων, v. 22). It is the marginal one, the one who would be reckoned 'unclean', who pushes Jesus to new possibilities. The disciples, scions of Israel, do not want to open up to new possibilities, but rather foreclose them. Dismissal of the Canaanite woman would keep things the way they have always been. The woman from the margin, however, will not settle for this. She lives a faith filled with new possibilities and hope for a vibrant future.

Jesus was changed by this woman's boldness. Just as God is impinged upon by Israel's pleas, so is Jesus impinged upon here. The Canaanite woman knows who Jesus is and holds him to it; she will not settle for a diminishment of the promise. She insists that Jesus be Jesus, and through her insistence she frees him to be fully who he is. Two dominant themes of Mt. 15.21-28 are healing (vv. 22, 27) and feeding (vv. 26-27). Jesus resists doing either. Immediately after his exchange with the Canaanite woman, however, Jesus moves on to heal (vv. 29-31) and feed (vv. 32-39) multitudes. Once again, we may regard this configuration of texts as more than happenstance. The woman's faith in Jesus reminds him of the fullness and vitality of the promise, and he moves forward to fulfill that promise.

Matthew 15.21-28 is a powerful story about the surprise of the gospel. Using the idiom of Israel's lament, Matthew narrates a story that shows the power and possibility inherent in boldly insisting that God be faithful to God's promises. In the voice of this marginal woman who would not be silenced even when no one seemed to listen, we hear the resilience of faith. The Canaanite woman's faith insisted on the fulfilment of the gospel promise, and Matthew asks that we, like Jesus himself, listen to her and be transformed through a faith like hers: persistent, vigorous, and confident in God's faithfulness to God's promises.

NOT WITHOUT MY DAUGHTER:
GENDER AND DEMON POSSESSION IN MATTHEW 15.21-28

Elaine M. Wainwright

While preparing this paper I experienced Barrie Kosky's *King Lear* presented by the Bell Shakespeare Company. In an interview recorded in the booklet accompanying the play, John Bell says: 'It's great to come back to it and have a second go. As with any great role, you need to work it again and again, just as a classical musician or singer works a particular repertoire.'[1]

This led me to reflect on my wish to revisit Mt. 15.21-28, the story of Justa, the Canaanite woman and her daughter.[2] Three times now I have turned my lens upon this story from different vantage points, and three times it has yielded to the re-working of it.[3] In this essay, I wish to turn attention to the most forgotten aspect of the story, the daughter of Justa and her demon possession. She is, in fact, the *raison d'être* for the story, and yet she is so often overlooked. This paper will explore that neglect of Justa's daughter and her demon possession

---

1. *Barrie Kosky's King Lear by William Shakespeare* (Queensland Theatre Company, nd).
2. The *Pseudo-Clementine Epistles* give the name 'Justa' to the Canaanite woman. I have chosen to use this name throughout this paper in order that in the reclamation of this story, the naming of the woman may lead to her story being remembered in contemporary Christian telling of the story. Unnamed characters tend to be forgotten more easily than those who have been given names, and female characters in the gospel story, especially; named female characters are fewer than named male characters. The naming of women characters, especially when that naming belongs within the Christian tradition, can assist in bringing them to the center of the Christian re-membering.
3. Elaine Mary Wainwright, *Towards a Feminist Critical Reading of the Gospel According to Matthew* (BZNW, 60; Berlin: W. de Gruyter, 1991); *eadem*, 'A Voice from the Margin: Reading Matthew 15:21-28 in an Australian Feminist Key', in Fernando F. Segovia and Mary Ann Tolbert (eds.), *Reading from this Place. II. Social Location and Biblical Interpretation in Global Perspective* (Minneapolis: Fortress Press, 1995), pp. 132-53; and *eadem, Shall We Look for Another? A Feminist Rereading of the Matthean Jesus* (Maryknoll, NY: Orbis Books, 1998), pp. 84-92.

and then, using an anthropological approach, it will examine the healing of the young girl or young woman within the context of the unfolding narrative of healing within the Matthean Gospel story. Particular attention will be given to gender and its interconnection with ethnicity within this story.

A Silent Voice is Further Silenced

Within the Matthean story-telling, it is Justa who gives voice to her daughter's demon possession: 'My daughter is severely possessed by a demon' (Mt. 15.22). Davies and Allison, in the most extensive historical-critical commentary on Matthew's Gospel, pay much more attention to the differences between the Markan and Matthean designation of the daughter than they do to the possible meaning of her mother's description.[4] Two recent commentaries by Donald Senior and Daniel J. Harrington pass over the reason for this story in silence.[5] There is no discussion of the designation 'demon possessed' as it is predicated of this young woman/girl, no questioning as to what this might mean in the unfolding of her story and that of her mother.

An examination of the most recent studies of Mt. 15.21-28 from a variety of perspectives yields a similar result. Two *Semeia* articles which approach the text from a postcolonial and an African perspective, giving attention to Christology and the action of the spirit or *Moya*, both completely ignore the description of Justa's daughter. More attention is given to the dogs that eat the crumbs than the young woman/girl.[6] J. Martin C. Scott undertakes both an historical-critical and a narrative reading of the gospel, but like most readings his focus rests on Jesus and Justa even though the article begins with an imaginative reconstruction of the young woman's story in her own voice.[7] It seems unnecessary to detail further this lacuna, this silencing of Justa's

---

4. W.D. Davies and Dale C. Allison, Jr, *A Critical and Exegetical Commentary on the Gospel According to Saint Matthew* (3 vols.; ICC; Edinburgh: T. & T. Clark, 1991), II, p. 548.

5. Donald Senior, *The Gospel of Matthew* (Interpreting Biblical Texts; Nashville: Abingdon Press, 1997), p. 131; Daniel J. Harrington, *The Gospel of Matthew* (Sacra Pagina, 1; Collegeville, MN: Liturgical Press, 1991), p. 235.

6. Jim Perkinson, 'A Canaanitic Word in the Logos of Christ: or the Difference the Syro-Phoenician Woman Makes to Jesus', *Semeia* 75 (1996), pp. 61-86; Musa W. Dube, 'Readings of *Semoya*: Batswana Women's Interpretations of Matt 15:21-28', *Semeia* 73 (1996), pp. 111-30.

7. J. Martin C. Scott, 'Matthew 15.21-28: A Test-Case for Jesus' Manners', JSNT 63 (1996), pp. 21-44.

plea for her daughter. Suffice to conclude that Richard H. Hiers may well be correct when he notes that 'Jesus' work as demon-exorcist has generally received little attention'[8] and hence the overlooking of Justa's daughter's plight belongs to this blindspot. Another explanation may be that of the summary given by Amy-Jill Levine in the paper delivered to the Colloquium on the Gospel of Matthew *in memoriam* of William G. Thompson in which she categorized two schools of scholarship on this pericope: the older son representing more 'traditional' malestream scholarship and the younger daughter who reads with the lenses of feminism, postcolonialism, and postmodernism. She states that '(w)here the son concentrates his attention on Jesus, the ultimate insider, in terms of Christology, miracle, and approval of the woman's faith, the daughter focuses on the woman's ethnicity, gender, and otherness'.[9] Attention has shifted, as Levine has pointed out, from sole focus on Jesus to an inclusion of Justa and her role in the story.[10] It has not yet moved to include that of her daughter or more particularly her demon possession.[11]

Within the Matthean text, however, in a way which differs from the work of interpreters, the designation of Justa's daughter as demon possessed has a place. It belongs with a number of other references to those whom Jesus encounters in the reign-of-God movement and whom first-century society named as demon possessed. Several times the participle, δαιμονιζόμενος or 'demon possessed', is used to refer

8. Richard H. Hiers, 'Satan, Demons, and the Kingdom of God', *SJT* 27 (1974), pp. 35-47 (35). The situation Hiers describes has, however, been rectified a little in recent times by Graham H. Twelftree, *Jesus the Exorcist: A Contribution to the Study of the Historical Jesus* (Peabody, MA: Hendrickson, 1993).

9. Amy-Jill Levine, 'Matthew's Advice to a Divided Readership', in D.E. Aune (ed.), *The Gospel of Matthew in Current Study* (Grand Rapids: Eerdmans, 2000), pp. 22-41.

10. I do not agree with Levine, 'Matthew's Advice', p. 13, when she seems to want to separate the Matthean telling of the story of Jesus from that of other characters like the Canaanite woman. This is to isolate Jesus from the reign-of-God movement in which he was embedded and to deny the role that others both within the reign-of-God movement and in the Matthean storytelling community played in the shaping of the Jesus' story and the significance, therefore, of their stories. For further development of this, see Wainwright, *Shall We Look*, pp. 14-17, 23-26.

11. In Wainwright, *Shall We Look*, p. 90, I do characterize the household constituted by Justa and her daughter as demon possessed but do not develop this further; I simply contrast it to the other household, the house of Israel. Also, in 'A Voice from the Margin', pp. 147-48, attention is given to the intimate link between mother and daughter and its significance for contemporary feminist subjectivity, but again, the demon possession is not explored.

generally to those considered to be afflicted by demon possession and who were, therefore, in need of healing (Mt. 4.24; 8.16; 12.22). It is also used in specific cases of demon possession—the two Gadarenes (8.28), the dumb demoniac (9.32), and Justa's daughter (15.22), in which case the participle is in the feminine form. There are also instances in which reference is made to the casting out of demons generally (7.22; 10.8 and 12.27) and to particular demons like that which possesses the epileptic boy (17.18). Within the specific references, Justa's daughter is the only female said to be afflicted with demon possession and hence in need of healing. The reader could assume, however, that the general references to those demon possessed could have included both women and men.

A Methodological Approach

Since both historical-critical and narrative approaches to Mt. 15.21-28 have failed to take account of the description of Justa's daughter, attention must be directed toward the development of a methodological approach which may enable the best exploration of the meaning-making process entailed in the label 'demon possessed'. Such an approach needs to be text based, as it is the language of the text which conveys meaning. When a literary approach is accompanied by social-scientific methodologies—especially a cultural-anthropological approach which examines the meaning-making associated with the language of sickness and healing generally and, in this instance, the language of demon possession—unique possibilities of understanding emerge. Within this approach, demon possession and its healing are not understood simply in terms of healer, recipient of healing, description of an illness or type of cure but within an entire socio-cultural system which is both semantic and symbolic. John Pilch notes in this regard that '(h)uman sickness as a personal and social reality and its therapy are inextricably bound to language and signification'.[12]

This hermeneutical approach to healing is particularly appropriate in a study whose focus is the gendering (see p. 13) of healing, given the recognition among feminist scholars that gender, like healing, is not a cultural 'given' but is being constructed in the process of human meaning-making.[13] The healing of Justa's daughter from demon possession will be examined in relation to other accounts of demon possession but also in relation to other healing accounts of women in

12. John J. Pilch, 'Understanding Biblical Healing: Selecting the Appropriate Model', *BTB* 18 (1988), pp. 60-66.
13. Margaret W. Conkey and Joan M. Gero, 'Tensions, Pluralities, and Engen-

the Matthean storytelling in order to determine how it is constructed in and by the text within a socio-cultural system. The model chosen for this comparative study is that of Arthur Kleinman.[14] I will use the five categories of Kleinman's cross-cultural criteria—institutional setting; characteristics of the interpersonal interaction; idiom of communication; clinical reality; and therapeutic stages and mechanisms[15]—allowing them to overlap somewhat as the analysis unfolds. As noted, I have already applied these to the three healing narratives of women in Mt. 8-9. An examination of the language and accounts of demon possession with particular attention to Mt. 15.21-28 will then enable some comparison to be made with other healing narratives and in relation to healing generally in the Matthean Gospel.

Demon Possession in the Greco-Roman World: A Brief Survey

To undertake this brief survey of demon possession in the Greco-Roman world is to undertake a difficult task, especially from a cultural-anthropological point of view which is based on an understanding that 'culture determines the meanings that humans attach to all that goes on in the world around them'.[16] It is cultural knowledge that gives meaning to the narrative world constructed by texts and yet, in relation to an ancient world like the Greco-Roman world, our access to that world is based so much on texts. Cross-cultural studies have, however, sought to piece together the somewhat fragmented picture we have of demon possession.

Roger Baker, in his work *Binding the Devil*, notes that one function of demons in the ancient world was as an explanation for 'anything

---

dering Archaeology: An Introduction to Women and Prehistory', in Joan M. Gero and Margaret W. Conkey (eds.), *Engendering Archaeology: Women and Prehistory* (Oxford: Basil Blackwell, 1991), pp. 3-30; Rosi Braidotti, 'What's Wrong with Gender?', in Fokkelien van Dijk-Hemmes and Athalya Brenner (eds.), *Reflections on Theology and Gender* (Kampen: Kok, 1994), pp. 49-67.

14. Arthur Kleinman, *Patients and Healers in the Context of Culture: An Exploration of the Borderland between Anthropology, Medicine and Psychiatry* (Comparative Studies of Health Systems and Medical Care; Berkeley: University of California Press, 1980).

15. Kleinman, *Patients and Healers*, pp. 207-208. I wish to note here that I have already applied these categories to a study of the healing accounts in Mt. 8-9, especially the healing of women; see ' "Your Faith Has Made You Well": Jesus, Women and Healing in the Gospel of Matthew', in Ingrid Rosa Kitzberger (ed.), *Transformative Encounters: Jesus and Women Re-viewed* (Leiden: E.J. Brill), pp. 224-44.

16. Susan R. Garrett, *The Demise of the Devil: Magic and the Demonic in Luke's Writings* (Minneapolis: Fortress Press, 1989), p. 6.

that threatens the new *status quo*—basic systems of organization, or the social order itself'.[17] Demons were likewise associated with that which threatened the well-being of the person in society: certain illnesses or deformities and even death.[18] The exorcising of demons, therefore, was linked very closely to healing and could generally be considered one aspect of the health-care system as it functioned in unique ways in ancient societies. Demon possession was one among a number of explanations for lack of personal or social health and well-being.

From a hermeneutical point of view, the construction of a world of demons in ancient Mesopotamia was carried over into Israel. Israel recognized evil spirits which could cause undesirable physical and social effects. As Dennis Duling notes, however, there is a 'paucity of exorcisms in the Jewish literature'.[19] Saul is tormented by an evil spirit which David's playing of the lyre is able to drive out (1 Sam. 16.14-23), and Raphael enables Tobias to overcome a demon in order that he might marry Sarah (Tob. 6.14-18). There are scattered references to evil spirits in Second Temple Jewish literature (*1 En.* 15.7-16.1; 40.7; 53.3; 56.1; 69.4-6; *Jub.* 4.22; 5.1). Duling has also explored the link between Solomon, son of David, and exorcism, especially in the *Testament of Solomon* and Josephus (*Ant.* 8.42-49).[20] As with healing in ancient Israel, the exorcising of evil spirits was the work of God.

When we look at the gendering of demon possession in Israel, it is difficult to draw conclusions because the paucity of evidence in this respect is even greater. In general, evil spirits seem to possess more men than women—Saul (1 Sam. 16.14), the Egyptian Pharaoh (*Genesis Apocryphon* 20.16b-32), the man from whom Eleazar drives out the demon (*Ant.* 8.42-49). The demon associated with Sarah in Tobit is one of the few exceptions, but it is not so much said to possess Sarah as to destroy those who marry her. While most exorcists are male, the woman of Endor can call on the spirit of the dead Samuel even though she is not recorded as driving out spirits (1 Sam. 28). In this, Israel

17. Roger Baker, *Binding the Devil: Exorcism Past and Present* (New York: Hawthorn Books, 1974), p. 21.
18. Baker, *Binding the Devil*, pp. 21-26, notes that in both Mesopotamia and ancient Egypt the demonic was associated with certain forms of sickness although these were not generally identified and cannot now be established with any degree of certainty.
19. Dennis C. Duling, 'The Eleazar Miracle and Solomon's Magical Wisdom in Flavius Josephus's *Antiquitates Judaicai* 8.42-49', *HTR* 78 (1985), pp. 1-25 (5).
20. Duling, 'The Eleazar Miracle', and 'Solomon, Exorcism, and the Son of David', *HTR* 68 (1975), pp. 235-52.

differs from Greece where it was mainly women who were said to be possessed; the demon was not generally characterized as evil but could be a god or goddess as with the Pythia of Delphi. Ruth Padel demonstrates, however, that the association of women with enclosure contributes to the cultural construction of women as demon prone and hence to the shaping of female gender.[21] In the Syrian-Galilean axis of the developing Matthean traditions toward the end of the first century, both cultural determinants may have been functioning in the meaning-making processes of this community in relation to possession.

A Demon Possessed Daughter: An Anthropological Study in Context

The *setting* for the story of Justa's daughter is, like most other healing stories in the Matthean Gospel, non-institutional. It is in the border regions between Israel and Tyre/Sidon, a place of ambiguity, of border-crossing or of marginalization.[22] Jesus has withdrawn there (15.21) following the challenge to his interpretation of the Law by some Jerusalem scribes and Pharisees, just as he withdrew following earlier controversy (12.15). In each instance that withdrawal is followed by an encounter with one who is demon possessed — a blind and dumb demoniac in 12.22 and Justa's daughter possessed of a demon in 15.22. Jesus' withdrawal in each instance is linked with an encounter with the demonic. If the demonic describes what is out of place — blindness and dumbness in 12.22 and no explanation for the designation in 15.22 — then when Jesus is out of his own place that is symbolized by his encounter with the demonic.

A number of aspects of the *characteristics of the interpersonal interaction* in this story need to be noted. First, Justa's daughter is not a character in the story or a participant in the interaction. She is spoken about by Justa (15.22) and the narrator (15.28). There is, therefore, no narrated interaction between herself and Jesus. The interaction takes place between Justa, her mother, and Jesus. The encounter is purely episodic in the unfolding narrative, as are most other healings. This characteristic is communicated in the majority of those accounts by way of verbs of movement, forms of ἔρχομαι, in order to convey that the encounter takes place briefly in the movement of the ongoing story. In this pericope, Jesus goes out into or toward the region of Tyre and

---

21. Ruth Padel, 'Women: Model for Possession by Greek Daemons', in Averil Cameron and Amélie Kuhrt (eds.), *Images of Women in Antiquity* (London: Croom Helm, 1983), pp. 3-19.
22. See Wainwright, *Shall We Look*, p. 87.

Sidon (ἐξελθὼν ἐκεῖθεν ὁ Ἰησοῦς εἰς τὰ μέρη Τύρου καὶ Σιδῶνος) while Justa comes out from the region (ἀπὸ τῶν ὁρίων ἐκείνων ἐχελθοῦσα).

The quality of the interaction between Justa and Jesus is formal. She comes as supplicant to the one constructed in the narrative as healer, albeit folk healer within Israel's health-care system and hence mediator of divine healing.[23] Justa addresses Jesus in the formal tones of previous male supplicants by using the titles κύριε ('Lord') and υἱὸς Δαυίδ ('Son of David'). She follows these with a formal plea: have mercy on me (cf. Mt. 8.2, 5-6; 9.18, 27).[24] The attitude of Justa to her daughter's demon possession is demonstrated in her pleas for mercy and help (15.22, 25) and her simple placing before this healer the plight of her daughter. In contrast to all the other healings and exorcisms as these have been recounted in the Matthean Gospel to this point, the supplicant and healer do not share the same attitude toward this healing.[25] Jesus not only ignores Justa and her plea (15.23) but places in her way two obstacles drawn from his tradition which is not a shared tradition given the ethnic designation of Justa as Canaanite. He claims that he was sent only to the lost sheep of the house of Israel (15.24) and that children's bread cannot be given to dogs (15.26). Jesus is 'out of place' and in this context interprets a healing confrontation with the demonic to be likewise 'out of place'.

Little can be deduced from this account of the *idiom of communication* of healing. It takes place at a distance and is in response to the mother's plea but only after she has entered into a challenge/riposte style debate with Jesus.[26] Readers/hearers of the story do not hear an explanation from Jesus as to why this demon possession and its healing have no place in God's *basileia*—which is at the heart of his ministry. Rather, the explanatory movement shifts to make Justa and by

---

23. Wainwright, 'Your Faith Has Made You Well'.
24. I have analyzed the use of these titles from a feminist-critical point of view in Wainwright, *Shall We Look*, pp. 90-91. In *A Feminist Critical Reading*, p. 237, I demonstrated that the language of Justa's pleas was the formal liturgical language of a number of Israel's psalms.
25. Amy-Jill Levine suggests in *The Social and Ethnic Dimensions of Matthean Salvation History: "Go Nowhere Among the Gentiles..."* (Studies in the Bible and Early Christianity, 14; Lewiston, NY: Edwin Mellen Press, 1988), pp. 111-12, that Mt. 8.7 should be read as a question which would mean that Jesus expresses a reluctance to grant the centurion's request. If this verse is read thus, it means that there is a parallel feature between Mt. 8.5-13 and 15.21-28: supplicant and healer do not share the same attitude toward the healing.
26. Wainwright, *Shall We Look*, p. 86, for a more extensive discussion of this aspect of the narrative.

implication her daughter 'out of place' because they are not 'of the house of Israel', not 'children' around the table but 'dogs' whose place is outside the *basileia* of God, non-recipients of the children's bread. It could be argued that by ignoring Justa's plea for her daughter to be freed from demon possession and by shifting the explanation from demon possession (the social labeling given to Justa's daughter) to Justa's status as 'outsider' (a social labeling given her by Jesus), Jesus links demon possession in this instance with the ethnic outsider.[27] Both Justa and her daughter are designated 'out of place', and Jesus who is likewise 'out of place' in this story must confront and struggle with both on the margins or at the border.[28] His retreat to traditions from the center is not accepted by Justa within the therapeutic expectations of the healing relationship. Justa's kneeling in front of Jesus and her turning of Jesus' words about the children's food back on him point to her responsibility for her daughter (15.25, 27). She refuses to leave without her daughter being healed.

In terms of the *clinical reality* of this healing, the setting is secular, but Justa's use of the therapeutic title 'Son of David'[29] and the religious title 'Lord' constructs a world of healing that is sacred. Justa's explanation of her daughter's condition is disease-oriented, but the debate with Jesus shifts the focus to an illness orientation and a struggle over insider and outsider status linked to the demon possession.[30] Given the sociocultural context of demon possession already established and its general lack of clear gendering, it would be difficult to establish here any specific interlocking of gender and demon possession as characteristic of the outsider status of Justa and her daughter.

---

27. Elsewhere I have argued that gender and ethnicity are intimately linked in this pericope when the focus has been on the interaction between Justa and Jesus (Wainwright, *A Feminist Critical Reading*, pp. 104-18, 244-47). The focus on demon possession and the earlier discovery of its apparent lack of gendering within Israel suggests that Jesus' refusal to heal this particular demon possession is linked in the narrative, especially given Mt. 15.24, with ethnicity.

28. The imagery of Jesus as boundary-walker in this narrative has been developed in Wainwright, *Shall We Look*, pp. 84-92.

29. For a full development of this see Dennis C. Duling, 'Matthew's Plurisignificant "Son of David" in Social Scientific Perspective: Kinship, Kingship, Magic and Miracle', *BTB* 22 (1992), pp. 99-116; and *idem*, 'The Therapeutic Son of David: An Element in Matthew's Christological Apologetic', *NTS* 24 (1978), pp. 392-410.

30. A cultural-anthropological approach to healing distinguishes between 'disease' as a biomedical explanation of a condition and 'illness' as a more coherent social and cultural explanation within a human meaning-making system. See Pilch, 'Understanding Biblical Healing', pp. 60-66.

The *therapeutic stages and mechanisms* in this story are clear. Justa's daughter is labeled as demon possessed, a label rich in cultural meaning in the Greco-Roman world of the first century as indicted above. This cultural label is manipulated by Jesus in this instance in a way that is not made visible to the reader, but as a result a new cultural label is sanctioned: the daughter who was demon possessed (v. 22) is now healed (v. 28). The verb used in this new cultural designation is ἰάομαι (to heal/cure)—the daughter is healed (ἰάθη ἡ θυγάτηρ) rather than demon possessed (ἡ θυγάτηρ μου κακῶς δαιμονίζεται). This verb ἰάομαι occurs much more rarely in Matthew than θεραπεύειν to designate healing (8.8, 13; 13.15; 15.28). It is, however, the same new cultural label given to the centurion's servant who is healed in a designation which parallels that of Justa's daughter:

καὶ ἰάθη ὁ παῖς [αὐτοῦ] ἐν τῇ ὥρᾳ ἐκείνῃ
[And the servant was healed at that moment] (Mt. 8.13)

καὶ ἰάθη ἡ θυγάτηρ αὐτῆς ἀπὸ τῆς ὥρας ἐκείνης
[And her daughter was healed from that moment] (Mt. 15.28).

The only other occurrence of this verb in the Matthean Gospel is in an Isaian quotation in 13.15. The noun ἰατρός is used by Jesus in what may well have been a parabolic statement: 'Those who are well have no need of a physician (ἰατρός) but those who are sick' (9.12). It is significant to note in this respect that the only Matthean use of the verb and its root is in relation to the new cultural labeling of two Gentiles—the centurion's servant and Justa's daughter.[31] The verb ἰάομαι was in common usage in the Greco-Roman world to describe healing. θεραπεύειν had a more general meaning 'to serve', but it was taken up as a key designation of healing in the Jewish-Christian communities of the reign-of-God movement.[32] The Matthean text seems to reflect those origins in its predication of these two verbs to recipients of healing.

Another Matthean story of demon possession supports this analysis. Like the story of Justa's daughter, that of the boy with epilepsy who is also constructed in the story as having a demon (17.15, 18), is

---

31. It is significant to note here that the blind and dumb demoniac whom Jesus heals in 12.22, the one encountered subsequent to his first withdrawal as noted above, is likewise designated as healed by Jesus with the use of the verb θεραπεύειν but the new cultural label used in relation to him is that he 'spoke and saw'. The verb θεραπεύειν is descriptive of the work of Jesus rather than the state of the healed man.

32. Albrecht Oepke, 'ἰάομαι', *TDNT*, III, pp. 194-215; and Hermann Wolfgang Beyer, 'θεραπαία, θεραπεύω, θεράπων', *TDNT*, III, pp. 128-32.

an encounter between parent and Jesus—in the case of the young woman, her mother, in the case of the young man, his father. The language of the request is almost parallel:

Ἐλέησόν με, κύριε…ἡ θυγάτηρ μου κακῶς δαιμονίζεται
Have mercy on me Lord…my daughter is severely posessed by a demon (15.22).

Κύριε, ἐλέησόν μου τὸν υἱόν, ὅτι σεληνιάζεται καὶ κακῶς πάσχει
Lord have mercy on my son, for he is epileptic and suffers terribly (17.15).

'Lord, have mercy on me', plus the description of the illness; she is severely possessed of a demon, and he is epileptic and suffers terribly. In the second instance, however, the parent supplicant is neither ignored nor culturally labeled. In both instances, however, a very similar new cultural label is given to the child:

καὶ ἐθεραπεύθη ὁ παῖς ἀπὸ τῆς ὥρας ἐκείνης
And the boy was healed from that moment (Mt. 17.18).

καὶ ἰάθη ἡ θυγάτηρ αὐτῆς ἀπὸ τῆς ὥρας ἐκείνης
And her daughter was healed from that moment (15.28).

The significant difference between these three stories of children/ servants being healed and the new cultural labeling of each which are paralleled is that the centurion's servant and Justa's daughter are clearly Gentile while the reader is more likely to assume that the man's son is constructed as Jewish because of the story's location and the absence of any other ethnic indicator. The healing of daughter and son are from demon-possession, and the servant from paralysis. It seems, therefore, that a particular cultural label is considered more appropriate for Gentile recipients of healing and another for Jewish recipients.[33] The social construction of the world of demon possession within the world of healing generally in the Matthean story telling also constructs a world of ethnic differences.

It is of interest in this respect to compare the healing of Justa's daughter with the healing of other women in the Matthean narrative. In an earlier study, I demonstrated that the new cultural labels given to the three women healed in Mt. 8-9 (serving/διηκόνει, being saved/ ἐσώθη and being raised/ἠγέρθη—8.15; 9.22 and 25)[34] shared in the

33. It is significant to note in this respect that no new cultural label is given to the two demon-possessed Gadarenes in Mt. 8.28-34.
34. The new cultural label of the woman with a hemorrhage is time specific as is that of Justa's daughter and the same phrase links the two—ἀπὸ τῆς ὥρας ἐκείνης.

semantic universe which characterized the transformative activity associated with the Jesus of that gospel narrative.[35] I argued that gender seemed to categorize healing in that males were commissioned to share in the healing ministry of the male healer Jesus (Mt. 10.8). Women were not so commissioned, but women's healed bodies configured the divine healing power mediated through Jesus. I did not, however, in that study examine the way in which healing constructed ethnicity as well as gender. This study has made it clear that it also constructs ethnicity in a way which intersects with and shifts the gender construction. The transformative re-labeling of Justa's daughter does not share in the symbolic universe associated with Jesus as does that of the other females healed in the Matthean narratives of healing to this point — Peter's mother-in-law, the woman with the hemorrhage and the ruler's daughter — all of whom are culturally Jewish.[36]

Conclusion

This study follows a previous one which examined the construction of healing and gender within the Matthean Gospel. It was shaped by the question of whether the demon possession/gender nexus could simply be considered to function in a way similar to the construction of healing and gender or whether it functioned differently. A medical-anthropological analysis of the story of Justa's daughter in Mt. 15.21-28 in which demon-possession and female gender are linked, using the same categories applied to the healing stories of women in Mt. 8-9, revealed a correlation between demon possession and ethnicity rather than gender. Such findings could then have been brought into dialogue with other studies of both Jesus and Justa in Mt. 15.21-28 in order that gender and ethnicity could be considered together in that story. This, however, is another project in which Justa will not be able to be considered without her daughter and both will need to be examined in relationship to Jesus who cannot be isolated from other characters, especially in this story in which the narrative interaction is central. This essay has simply prepared the way for such further investigation.

---

35. Wainwright, 'Your Faith Has Made You Well'.
36. It has been demonstrated above that ἰάομαι could not be considered central to the symbolic universe of Jesus' transformative ministry.

THE CANAANITE WOMEN IN MATTHEW

Stephenson Humphries-Brooks

Three stories begin our journey into Matthew.

Rachab

The first, 'And Salmon caused the conception of Boas from Rachab' (Mt. 1.5a), consists of only a part of a line of text.[1] It is, however, a complete sentence containing subject and verb. The narrative, while minimal, is enough to qualify as story.

The subject of this story grammatically is 'Salmon', a man about whom we know little. The inclusion of 'Rachab' as the mother out of whom Boas comes, the object of the preposition, gives whole new information. As others have noted, the inclusion of just four particular women in the genealogy of Jesus stands out enigmatically from the list whose other occupants are universally fathers.[2] The NRSV emphasizes this fact of fatherhood by translating the verse as: 'Salmon the father of Boaz'. The verb meaning 'to impregnate' or 'cause to conceive' becomes a governing noun, 'the father'. So, the translators recognize the women's roles even less than the original does.

Who then is this grandmother of Jesus and why does the text emphasize her story by seating her on the threshold of the audience's consciousness and thereby making her 'liminal'? Her full story occurs in Josh. 2. The author of Matthew transliterates her Hebrew name, רחב, into Greek, Ῥαχάβ, unlike the other New Testament (Jas 2.25; Heb. 11.31) and early church authors, who use Ῥαάβ. Therefore, I transliterate her name as 'Rachab' rather than the more standard 'Rahab'.

---

1. All translations are mine unless otherwise noted.
2. E.g. Raymond E. Brown, *The Birth of the Messiah: A Commentary on the Infancy Narratives in Matthew and Luke* (Garden City, NY: Doubleday, 1977); Stephenson Humphries-Brooks, 'Matthew', in Watson E. Mills and Richard F. Wilson (eds.), *Mercer Commentary on the Bible* (Macon, GA: Mercer University Press, 1995), pp. 939-74 (946).

In the Matthean genealogy, she occurs out of place historically. The Hebrew Scriptures never associate her with the line of David.[3] According to Rabbinic texts, she married Joshua (*Midr. Qoh.* 8, 10). She is also mentioned with Jethro and Ruth as examples of the presence of God's spirit among the nations (*Pes. R.* 167b).[4] In Matthew she occurs, anachronistically, at least two generations too late as the mother of Boaz.

Joshua 2 gives us Rachab's story in full. Hers is one of the longest and most carefully developed stories in Joshua. The plot, as in most biblical Hebrew narrative, occurs strictly chronologically, without analepsis or prolepsis. Joshua sends two spies to Jericho, where they spend two nights in the house of a prostitute, Rachab. The king of Jericho, who has been warned of their mission, seeks them. Rachab hides them, and she asks them that she and her household be spared when Israel invades. They swear to do as she asks. She lets them down through an outside window of the house that is in the city wall and ties a crimson cord in the window as a sign of their oath. Later, the narrative informs us that the promise was kept: 'But Rahab the prostitute, with her family and all who belonged to her, Joshua spared. She has lived in Israel ever since...' (Josh. 6.25, NRSV). Rachab then disappears from canonical Hebrew storytelling.

As in most stories, however, the plot neither provides the whole meaning nor exhausts the possibilities for expansion and extension of the audience's understanding. Characterization plays a large role. In biblical Hebrew narrative, characterization occurs predominantly by dialogue. Occasionally, we receive commentary from the third-person narrator, but usually the narrator leaves the audience to judge a character, her feelings and motives, based upon what she says and how she acts.

Rachab's actions and speech dominate her story. She hides the spies; she helps them escape. In Josh. 2.9-13 she gives the reasons for her actions. First, she knows the history of God's acts with Israel: Yahweh dried up the Sea of Reeds, utterly destroyed the Amorite kings Sihon and Og, and has given Jericho into Israel's hand. In this history, she correctly reads the intent of Yahweh to make the inhabitants of Canaan a whole burnt offering, a thing devoted to destruction, a purification, a cleansing, חרם (Lev. 27.29). As a matter of survival she wishes to avoid the ethnic cleansing of Israel's God.

Second, she recognizes the universal sovereignty of this God (v. 11b). Therefore, her speech may be read as a confession of her faith in the

---

3. Brown, *Birth*, pp. 71, 60.
4. See further Str-B, I, pp. 20-23.

God to whom Israel traces its ethnic and national identity as well as to the God who universally creates and rules. It is both a geopolitical and transcendent declaration.

The story contains many surprises, not least of which is Rachab's profession. She is a prostitute. In Hebrew the word is זונה. The Hebrew text designates her as a 'secular' prostitute as opposed to a קדשה, whose status might have included sacral or ritual connections.[5] The Greek text of the LXX uses πόρνη, 'buyable female', and so distinguishes her from an ἑταίρα, 'female companion'. To a Greek-speaking audience, such a designation indicates Rachab as a commodity. Her sisters are available in the brothels and slave markets of the entire Mediterranean Basin. She is a desired and consumable object from whom males may expect services for pay.[6] To such a one the spies turn for sexual satisfaction.

The text represents Rachab's status spatially as well: the house is 'in' or perhaps 'on' the outer city wall: the Hebrew preposition allows either interpretation. The detail becomes necessary to the plot because she is able easily to effect the escape of the spies by virtue of this architectural detail. The impact of the text, however, should not be limited to this simple detail. Ancient cities were built hierarchically. The king's palace and the temple occupied the highest and most inner area of the city. Excavations of Canaanite sites generally indicate a progressive impoverishment of material culture as one moves to the outside of the city.[7] In other words, the wealthy ruling class lives in the safest area of the city, frequently an acropolis, fortified against foreign invaders who have archers and siege machines. Equally, they fortify themselves against uprisings by peasants or slaves who work in their fields. The Jerusalem of David and the Samaria of Jeroboam I will duplicate their Canaanite predecessors in this architectural spatialization of social value.

Rachab the prostitute is, therefore, among the lowest of status. Barely within the protection of her city, she exists liminally. Indeed, the miracle is that in the sack of Jericho her house—although part of the city wall—escapes destruction: a detail neither unintentional by

---

5. Elaine Adler Goodfriend, 'Prostitution', *ABD*, V, pp. 505-10.
6. Madeleine M. Henry, 'The Edible Woman: Athenaeus's Concept of the Pornographic', in Amy Richlin (ed.), *Pornography and Representation* (New York: Oxford University Press, 1992), pp. 250-68 (263).
7. The tendency seems typical of all city building in the Mediterranean Basin during the ancient period. See 'Samaria', 'Jerusalem', 'Megiddo', 'Hazor', 'Jericho', in Ephraim Stern (ed.), *The New Encyclopedia of Archaeological Excavations in the Holy Land* (4 vols.; New York: Simon & Schuster, 1993).

the Hebrew storyteller nor lost on later ancient readers (see, e.g., Heb. 11.31).

From the perspective of the Torah, the profession of prostitution is abhorrent. Specifically, fathers may not make their daughters into prostitutes (Lev. 19.29). A priest may not marry a prostitute (Lev. 21.7, 14). The child of an illicit union may not enter the congregation of Yahweh (Deut. 23.2). The story of Rachab constitutes, therefore, an incredible dispensation in the will of Yahweh. First, she is a member of the condemned Canaanites who are to be offered as a whole burnt offering of purification of the land to God. Second, she is a member of one of the most detested professions within Torah-centered Judaism. Josephus, writing at about the same time as the author of Matthew, retells her story and calls her an 'innkeeper', perhaps softening for his Greek audience the charge of πόρνη, although innkeepers were known as pimps and prostitutes throughout the Greek and Roman world (*Ant.* 5, 7). The author of Matthew, unlike the authors of James and Hebrews, does not call her a 'prostitute', possibly for similar reasons.

The story raises Rachab above the level of silent object of God's decision to the level of acting subject who engages theologically with the spies and thereby binds their God of war to an oath. She is the head of the household who provides for the security of her family, including her mother and father. She fulfills the role ideally reserved in Jewish, Greek, and Roman patriarchal societies for the father, the male head of the household. She acts in a faith defined by her own seizure of the initiative to wrest graceful action from God. The author of Hebrews reads this story as reflecting her faith (Heb. 11.31). Likewise, the Epistle of James emphasizes her faithful action in saving the spies (Jas 2.25). None notes that Rachab forces divine dispensation by her own act. A woman's initiative becomes theologically subsumed by later male interpretation.

The trace of the story in the Matthean genealogy recalls to the audience these elements. Genealogies in literature function to allow for the acceleration of story time by appeal to the collectively remembered past. To join the audience of Matthew we must re-remember what perhaps we have been trained to forget. Unlike Raymond E. Brown, who states, 'Thus there is little likelihood that Matthew's readers would have understood the women as sinners', I think, rather, that the author of Matthew depends on the audience's perception of Rachab as a sinner.[8] The effect of the text requires that we see the extreme marginality of Grandmother Rachab.

8. Brown, *Birth*, p. 72.

The Canaanite Mother[9]

The second reads as follows:

> Jesus left that place and went away to the vicinity of Tyre and Sidon. Just then a Canaanite woman from that region came out and started shouting, 'Give me mercy, Lord, son of David; my daughter is evilly possessed by a demon'. But he did not answer her a word. And his disciples came and urged him, saying, 'Send her away, for she shouts after us'. But he answered saying, 'I was not sent, except to the lost sheep of the house of Israel'. But she came and prostrated herself before him, saying, 'Lord, help me'. But he answered saying, 'It is not good to take the bread of the children and throw it to the dogs'. But she said, 'Yes Lord, for the dogs eat the crumbs from the table of their lords'. Then Jesus answered her, 'O woman, huge is your faith; let it be for you as you wish'. And her daughter was healed at that instant (Mt. 15.21-28).

The use of 'Canaanite' rather than 'Syrophoenician' as in Mk 7.26 emphasizes that the woman comes from an ethnicity Israel traditionally viewed as worthy of extermination (see Josh. 12.20). It also links her to the story of Rachab. The story of the Canaanite woman shows that Jesus himself can initially fail to perceive faith and, thereby, refuse access to the kingdom to those to whom he was sent. Jesus, an Israelite man, allows himself to be duped by the appearance of this supplicant as a woman and a non-Israelite.

Jesus refuses to hear her petition and strives to silence her by ignoring her (v. 23a). But the woman demands a hearing for her daughter's need. In the translation I have rendered her ailment as 'evilly possessed by a demon'. The word on which this translation depends, κακῶς—usually translated as 'to be ill' (with ἔχειν) or 'to suffer severely'—also indicates moral wrong or wickedness.[10] The use here in the context of Matthew bears the entire field of meaning. Demons in Matthew and their torments are not merely physical but the oppression of the Evil One against God's creatures. The language of the Canaanite woman implies the tie between her daughter's illness and the brokenness of creation (see, e.g., 12.22-32).

The disciples become upset at her noisy importunity and plead for Jesus to send her away (v. 23b). The male Israelite householders strive

---

9. In this section I develop further a line of interpretation of the Canaanite mother begun in earlier work. See my 'Indicators of Social Organization and Status in Matthew's Gospel', in Eugene H. Lovering, Jr, *SBLSP* 30 (1991), pp. 31-49 (41); 'Matthew', pp. 960-61.

10. BAGD, p. 398.

to silence and assign to the margins the supplicating Canaanite mother.[11]

Jesus finally engages in conversation with her after reiterating his statement of mission in the same words as Mt. 10.6. Matthew depicts Jesus' earlier mission up to that point as universal.[12] During that mission Jesus recognizes and heals women supplicants from Israel as well as men of both Israel and non-Israel (Mt. 4.25; 8–9). Compare especially Jesus' treatment of the centurion in 8.5-13. Here, for the first time, Jesus confronts a non-Israelite woman.[13]

Jesus' journey into Tyre and Sidon indicates an intention to transcend the borders of the Israelite homeland. With his mission, therefore, we might anticipate, based on his previous behavior, that here Jesus himself will move beyond the ethnic and national boundaries imposed since 10.5. Such a return would confirm the earlier indications in Matthew of a universal mission.

The speech and action of Jesus do not accord with either his own actions or speeches elsewhere and therefore disconfirm our expectations.[14] The woman, however, proves to be a better theologian than Jesus himself. She willingly identifies her utter abasement as a crumb-licking dog and refers to the 'lords' table' from which she begs scraps. This phrase usually is translated, as in the NRSV, as 'masters' table' and taken to refer to Israel as the children. Such a reading becomes problematic since the narrative previously condemned Israel as unrepentant (11.20-24).

In Matthew, the singular 'lord' occurs as a confessional title used by supplicants of Jesus. Jesus recognizes in this title the presence of faith. The woman uses this form of supplication in 15.22, 25, 27. By using the plural, the woman shows that she recognizes not only Jesus but also God as her lord. I read the plural τῶν κυρίων αὐτῶν in v. 27 as 'their lords'; it is a reference back to the confessional κύριε, 'lord', of

---

11. In a forthcoming book, *Rachab's Daughters: Gender, Ethnicity, and Reading in Matthew*, I show how the social status of the disciples and Jesus as male, Israelite, householders is developed and deconstructed by the author of *Matthew*. It must remain for that work to place the story of the Canaanite Mother in its broader literary and theological context. I offer an exploratory probe of this thesis in 'Indicators'. See also 'Matthew', p. 939, and comments on specific passages.

12. Humphries-Brooks, 'Matthew', pp. 948-49, 954-55.

13. This line of interpretation is more extensively developed in *Rachab's Daughters*. See also the relevant passages in 'Matthew'.

14. On the importance of the speeches in establishing the audience's expectations see my 'Spatial Form and Plot Disruption in the Gospel of Matthew', *Essays in Literature* 20 (1993), pp. 54-69.

144   A Feminist Companion to Matthew

the same sentence and not a reference to 'the children'. The bread not the table, according to Jesus' initial statement, belongs to the children. These children according to his interpretation are the 'lost sheep of Israel'. The Canaanite woman's theology is superior and in keeping with the claim in Matthew that the eschatological banquet belongs to God and the Son of Man (e.g. 22.1-14; 25.1-13). Therefore, this theological, christological, and eschatological-apocalyptic insight prompts Jesus' recognition of the woman's faith, not her 'conformity to the heavenly plan of salvation history'.[15] She understands the table as the table of the final banquet presided over by God and the Son of Man that includes all, despite accidents of ethnicity, gender, or status. Her theology moves beyond Grandmother Rachab. Her interpretation accords with Jesus' own interpretation of the faith of the centurion in 8.10-13. Just like Rachab, her understanding can, according to the world of the text, come only from God.

Jesus pronounces her faith and heals her daughter. The author does not shrink from showing Jesus as learning from a woman of an inappropriate ethnicity. The text highlights both status as woman and as non-Israel in order to show the apocalyptic faith that comes from the kingdom of heaven and that destroys all historical claims to prerogatives within the kingdom. Jesus himself in Matthew can be educated by such faith.[16]

The story of the Canaanite mother shows that social status can initially bind Jesus, as a character. He comments directly on the woman's utter lack of any status whatever by designating her as a dog (v. 26), only to be made aware, by deft argument, of the faith of a non-Israelite woman. The woman here proves to be a better theologian than Jesus by illustrating her utter abasement and need in willingly identifying herself as the crumb-licking dog and implicitly recognizing God, in Jesus, as her master.

The Canaanite mother is the only character in Matthew, and perhaps in the four canonical gospels, to win a theological argument with Jesus. She is the type of the perfect mother. She, like Rachab, appears as the head of the household: no husband aids her petition (cf. the story of the leader's daughter in 9.18-26). She provides for her

15. Amy-Jill Levine, *The Social and Ethnic Dimensions of Matthean Salvation History: "Go nowhere among the Gentiles..." (Matt. 10.5b)* (Studies in the Bible and Early Christianity, 14; Lewiston, NY: Edwin Mellen Press, 1988), p. 152.
16. Cf. Elisabeth Schüssler Fiorenza, *In Memory of Her: A Feminist Theological Reconstruction of Christian Origins* (New York: Crossroad, 1983), p. 138; Christiana de Groot van Houten, 'Pondering the Word', *Perspectives* (August/September 1994), p. 24.

daughter access to the gracious will of God. By the healing, her daughter is liberated from the Evil One.

Herodias

The third:

> At that time Herod the Tetrarch heard news of Jesus, and he said to his boys, 'This is John the Baptist: he has been raised from the dead and for this reason the Powers are at work through him'. For Herod, having arrested John, bound him and put him in prison because of Herodias, the wife of his brother Philip. For John said to him, 'It is not for you to have her'. And although he wanted to kill him, he was afraid of the crowd, because they considered him like a prophet.
> When Herod's birthday came, the daughter of Herodias danced at the party, and she pleased Herod. Therefore, he swore with a mighty oath that he would give her whatever she might ask. But, coached by her mother, she said, 'Give me here on a platter the head of John the Baptist'. And, although the king was distressed, because of the oaths and the guests, he commanded that it be given. Then, sending word, he had John beheaded in prison. And his head was brought upon a platter and given to the young girl, and she brought it to her mother. And his disciples came and took the body, and they buried him. Then they went and told Jesus. When Jesus heard this, he withdrew from there in a boat into a deserted place to be alone (Mt. 14.1-13a).

Our third story does not fit with the previous two on first inspection. The story of Herodias and her daughter does not involve an immediately positive evaluation of each female. In the history of biblical interpretation and Western art both Herodias and her daughter (Salome is the name supplied by Josephus) are villianized, eroticized, and roundly condemned. They are bad girls, femmes fatales on a par with Lady Macbeth, Catherine D'Medici, and M'Lady.[17] Unlike Rachab and the Canaanite mother, Herodias appears to oppose the will of God. She is not Canaanite. She is in status an elite, royal, and evil. Why then include her story?

I argued above that the Canaanite mother and her daughter escape the dominance of Israelite male householders by direct revelation of the will of God to the mother's faith. The Canaanite mother becomes a doorway for God's power. The liminal opens a door and lets God in.

---

17. Two feminist treatments of the dancing daughter/Salome greatly influence my work. See Janice Capel Anderson, 'Feminist Criticism: The "Dancing Daughter"', in *eadem* and Stephen D. Moore (eds.), *Mark and Method* (Minneapolis: Fortress Press, 1992), pp. 103-34; Alice Bach, *Women, Seduction, and Betrayal in Biblical Narrative* (Cambridge: Cambridge University Press, 1997), pp. 224-62.

By contrast, Herodias and her daughter are deeply embedded in patriarchy and phallocentricity. Their presence in Matthew links them obversely with Rachab and the Canaanite mother. They expose the pernicious weaknesses of patriarchy and phallocentricity and the theologies attendant thereupon.

The narration of the plot focuses attention on Herod and John the Baptist, who are the two poles of narrative tension. The polarity is resolved by the action of Herodias (v. 8). The story is circumscribed by the action of Jesus (vv. 1, 13a).

Herod hears of Jesus and concludes he is John the Baptist, resurrected. By analepsis the narrator fills the audience in on the events leading to John's death. Herod arrests and imprisons John. On Herod's birthday the daughter of Herodias dances. Herod swears to give her whatever she asks. Coached by her mother, she asks for the head of John the Baptist. The king commands that it be done. He sends to the prison and has John beheaded. The head is given to the girl, who gives it to her mother. John's disciples come, take his body, and bury it. They tell Jesus. Jesus withdraws.

This summary of the events of plot focuses attention on the acting subjects of the main verbs within the Greek text and English translation. Such an approach goes a long way toward making it apparent that Herod is the primary actor in the story. He is the subject of almost every main verb. The daughter 'danced' and 'brought'. The mother 'coached'. John 'said'. The disciples 'came', 'took', 'buried', 'went', and 'told'. The remainder of the action, 14 verbs in the Greek, is Herod's. The women have three verbs by comparison. Grammar reveals the embeddedness of Herodias and her daughter in the male discourse of elite, patriarchal, phallocentric power. Even though they are essential, they remain liminal, circumscribed, confined by the narrator's language itself.

Plot is of course not the whole story. Characterization conforms to the plot. The two main characters are Herod and John. They alone receive the privilege of revealing themselves by direct discourse. The narrative leaves little ambiguity about who they are. It gives priority to male identity.

Herod speaks to his 'boys'. The term translated 'boys' means male servants or slaves. They are his intimates, those who share in his theologizing. The narrator mentions no women. The male club theologizes about Jesus, and that theology is inadequate. Herod understands Jesus to be a servant of the 'Powers' (δυνάμεις). This is not the usual word for demons, the δαιμόνες who inhabit the sublunar cosmos, but some reference to cosmic powers must be involved. The narrator does not clarify whether, in Herod's opinion, these Powers are God-given. The audience can guess, however, that Herod regards Jesus as fearful just as he regarded John. He theorizes that Jesus is John raised, a clear mistake. Jesus is baptized by John in fulfilment of God's righteousness (3.1-17). The conclusion of that scene is the revelation from the heavens of the sonship of Jesus. Herod's is a false conclusion from inadequate information. The boys are theologically ill-informed.

The narrator gives Herod's internal motivations (vv. 3-4). Herod wants John dead but fears the crowds who regard John as a prophet. The cause of his animosity is John's challenge to his marriage to Herodias, his brother's wife. Characterization increases the tension provided by the plot. Herod, the weak tetrarch, cannot get what he wants. He leaves John in prison.

By indirect statement, the text shows Herod swearing an oath. The taking of an oath places him in opposition to Jesus, who has taught in Matthew against any oath-taking as being from the Evil One (5.33-37). The size of the oath coupled with the daughter's dance may indicate further that Herod has violated his own stepdaughter in terms of Jesus' teaching. Jesus condemns the lustful look and assigns responsibility and condemnation exclusively to the men apparently regardless of the circumstances (5.28). If we move from the literary to the social-historical level of a general Greco-Roman audience informed by the perspective of patriarchal Greek or Roman morality, Herod is a bad father. He exposes his stepdaughter to the revels of a *symposium* and so treats her like a hired mistress (ἑταίρα) rather than a protected female member of his household. She appears in the role of a purchasable party doll, in the escort service of the ancient world. Not only is Herod a patriarch, a phallocentric male, he is an evil one by anyone's measure.

The narrator calls him a king (v. 9). The title along with his name links him clearly to Herod in Mt. 2. That Herod, also murderous in intent, was not afraid to resolve his distress by murdering all the children under the age of two in Bethlehem. This second Matthean Herod finally resolves his distress and acts as a king, but not without the help of his queen, the mother of the daughter for whom he lusts.

Herod is the direct cause of John's death. His desire to kill John (v. 3) is finally fulfilled (vv. 9-11), but the prospect of the death of John does not relieve his mental state of conflict. The Greek word λυπηθείς, rendered 'distressed' above, can also mean 'sad' or 'grieved' (so the NRSV) in v. 9.[18] In view of Herod's fear of the crowd in v. 4,

---

18. BAGD, p. 481.

148   *A Feminist Companion to Matthew*

however, mental agitation, the return of fear, not grief or sadness should be understood. The story in Matthew in no way indicates that John and Herod somehow became friends during the imprisonment (cf. Mk 6.20). The characterization of Herod accords with his action in plot. He is an evil, unjust king who acts out of reprehensible passions including fear and lust. He is condemnable by both ancient and modern audiences at multiple levels.

The second agent, the second pole along which the plot action is deployed, is John the Baptist. Understanding him depends to a larger degree than does understanding Herod upon what the audience brings to his characterization because the narrator draws him less clearly.

John is the circumscribed object of Herod's murderous intent in much the same manner as the daughter becomes the object of Herod's lust. He acts as subject only by direct speech once: 'It is not for you to have her'. The basis of his judgment is ambiguous. Within Matthew the statement conforms to the saying of Jesus on divorce in 5.32, 'anyone who divorces his wife except for the matter of πορνεία and marries another makes her to commit adultery, and whoever marries a divorcée commits adultery'. If the audience knows what Josephus knows, that Herod divorced his first wife in order to marry Herodias and that Herodias divorced her first husband in order to marry Herod (*Ant.* 18.109-15, 136), then the story makes further sense. Or, the basis of John's condemnation may be the Levitical injunctions, 'You shall not uncover the nakedness of your brother's wife (Lev. 18.16). If a man takes his brother's wife, it is impurity; he has uncovered his brother's nakedness; they shall be childless' (Lev. 20.21, NRSV). Josephus appears to have this understanding in his account of the marriage of Herodias and Herod. He points out that 'she parted from a living husband', the brother of Herod by the same father (*Ant.* 18.136). He considers Herod and Herodias as a part of the Herodian line that comes to grief, without children, because of their impiety. Salome, the daughter of Herodias's first marriage, according to Josephus, also has a fruitless union with her uncle Philip.

Since Matthew also contains the notion about the brother, it is possible that the audience is assumed to think somewhat along the lines of Josephus's reasoning. If the audience knows Leviticus and the Herodian family history, then they may think along these last lines of interpretation. John then represents the Torah. If, on the other hand, the audience only knows Jesus' teaching, they think along the lines of Jesus in 5.32 and align John with Jesus' commandments rather than Torah. The text may presuppose a combination of these positions or other unrecoverable permutations of attitudes.

In either case, the story presents John consistently with his portrayal in Mt. 3.1-17, where he is an eschatological prophet dressed like Elijah (2 Kgs 1.8). Jesus himself declares John to be Elijah, the eschatological prophet who will come at the end of time (Mt. 11.2-14). Enigmatically, in that passage, Jesus places John/Elijah lower than the least in the kingdom of heaven.

The current story highlights the importance of the relationship of Jesus to John by the withdrawal of Jesus in 14.13. The movement creates a chronological aporia in Matthew since the description of the death of John is a flashback, an analepsis, by the narrator to explain the comment of Herod on Jesus. Hence we cannot tell whether the events of 14.13ff. occur immediately after the death of John, and perhaps prior to Herod's comment in v. 2, or whether 14.13-34 occur after Herod's comment. The temporal ambiguity unhinges a clean progression of plot. This conforms to Matthean narrative techniques throughout the Gospel.[19]

The two final characters complete the triangle. Together they constitute the subject whose action resolves the complications of plot and leads to climax and dénouement. In their characterization, both Herodias and her daughter remain confined by patriarchy and phallocentricity both socially and theologically.

First, Herod acts upon Herodias. According to the view of divorce promulgated by Jesus in Mt. 5.27-28, 31-32, she is the victim of Herod's lust. She acts, but the narrator gives only the cryptic note that she 'coaches, instructs, or incites' her daughter to ask for John's head. The narrator in Matthew gives no reason for her thinking or motivation.

What should the audience presume? What should we supply? If we restrict ourselves to the world of Matthew, then her behavior is troubling. Within the entire text of Matthew she is the only evil female, the only woman with murderous intent. Her status is that of a queen, royal, urban, presumably Israelite elite.[20] Her name, like Herod's, reminds us of the Herod of Mt. 2.

If we move outside Matthew, we can add other details. Josephus says she is the grand-daughter of Herod the Great, and daughter of Aristobolus. Thus, she is the niece of both of her husbands, although Aristobolus is only their half-brother (*Ant.* 18.11).[21] Indirectly, Josephus hints that she may not be quite a true Israelite. He reports prior

---

19. Humphries-Brooks, 'Spatial Form'.
20. On the question of characterization and status in Matthew, see Humphries-Brooks, 'Indicators'.
21. Anderson, 'Dancing Daughter', p. 120. *ABD*, III, pp. 174-76.

150   *A Feminist Companion to Matthew*

to the story of Herod and Herodias that the Herodian line is Idumean. This last point, however, is not emphasized of Herodias by Josephus and has no indication in Matthew. According to Josephus she remains a faithful wife to Herod. She goes into exile with him after his deposition by Gaius.

Mark states that she was the one who desired John dead, not Herod, and thereby makes her action a pre-conceived plot to incite Herod to the execution (6.19). Matthew, however, never refers directly to Mark nor gives any indication that the audience should know Mark's story for comparison. Matthew never refers by name to any other early Christian writing; hence it is difficult to know to what extent an audience is expected to know the content of Christian texts contemporaneous with or earlier than Matthew. Other interpreters and audiences familiar with Mark frequently read Herodias in Matthew through Markan eyes and impute to her the motives assigned to her in Mark. I want to concentrate for the present on the text in Matthew.

Clearly, Herodias cannot be understood without considerable work by the audience. What we bring to the text determines our understanding of her behavior. She constitutes the second, female side of the same king-queen, Herod-ias. She is the sentient planner who fulfills his desire. This much is evident from the text as it stands. There is no eroticization, as in the art of Aubrey Beardslee, of her desire for John's head. She remains open, anecdotal, in Matthew. Her action is a chance action, the occasion for it apparently unexpected but exploited when presented. She is a reminder of the extent to which the historical never unravels according to the inevitability of history.[22] She remains opaque, ambiguous, but clearly within the structures of patriarchal social organization and phallocentric power exchange.

The second supplementary actor in the story is the daughter of Herodias. Matthew contains no name for her, in keeping with a general pattern of unnamed daughters and children: no child, save Jesus, is named; no daughter given a person by naming. Tradition supplies 'Salome' from Josephus; some manuscripts of Mark call her Herodias.

If her dance is at all erotic, the text does not eroticize it. If the party is an elite *symposium*, then the male guests understand her as fair sexual game regardless of her own motivations or intentions. Of recent interpreters in film, Pier Pasolini shows the dance as chaste and

---

22. Joel Fineman, 'The History of the Anecdote: Fiction and Fiction', in H. Aram Veeser (ed.), *The New Historicism* (New York: Routledge, 1989), pp. 49-76.

demure; Ken Russell as homoerotic. Matthew fuels the imagination of modern art, but the narrator refuses lurid speculation.[23]

How old is she? She is 'daughter' (θυγάτηρ) and 'girl' (κοράσιον): a girl, perhaps pubescent, but sexually inexperienced, a virgin more than likely. Given that the average age for marriage in ancient society was somewhere between 12 and 15 for girls, then she is an early adolescent. She is sexually ambiguous and marginal. She stimulates her stepfather. We do not know her intentions.

The terminology for the daughter as also κοράσιον occurs earlier in Matthew in the story of the healing of the ruler's daughter and the woman with the flow of blood (9.18-26).[24] In that story, the girl is the special subject of God's grace through Jesus' healing. The request comes from the father, although the entreaty need not be as insistent or heart-wrenching to the audience as the Canaanite mother's. No faithful mother intercedes for the daughter of Herodias.

She is the daughter of Herodias like the daughter of the Canaanite woman. She is the 'young girl', 'apple of the eye' of Herod, like the young girl who is the beloved daughter of the ruler. According to other Matthean patterns of story, she is worthy of protection and healing. (Jesus also refers to the woman with the flow of blood as 'daughter'.) The audience might well expect a happy outcome to this story. The audience certainly regards the daughter of Herodias with sympathy.

In those other and parallel stories, however, the unnamed daughter is the beneficiary of faith, either her own (the woman with the flow of blood) or her parent's (Canaanite mother, ruler). No benefit or protection comes from God to the daughter of Herodias. She remains victim of her father's desires and her mother's plot. The narrator does not mention faith. If Herodias is circumscribed by patriarchy and phallocentricity, her daughter is nearly erased by the same.

The daughter's dance, from the daughter's perspective, is ambiguous. Matthew gives no indication of her motivation, her state of dress; the text refuses to enlighten the audience's prurient interest, unlike most male interpreters who assign to the daughter some form of intentional sexual content. Men, after all, must be encouraged to sexual

23. Pier Paolo Pasolini, *Il Vangelo secondo Matteo* (Arco, 1964); Ken Russell, *Salome's Last Dance* (Vestron, 1988). Russell's film shows the staging in a London brothel of Oscar Wilde's play. On the reception of Salome as a character in art and film, see further Anderson ('Dancing Daughter') and Bach (*Seduction*).

24. The Greek of Matthew does not identify the ruler as the ruler of the synagogue. Editors of the NRSV have emended the text to make it conform to Mk 5.22.

excess, licentiousness, by female behavior.[25] In Matthew, of course, as demonstrated above, Jesus' own teaching denies this link. Lust and adultery are male generated, not female, because only the male powerful can be held responsible in a phallocentric society (Mt. 5.27-32). The narrator does not hold the daughter responsible for the possible incitement of male desire.

The daughter is surrounded by male action, and her speech is dictated by her mother: 'Give me here on a platter the head of John the Baptist' might as well have come from Herodias herself. Herodias is responsible for the presentation of John as food.

Literary analysis leads to the conclusion that three characters—Herod, John, and Herodias—configure the action. The daughter never becomes an independent, acting subject; she remains an object. Herod and John establish the two poles of desire that control the plot. Herodias resolves the polarity by bringing the prophet to defeat and the king, her husband, to success. In this triangle of king-prophet-queen lurks recognition of a third Canaanite woman in Matthew.

The story of Ahab-Elijah-Jezebel provides the *typos* for understanding Herod-John-Herodias. An examination of that story provides the key to understanding Herodias's bizarre request for a head on a platter. It also suggests a line of interpretation that allows us to place Herodias and her action within the textual and theological world of Matthew. This line of interpretation, as those suggested by Rachab and the Canaanite mother, can only be outlined in the present essay.

The text implies that there must be an explanation of how Herodias interacts with the theological culture of the author of Matthew and finally how she along with other Canaanite women interacts in our own. In what follows I have been guided by the work of Phyllis Trible in 'Exegesis for Storytellers and Other Strangers'.[26]

The narrator reports that the people regard John as a prophet. This characterization accords with Jesus' own direct statement that John is Elijah, 'the one who is about to come' (Mt. 11.14). Jesus identifies John, prior to John's death, as the eschatological appearance of Elijah, the anticipated final prophet. When Jesus says that John is Elijah, there is no indication to the audience that he speaks metaphorically. He says that John is (really) Elijah, who has descended from the heavens to inaugurate the final days. John's action in Mt. 3.1-17 is consistent with

---

25. See Anderson, 'Dancing Daughter', pp. 121-24.
26. Phyllis Trible, 'Exegesis for Storytellers and Other Strangers', *JBL* 114 (1995), pp. 3-19.

this judgment in that it matches the depiction both physically and theologically of Elijah by the Deuteronomistic historian.

The story of Herodias shows a king troubled by his own desire and fearing to fulfil it. The queen overcomes this situation on the king's behalf. A similar plot structure occurs in 1 Kgs 21.1-28. In that story Ahab broods because he cannot acquire the vineyard of Naboth. Ahab is the Israelite king of the Northern Kingdom based in Jezreel, and so is comparable to Herod the tetrarch of Galilee. Their kingdoms overlap geographically. Ahab 'lay down on his bed, turned away his face, and would not eat' (1 Kgs 21.4b). The Hebrew narrative more precisely than Matthew shows the external manifestation of the frustration of desire. In full detail it also tells of Jezebel's actions (1 Kgs 21.8-16). By a murderous plot the queen attains the king's desire. Ahab takes possession of the vineyard after the death of Naboth; Herod has John killed.

Unlike Herodias, Jezebel is a fully developed character in the narrative of 1 Kings. Trible examines her in detail and shows her proper opponent is Elijah. Thus, the triangle of king–prophet–queen, with regard to the Hebrew story should be amended to prophet–queen–king thereby giving attention to the polarity of Elijah–Jezebel.

A few points of Jezebel's characterization and action flesh out this broad typology and let us see the ways in which the text of Matthew interacts with and modifies the tradition. Ahab marries Jezebel inappropriately (1 Kgs 16.31). She is Phoenician, Canaanite. Shortly thereafter, according to the narrative, Hiel of Bethel rebuilds Jericho, at the cost of his son (16.34). The audience understands this action to be a result of Ahab's alliance with Canaanite culture through his wife. The narrator reminds the attentive listener of Joshua's curse: 'Cursed before the Lord be anyone who tries to build this city—this Jericho! At the cost of his firstborn he shall lay its foundation and at the cost of his youngest he shall set up its gates' (Josh. 6.26, NRSV). The curse follows immediately the conclusion to Rachab's story in Josh. 6.25. The Hebrew narrator contextually links the curse of Joshua and the salvation of Rachab. The narrator also links the introduction of Jezebel and the violation of the curse. Narrator expands upon narration, layering interpretation by referentiality.

Jezebel, the Canaanite princess, stands juxtaposed to the faith of Rachab the Canaanite prostitute in the Hebrew narrative. The author of Matthew explores these linkages. The author as interpreter does not move simplistically from type to anti-type, but rather uses the complexity of scripture to enhance the referentiality and layered meaning of Matthew. Such richness of story creates the richness of theology in

Matthew. The author prefers to interpret the Law and the Prophets by story rather than by the relative theological poverty of dogma/ doctrine. The first theological strategy is generated by the faith of the liminal; the latter by the desire to control and circumscribe that faith. The author of Matthew does not write commentary on the biblical narrative, but rather new story.

In all of these texts, ethnicity, class, and gender play integral roles. The Canaanite grandmother of Jesus is created and linked to Jezebel through ethnicity and place. But, Jezebel comes from the palace, not the wall. She is royal, while Rachab is a prostitute.

For the death of Naboth, Jezebel will die, says Elijah. Prophetic word delivered to the king singles out the queen for a punishment otherwise reserved for the king's heirs (2 Kgs 10.11): 'The dogs shall eat Jezebel within the bounds of Jezreel' (1 Kgs 21.23). The triangle prophet–queen–king results in the consumption of the queen as dog food (2 Kgs 9.30-37).[27] The prophet, Elijah, however, goes to his apotheosis, carried by a chariot into the heavens (2 Kgs 2.1-12). In later times he will be anticipated by many, including Jesus in Matthew, to return at the end time.

Matthew bewilders us readers of the Hebrew story by its new appropriation of the theology of annihilation. Herod marries Herodias inappropriately. Herodias gains for her husband what the king wants but is too distressed to acquire himself. The triangle is structured as king–prophet–queen, a modification that prioritizes the action of the king. The elite Herodian princess, however, accomplishes what her foremother, the Canaanite Jezebel, could not. Here in the last days John/Elijah dies and is presented as food, just as Jezebel was presented as food in the former days. We never learn Herodias's destiny from Matthew. The pattern of judgment-apotheosis, failure-success, female elite-male prophet that shows an economy of vengeance and justice appropriate to the Law of God as depicted in the Elijah/Elisha-Jezebel story is ruptured and fragmented by the story in Matthew. This rupture in the theological world to which Matthew appeals opens the way for reflection and reformulation.

> In behavior and mode of being Elijah and Jezebel become mirror images that haunt the ages. To have one is to have the other. Wherever he appears, she is there. She haunts not only him but all that he represents in the saga of faith. To understand their inseparability is to find her on the Mount of Transfiguration and to invoke her at the Seder meal. To understand their inseparability is to perceive the limits of polarized

---

27. Trible, 'Exegesis for Storytellers', pp. 15-19.

thinking and so alter the strictures of theological discourse. Though we may find the convergence repugnant, we can be sure we are heirs to it, indeed that we participate in it.[28]

At the Threshold

These three stories have remained liminal, at the threshold of modern interpretations of Matthew. We are unable to come to terms with their theological implications, rooted as they are in assumptions about revelation. For here, the revelatory moment is located in the doorway. And the doorway, the liminal revelatory moment, opens onto our own assumptions about gender, ethnicity, and social status and how such positionings affect our construction of God. These three stories block and fragment meaning.

One thing is certain, however: seen literarily, authorially, and theologically, Rachab is successful. The Canaanite mother is successful. Most disturbingly, Herodias is successful. This last stands as the divine agent of death against prophetic extremism and religiosity. By the inclusion of this last Canaanite woman, the author accomplishes a profound swerve in the theological reading of the Law and the Prophets. Herodias, as it were, ends the fabula of an Israelite prophetic history which stands for monotheistic absolutism resulting in holy war, genocide. She is the end of what we call the Deuteronomic History whose theology of חרם would have destroyed even Rachab had not she opened a lacuna in the divine will.

John, therefore, is the end of the Prophets and the Law, in some sense. He cannot enter the kingdom because his theology is among those who take the kingdom of heaven by force, as did his predecessor Elijah (Mt. 11.1-14). John's death as the death of the final Elijah frustrates the anticipation of an ethnically pure theocratic, patriarchal, and phallocentric messianic reign. From this point on, Jesus' destiny will not lie in Matthew in continuity with this element of theology. Rather, Matthew will identify Jesus, read Jesus, through other prophetic strains derived from Jewish tradition, especially the universalism of Isaiah. At least these are the lines along which interpretation of Matthew lies if we take the presence of Herodias seriously.

How does this familiar story look to us, now? By raising simple questions of ethnicity, gender, status, the reading of Matthew is problematized. Matthew must be read in conversation with these Canaanite women, a conversation initially refused by Jesus himself, as we have seen.

28. Trible, 'Exegesis for Storytellers', p. 18.

I must close with remarks on the work of the author, the historical person who composes Matthew. This essay has shown that the author is highly aware of and presumes an audience awareness of Jewish Scriptures and traditions of use and interpretation. We simply cannot understand Matthew unless we try to understand the ways in which the author/audience appreciate and interpret the Law and the Prophets. I suggest that the author approaches Jewish Scriptures typologically, allegorically, and eschatologically. This hermeneutic may be seen in the teachings of Jesus in Mt. 13.

The use of Jewish Scriptures and tradition is an aspect of the distinctive poetics which informs the author. Matthew both conforms to and exploits audience expectations. To what extent are these elements self-conscious on the part of the author and to what extent nonconscious?

Finally, explorations into the poetics of Matthew will help us to appreciate the presence of Rachab and her daughters in Matthew. Alice Bach reminds us 'that biblical narratives are written by men with an ideal audience of men'.[29] The Canaanite women in Matthew shift the normal 'male gaze' to a distinctly female one. Beyond this essay lie the further explorations of Matthew which will establish whether this female gaze is indigenous to the production and earliest performance of the text of Matthew or whether it is a fruitful contemporary starting point for reading against the text. Perhaps it is both.

---

29. Bach, *Seduction*, p. 128.

ABSENT WOMEN IN MATTHEW'S HOUSEHOLDS

Anthony J. Saldarini

In her feminist reading of the Gospel of Matthew, Elaine Wainwright correctly criticizes my reconstruction of the late first-century Matthean community for emphasizing its emerging coherent world view without listening 'for the voices of resistance within the developing coherence'.[1] In contrast, she tries to listen to the Gospel with the ear of a first-century woman who was a member of Matthew's community. (Matthew's 'community' was probably a household church or a group of household churches somewhere in greater Syria.[2]) Wainwright argues that the author of Matthew, writing for both the men and women of his community, must implicitly or explicitly address the needs and concerns of female members and thus affirm or dispute the attitudes and views of women. She also employs a second strategy for interpreting the gospel for women. The Matthean narrative and teachings provide sites where modern women readers may enter 'the narrative, open to the creative possibilities' in the text,[3] to uncover 'the possibilities of ongoing open-ended interpretation... The ἐκκλησία of women and its *poiesis* of Jesus is one possible site in which such possibilities can be realized'.[4]

---

1. Elaine M. Wainwright, *Shall We Look for Another? A Feminist Rereading of the Matthean Jesus* (Maryknoll, NY: Orbis Books, 1998), pp. 41-42, responding to Anthony J. Saldarini, *Matthew's Christian-Jewish Community* (Chicago, IL: University of Chicago Press, 1994). See also Wainwright's earlier study, *Towards a Feminist Critical Reading of the Gospel According to Matthew* (BZNW, 60; Berlin: W. de Gruyter, 1991).
2. Saldarini, *Community*, pp. 3, 26, 120-23. For an explicit argument for Galilee or its immediate environs as the social location of Matthew and his community, see J. Andrew Overman, *Matthew's Gospel and Formative Judaism: The Social World of the Matthean Community* (Minneapolis: Fortress Press, 1990) and Anthony J. Saldarini, 'The Gospel of Matthew and Jewish-Christian Conflict in Galilee', in Lee Levine (ed.), *Studies on Galilee in Late Antiquity* (New York: Jewish Theological Seminary, 1992), pp. 23-38.
3. Wainwright, *Shall We Look*, p. 66.
4. Wainwright, *Shall We Look*, p. 83.

Though Wainwright has effectively made a case for her mode of interpretation, she must read against the grain of the narrative. Why do women not leap out of the gospel to modern readers sensitized by the women's movement and feminist discourse? What has the author of Matthew done to conceal women and why?

Chapters 18–20 provide a test case for the treatment of women and for its author's lack of specific interest in them as members of the community. These chapters attend to intra-communal relations: care for one another, resolution of inner communal conflicts, and forgiveness in ch. 18; marriage, children, and wealth in ch. 19; and the relationship of day laborers and slaves/servants to masters in ch. 20. All these topics regulate inner communal or household relationships and thus implicitly reflect the author's interest in and perceptions of household and communal order. The topics in chs. 19 and 20 also appear in Greco-Roman household codes[5] and in inscriptions concerning Greek voluntary associations.[6] The concern for rebuking and forgiving sin and the procedures for resolving disputes in ch. 18 appear in the Dead Sea Scrolls.[7] Within this framework the author of Matthew consciously modifies the relationships among members of his households in the light of Jesus' teachings. Against the cultural dominance of the male head of the household, he teaches that members must serve one another and that like children they should subordinate themselves to others.[8]

Though the author of Matthew attends to the household as a reality and as a metaphor for the whole community, women appear or are mentioned rarely in these chapters, and only once does a woman have an active role.[9] When we speak of households, *we may*, with Wainwright, imaginatively include women as integral and essential members, as daughters, young women, wives, mothers, widows, and single women (Mary Magdalene, 27.56, 61; 28.1) and as followers of

5. Warren Carter, *Households and Discipleship: A Study of Matthew 19-20* (JSNTSup, 103; Sheffield: JSOT Press, 1994), pp. 17-22 and *passim*.
6. John Kloppenborg, 'Collegia and *Thiasoi*: Issues in Function, Taxonomy and Membership', in John S. Kloppenborg and Stephen G. Wilson (eds.), *Voluntary Associations in the Graeco-Roman World* (London: Routledge, 1996), pp. 16-30.
7. The Community Rule (1QS 5.24–6.3) and the Covenant of Damascus (CD 9-10).
8. Carter, *Households*, *passim*, notes that the Matthean community and constituent families embrace the kind of equality commonly found in new movements and sects and stress even more than the dominant Jewish and Greco-Roman societies stability and continuity in their households in order to survive.
9. Interestingly, Carter's very helpful study, which systematically expounds Matthew's views, lacks a sustained discussion of women just as the Gospel does.

Jesus. But why does the author of Matthew presume rather than speak of their presence? Why are women almost completely absent as actors in chs. 18-20? A brief analysis of this material will demonstrate that the evangelist addresses his instructions to and shapes his narrative for men who have the social power in his world. In accordance with the teaching and actions of Jesus he modifies traditional male roles to orient them away from the competition for social power and honor and toward a low and marginal social status symbolized by children and slaves. He encourages them to serve their fellow family and community members rather than exercise power over them, and women would presumably benefit somehow from this adjustment of social relations. However, the author does not explicitly attend to their experiences, perceptions, or needs, nor does he empower women as independent centers of power equal to men. Thus the shifts in household relations suggested by Matthew remain very much under male control, even if motivated by love patriarchy and the humility and sufferings of Jesus Christ.

Communal Relations in Matthew 18

Jesus' teaching ('sermon') on inner communal relations in ch. 18 contrasts children, who are the least powerful and most dependent members of society, with adult males, who are the most powerful. The disciples begin a public conversation with Jesus by asking about the greatest in the kingdom of heaven. Jesus responds by calling a child (παιδίον) into their midst as a case in point (18.1-2). They must somehow become like children, specifically by humbling themselves, and in an appended comment, by welcoming children (into their midst?) in Jesus' name (18.4-5). The author repeats and reinforces this metaphor in the household code in the following chapter. Jesus rebukes his disciples for resisting people's efforts to have him bless their children (19.13-15) and declares enigmatically that the kingdom of heaven (God's powerful rule over all creations) belongs to children. In these passages children serve as a symbol for those who lack power and social status in the household and ancient society. Matthew will argue for increasing mutually supportive relationships among household members and decreasing subordination through the exercise of power.

Ancient society generally treated children as dependents and as unfinished adults[10] who were socially embedded in their parents,

10. Carter, *Households*, p. 98.

especially their fathers, and thus subordinated and marginal to society.[11] Even children in rich families, though destined to exercise social and political power and influence and raised with all the advantages of wealth, lacked social rights and status independent from their parents. Matthew's Jesus challenges the disciples and men to give up their quest for and exercise of control over subordinates such as children in favor of 'humility'. Humility is an ancient virtue proper to ancient hierarchical, aristocratic society. It encouraged an appropriate recognition of one's social and political superiors and of one's inherited, subordinate place in society. The Greek verb used here, ταπεινόω, also has a negative meaning applied to the lower classes of society with the connotation of debasement, poverty, obscurity, low estate, etc. Modern, individualistic society which stresses self-worth and the dignity and rights of individuals tends to reject humility as a virtue. Similarly humility militates against the modern goal of competitive self-betterment.[12] Matthew (18.4) advises men to forego the exercise of their dominant roles and the acquisition of honor which goes with it in favor of occupying a low place in the social and power structure by being humble like children. Similarly, in the instruction on leadership (Mt. 23.1-12) the author rejects leadership's public places of honor, salutations and titles (rabbi, father, master). He concludes by connecting greatness with service, not station, power or honor, and by decreeing that 'whoever humbles himself (ταπεινωθήσεται) will be exalted' (23.12).

The low status and powerlessness of children mirrors the place of the new, small Matthean community within the larger, late first-century Jewish community and even more so within Greco-Roman society. The Matthean community has experienced itself as uninfluential, unaccepted, and oppressed by the majority of the population. The next paragraph of ch. 18 reflects this social world and transforms the

---

11. Carter, *Households*, pp. 108-13, points out that some first-century literature testifies to a growing affection for children. In lived fact, we may surmise that parents loved, cherished, etc., their children, but this does not alter public, traditional views of children which greatly influenced society. As W.D. Davies and Dale C. Allison, Jr, point out (*A Critical and Exegetical Commentary on the Gospel According to Saint Matthew* [3 vols.; Edinburgh: T. & T. Clark, 1991], II, p. 759), ancient literature, contrary to much modern exegesis, does not propose children as models to be imitated or praise 'child-likeness', much less engage in romantic, sentimental idealizations of innocent childhood.

12. Bruce J. Malina, 'Humility', in John J. Pilch and Bruce J. Malina (eds.), *Biblical Social Values and their Meaning: A Handbook* (Peabody, MA: Hendrickson, 1993), pp. 107-108.

metaphor of the child (18.2-5; 19.13-15) into a symbolic name for the members of the community, 'little ones' (μικροί in 18.6, 10, 14).[13] Jesus warns community members and perhaps by implication outsiders too against causing 'one of these little ones who believe in me to sin' (18.6) and 'despising one of these little ones' (18.10) because 'it is not the will of my Father who is in heaven that one of these little ones should perish' (18.14). The little ones are socially powerless and dependent on God and the love and care of one another. The very name encourages community members to care for one another and resolve disputes which might drive someone from the group. They exercise authority communally (18.15-17) without recourse to highly structured leadership roles (23.1-12).[14]

Does the narrative presence and metaphoric use of children at the beginning of ch. 18 suggest the presence of women among the disciples who initiate the conversation with Jesus about the greatest in the kingdom of God? Some have explicitly limited the disciples to the twelve,[15] and many simply assume that the disciples are men. However, Matthew uses the category 'disciple' in a vague inclusive sense[16] so the disciples here and elsewhere may include women. Conversely, the presence of a child in the narrative does not require women in the audience (contrary to some cultural stereotypes which associate

13. Davies and Allison, *Matthew*, II, p. 763.
14. The Matthean community may be on the way to institutionalization. The author refers to prophets, sages, and scribes in 23.34. Elsewhere he refers to prophets, scribes, and teachers frequently. Dennis Duling argues that a group of scribes in some sense lead the Matthean community. See his 'The Matthean Brotherhood and Marginal Scribal Leadership', in Philip F. Esler (ed.), *Modelling Early Christianity: Social-Scientific Studies of the New Testament in Its Context* (Routledge: London, 1995), pp. 159-82 (178-80).
15. Raymond E. Brown, *The Death of the Messiah: A Commentary on the Passion Narratives in the Four Gospels* (2 vols.; New York: Doubleday, 1994), II, pp. 1155-57. His argument that the women looking at the crucifixion 'from afar' (Mt. 27.55) implies rejection of Jesus because Peter followed Jesus 'from afar' to the high priest's house (Mt. 26.58) ignores the social situations, the public status of men versus women, and the contrasting actions of Peter, who explicitly denies knowing Jesus, and the women, who witness Jesus' crucifixion and go to his grave after the Sabbath.
16. The twelve, called disciples (Mt. 10.1) and apostles (10.2), function as a symbolic group related to Israel; they are all male. However, at the beginning of the Sermon on the Mount (5.1), where disciples are first mentioned, the Gospel does not identify the members of the group of disciples with precision. In general, the often-used word 'disciple' refers to those who regularly listen to and travel with Jesus (5.1; 8.23; 9.12; 12.1, etc.). Disciples probably included women as well as men.

children with women). The power question about the 'greatest' may sound like a male question, but women could be interested in power as much as men. Later in this series of chapters the mother of the sons of Zebedee asks for power for her sons in Jesus' kingdom (20.20-21, treated below).

In ch. 18, however, a number of male, but no female, characters appear to clarify Jesus' teaching about humility and forgiveness: a man with a hundred sheep (18.12), 'brothers' who have conflict within the community (18.15-17, 21), and male slaves/servants who are in debt (18.23-34). A woman appears once, in the parable of the unforgiving slave/servant. The king/householder[17] threatens to sell a slave/ servant along with his wife and children to repay the debt (18.25).[18] But the debtor's wife exists only as a pawn in the economic law of the first century, embedded in her husband and father of the family to such an extent that her life must service his debt.

The presence of a child at the beginning of ch. 18 suggests that adult men and women with their children were listening to Jesus teach when his disciples asked him about the greatest in the kingdom. Perhaps, but the women have no role, voice, or visibility. Fundamentally the author of Matthew adjusts social relationships and roles by contrasting adult male householders with children and slaves without explicit reference to women as actors, symbols, or beneficiaries.

The Household Code (19.1–20.16)

Chapters 19 and 20 comment upon a series of relationships which held the ancient household together. Yet, here too women are strangely neglected. Chapter 19 takes up the question of marriage and divorce but still omits women's perspectives, concerns, and roles in the household. The contents of chs. 19, 20 clearly resemble the household codes found in Greco-Roman sources and in the New Testament (Col. 3.18–4.1; Eph. 5.22–6.9; 1 Pet. 2.11–3.12).[19] Colossians treats in this order the

---

17. The parable begins by identifying the lead character as a king (18.23) who is then addressed as and called 'Lord' (18.26, 32). Granted the convention of parables about kings, the substance of this narrative fits better a rich householder of an estate dealing with his highly placed slave-manager.

18. The debt of 10,000 talents, more than the yearly taxes of a Roman province, is impossible. For an argument that the story contained an originally reasonable level of debt, which the sale of the debtor's family might have satisfied, see Davies and Allison, *Matthew*, II, pp. 795-96.

19. See Carter, *Households*, for a comprehensive and influential study and Davies and Allison, *Matthew*, III, pp. 1-3 for a précis that accepts Carter's approach.

reciprocal duties of (1) husbands and wives; (2) parents and children; and (3) slaves and masters. Strikingly, Mt. 19.1–20.28 treats a similar list of topics: the husband's obligations concerning marriage and divorce; eunuch-like celibacy, either to work for the kingdom of God or to keep from remarrying after a divorce; children; wealth; and slavery. But equally striking is the absence of the duties of wives toward their husbands from the list. Wives would benefit on the whole from the husbands' obligation not to divorce except in cases of sexual irregularity of some kind (πορνεία in 19.9) because ancient society located women economically and socially in a household headed by a male. Matthew's regulation constrains men from disrupting the supportive household relationships for trivial or selfish reasons. (The prohibition of divorce does not address wife abuse or failure to provide responsibly for the family.) But even granted potential benefits to women through the prohibition of divorce, Matthew does not articulate or attend to women's own needs, deprivations, duties, and rights.

True to traditional Near Eastern marriage customs, the *man* takes the woman as his wife, leaves *his* parents, and joins closely (κολληθήσεται in 19.5 quoting Gen. 2.24 from the Greek) *to her*. Similarly, if the marriage ends, he divorces her (19.3, 8-9, relying on Deut. 24.1).[20] Thus the man controls the traditional marriage and can cause a variety of hardships for his wife by controlling or leaving her. The solution proposed by Jesus' core teaching and by Matthew's elaboration of it requires that the *man take care of* his wife by living out his social and financial obligations to her, as was noted above. This plan eliminates divorce (except in cases of sexual irregularity) and thus protects the wife from all the economic and social disruption suffered by women abandoned by their husbands in a society that has little place for independent women.

Ancient society understands marriage as a public, social, economic union rather than the private, romantic, emotional union of the modern West. Though the man and woman are joined together as one flesh by God (19.6-7) in a way that suggests intimate, sexual, and emotional ties, in the end men still control the marriage. The disciples protest the difficulty of a *man* marrying if he cannot divorce under the usual circumstances (unhappiness; marital conflict?). Matthew's Jesus

---

20. Carter, *Households*, p. 80, claims that a woman could divorce her husband in the biblical tradition under certain circumstances. But he misinterprets the passages he cites. They deal with a woman's right to property, etc., but do not allow her to divorce her husband. Mk 10.12 envisions a woman divorcing her husband, but this view comes from Greco-Roman society.

responds with a greater challenge of celibacy (using the male metaphor of a eunuch), either for those men whose marriages have ended in divorce or for those men who have chosen to remain unmarried to work for God's kingdom. Jesus admits that only some men can accept this teaching, even as he recommends it (19.11-12). The discussion concentrates entirely on the actions and difficulties of the male without any direct mention of wife or children. Certainly women's roles and welfare can be extrapolated from the rules and instructions given to men, but Matthew does not address women.

The author's lack of interest in women follows from his focus on the males as the center of power in his society. In his concern to change societal norms so that they accord with the rule of God ('the kingdom of heaven'), Matthew curtails severely male prerogatives in marriage and immediately afterwards proposes the powerless status of children as a model for participation in the kingdom of heaven (19.13-15; see the earlier teaching in 18.2-5). This turns the traditional eastern Mediterranean household and its social relations on their head: 'divorce is wrong, children are to be honored, [and to anticipate] wealth is an obstacle to virtue, true greatness is readiness to offer God and others the service of a slave'.[21] Contrary to the modern stress on human rights and dignity in order to raise the status of the oppressed, Matthew works to lower the powerful, dominant position of the wealthy over the majority of the population which was poor and to restrict the traditional power of men over women. Thus his treatment of typical household relations has focused on divorce which disempowers women and children. He next initiates a larger discussion both of wealth which a rich young man wishes to conserve (19.22) and an atypical householder wishes to disburse (20.14-15) and of service/slavery on behalf of others for which Jesus provides the model (20.27-28).

The story of the wealthy young man who wishes to do 'something good' (τί ἀγαθόν) to acquire eternal life (19.16-31) and the parable of the householder who pays his day laborers equally for unequal work (20.1-16) severely relativize the importance of wealth for the survival of the household. The author of Matthew signals the reversal of values by concluding both stories with sayings about the first being last and the last first (19.31; 20.16). In antiquity the stability and continuity of families depended mainly on a steady food supply derived from arable land. The more land, the more secure and powerful the household and family. However, since people had to share a limited amount of

---

21. Davies and Allison, *Matthew*, III, p. 2.

arable land, the wealth of one household implied the poverty of others. This theory of limited goods cast suspicion on wealth and pressured the rich to give their surplus to the poor.

Jesus' response to the inquiry from the pious young rich man concerning 'something good' radicalizes his search. Already in control of 'many possessions' (κτήματα πολλά in 19.22) and observant of the commandments (19.17-20), he wants more: he wants to do something good to acquire eternal life (19.16). The choice of language here suggests that the young man sought eternal life as a commodity to be possessed. But Jesus sharply contrasts earthly wealth with 'treasure in heaven' (19.21) and recommends divestiture in favor of the poor and following, that is, becoming a disciple. The advice is so revolutionary that the young man withdraws (19.22), and Jesus' disciples nervously demand an elaborate explanation (19.23-30). And well they might. Though this instruction has inspired Christian monks, nuns, and saints for centuries, it disrupts and endangers the continuity and security of families and households. Carter correctly argues that abandonment of wealth signifies a transition from the typical household and social structures of ancient society to the 'new age' or 'renewal of all things' (παλιγγενεσία in 19.28). The Matthean community sees itself as marginalized in relationship to society at large and as dependent on God.[22] Thus abandonment of wealth serves Matthew's main concern, the kingdom (rule) of God in the community now and at the end of the world.

Significantly, a lone rich young man appears in the instruction concerning total dedication without the support of possessions. The text does not allude to or grapple with the typical male responsibilities for feeding and sheltering a wife and children, nor aged parents, nor slaves and other dependents. Though ancient literature sometimes portrays the wealthy as selfish, self-indulgent, and unjust, a well-run, prosperous household supported and benefited many people including women and others who were dependent on elite men in ancient society. Thus society required men to amass power and wealth in order to care for their dependents. The Gospel of Matthew inverts these values by discouraging the pursuit of honor,[23] power, and wealth with the result that the followers of Jesus in Matthew's community should share significant risk in following Jesus. As in previous sections

22. Carter, *Households*, p. 145, and in the whole of ch. 5.
23. For the exceedingly broad and important dimensions of this fundamental cultural perspective, see the recent book by Jerome Neyrey, *Honor and Shame in the Gospel of Matthew* (Louisville, KY: Westminster/John Knox Press, 1998).

of chs. 18 and 19, this discussion presumably encompasses women. Peter had a family (8.14-15), and probably other male disciples did too. Women followed Jesus in Galilee and when he went to Jerusalem (27.55). Matthew seeks to disrupt and transform the stable, hierarchical family relationships so that men take on roles of service usually relegated to women, slaves, and other subordinates. However, this change may come at the price of less material security in some cases. Matthew does not pay explicit or nuanced attention to the status, social disabilities, and needs of women who most often suffered the ill effects of household or communal instability and impoverishment. Rather, he concentrates on changing the men who control power and wealth.

The discussion of householders and wealth continues in the parable about the day laborers hired by a householder to work in his vineyard (20.1-16). This story of hired workers substitutes for the standard discussion of master/slave relations in the household codes. Ordinarily slaves were exhorted to work hard and obediently and masters were counseled to act justly and without cruelty toward their slaves. In this parable the normal expectation is a standard day's pay (a *denarius*) for an ordinary day's work. But the master overturns the norm of measure for measure by paying a day's wage for an hour's work as well as for 12 hours' work. All the workers and their families benefit by receiving enough to feed them for that day, and the householder betters the lives of the workers hired near the end of the day by generously giving them sufficient resources out of his abundance. The families of the workers, including women, presumably benefited from this adjustment of economic norms of justice, but the voices of women and other dependents remain silent and the effect of this policy on them invisible. Matthew analyzes and instructs the men who control the public marketplace in order to advocate generous, reciprocal relationships.

Slavery as a Norm

The author of Matthew continues the interaction between Jesus and his disciples in order to reveal the basis for his reorganization of household and social relationships in the community. For the third time Jesus tells his disciples that he will be executed and rise from the dead in Jerusalem (20.17-19; cf. 16.21; 17.22-23), and then he instructs them about their own suffering (20.20-28). Unsurprisingly, the author of Matthew proposes Jesus as the model for a life spent in service and self-giving, like that of a slave. (The Greek word δοῦλος is usually translated by the less offensive term 'servant', but both slave and servant denote the lowest social status and subordination of one human to the wishes of another.) Rather than engaging in power struggles and seeking to dominate his enemies, Jesus accepts God's will that he die for others. The powerless, disenfranchised main figure in the narrative corresponds to the Matthean community which is socially marginalized or under the threat of social marginalization because of its conflicts with the larger Jewish community in the late first century.[24] Ironically, two of Jesus' disciples, the sons of Zebedee, (through their mother) seek preferment when Jesus takes power at the end. Jesus responds by hinting to them that they will suffer as he will and by explicitly instructing them not to seek power, but to be slaves/servants to one another. At the beginning of ch. 18 the status of a child undermines the socially normative quest for honor and power in favor of humility; similarly here at the end slavery symbolizes subordination to one another and reciprocal service. The author of Matthew continues his attack on the attitudes, norms, and behaviors which govern the males who dominate society.

Just at this point, at the end of extensive teaching on households, a woman finally appears, briefly, as an actor. The mother of the sons of Zebedee, that is, of Jesus' disciples, James and John, intervenes on her sons' behalf (20.20); she asks that they receive preferential treatment when Jesus takes power in God's kingdom later on. But why does Matthew introduce her here and once again in the crucifixion scene? She is mentioned in no other Gospel in any capacity, even though her sons along with Peter appear a number of times in special situations. In the Gospel of Mark's version of this story the brothers James and John request preferment from Jesus directly (Mk 10.35). Commentators usually suggest that the author of Matthew has introduced the mother to make the disciples look better than they do in Mark: the mother initiates a naive request which Jesus deflects by saying that they 'do not know what they are asking' (20.22). However, the presence of the mother does not remove the brothers from the center of the story since Jesus immediately confronts and instructs them and then the rest of

---

24. Marginalization refers to the status of those people or groups at or near the bottom of the social hierarchy. It especially refers to people excluded from participation in social roles in which they might be expected to participate according to generally accepted social criteria. See Duling, 'Matthean Brotherhood', p. 180.

168   *A Feminist Companion to Matthew*

the disciples,[25] and they all receive the same challenge: to suffer with Jesus and to serve one another rather than seek power (20.22-28).

The designation of this woman as the mother of the sons of her husband Zebedee illustrates the embedded social position of women in antiquity and especially in the Matthean narrative. Her name is not given.[26] Rather, she is named and defined by her family relationships, in this case, her sons, who themselves are not named here, but defined by their relationship to their father, Zebedee. The household head is the father and husband, Zebedee. His sons are identified by their relationship with him and their mother by her relationship to the sons. As has been noted before, society treats women and children as embedded in the male head of the household.

The mother of the sons of Zebedee appears one more time, along with other women at the cross (27.53-55). Her later activity throws light on her earlier request and on her very appearance with her sons earlier in the Gospel.[27] All four Gospels have a tradition that women from Galilee followed Jesus. In Mark a group of women observe the crucifixion. They include (by name) Mary Magdalene, Mary the mother of James the younger and Joses, and Salome. They and others had come from Galilee to Jerusalem with Jesus, ministering to him (Mk 15.41; cf. Mt. 27.55); they watched Jesus' execution from a distance (Mk 15.40; cf. Mt. 27.55). Matthew substitutes the mother of the sons of Zebedee for the otherwise unknown 'Salome' (27.56)[28] in order to complete her role in the narrative begun in ch. 20.

    25. Davies and Allison, *Matthew*, III, pp. 86-87, discount the usual explanation and offer a few subtle biblical parallels, but do not illuminate the situation.
    26. Harmonizing interpretations have identified the mother of the sons of Zebedee as the woman Salome, mentioned in parallel passages in Mk 15.40 and 16.1. Some commentators have further identified Salome (= the mother of the sons of Zebedee) as the sister of Jesus' mother, mentioned in Jn 19.25. These identifications are highly speculative. More importantly, they are irrelevant to the Matthean narrative which does not present the mother of the sons of Zebedee as a relative of Jesus or as a distinct character with her own name.
    27. Besides the standard commentaries, see Wainwright, *Shall We Look*, pp. 105-10; eadem, *Feminist Critical Reading*, pp. 137-43, 293-99.
    28. The second woman in Matthew is identified as the mother of James (dropping Mark's identifier 'the younger') and Joseph (a variant of Mark's 'Joses'). The Gospel of John, an independent tradition, places a group of women near the cross: Jesus' mother (whose name is not given in John), her sister Mary, the wife of Clopas, and Mary Magdalene. Matthew and Luke both modify the Markan tradition. The Gospel of Luke expands the Markan tradition by referring to a group of Galilean women who provided for Jesus and identifying its members as Mary Magdalene, Joanna the wife of Chuza, Herod's steward, Susanna, and many

What then does the mother of the sons of Zebedee symbolize? She, along with the other women, had followed Jesus in Galilee and from Galilee to Jerusalem. When she asks Jesus to give her sons power (20.22), they are all in 'the region of Judea beyond the Jordan'.[29] She has followed Jesus from Galilee to Jerusalem and is in a substantial sense a disciple.[30] But like many women in the Gospels, she has no name. She and the other women function as a counter-group of disciples ironically contrasted to the male disciples who appear throughout the Gospels. The men abandon Jesus and flee in fear (26.56, 69-75), but the women stay with Jesus until his death and visit his tomb afterwards (27.53-55; 28.1-10). They quietly do what the prominent disciples should have done. Matthew sharpens this contrast through the partially identified, but unnamed, mother of the sons of Zebedee. Jesus had challenged her and her sons to drink the cup which he had to drink (20.22); they did not, but strikingly, she, the very one who made the inappropriate request for power for her sons, did in the end drink of the cup by standing with Jesus at his execution.[31] She responded to Jesus' teaching in sharp contrast to her sons and the rest of the twelve, who did not.

Has the author of Matthew suddenly changed his perspective and moved women to the center of his narrative? At best the appearance of the mother of the sons of Zebedee comments subtly on the failures of the disciples. 'Subtly', that is, she appears only twice and briefly; 'comments', that is, Matthew's focus remains on the men in the story,

---

others (Lk. 8.2-3). Luke then refers to these Galilean women as a known group at the crucifixion and burial (Lk. 23.49, 55). Some of these same women in all four Gospels reappear to witness the empty tomb. Only Mary Magdalene is present in all four sources. The other names vary within the common, stable tradition that some women witnessed Jesus' death and his empty tomb. For a recent discussion of these traditions, see Brown, *Death*, II, pp. 1013-19, with a chart, and *Death*, II, pp. 1152-55.

29. See Davies and Allison, *Matthew*, III, p. 7, for the difficulties of this geographic expression. Trans-Jordan is Perea and strictly speaking this is not part of Judea, but since it had been ruled by Herod the Great and was at this time (c. 30 CE) ruled by his son Antipas, people may have thought of it as 'Jewish territory' and so Judea in a very loose sense.

30. On disciples and following, see Jack Dean Kingsbury, 'The Verb *akolouthein* ("to follow") as an Index of Matthew's View of his Community', *JBL* 97 (1978), pp. 56-73.

31. On the danger faced by those associated with crucified felons, see Luise Schottroff, *Let the Oppressed Go Free: Feminist Perspectives on the New Testament* (Louisville, KY: Westminster/John Knox Press, 1993), pp. 168-69.

in this case the eleven male disciples whom Jesus will authorize to make disciples of all nations (28.16-20).

Matthew does not exclude or attack women, but he does not reimagine their place in society either. He seeks to reshape society and his community according to the teachings of Jesus from the top down, working through male heads of the community and its households. We may imagine and argue that women took part in that process and that women benefited from the emphasis on men taking on the social roles of slaves/servants within the community and society, rather than as dominant authorities using the resources of women and slaves. However, we must imagine it and fill in the gaps which Matthew leaves.[32]

---

32. Wainwright, *Shall We Look*, p. 120, puts this task well. 'Narrative, metaphor, and the imagery that have been used to construct Jesus have been and can be interpreted in ways that are oppressive and that construct meaning simply to support the status quo. On the other hand, a feminist reading of that imagery within the creative meaning-making potential of narrative and attention to the agency of those previously silenced has yielded not only other ways of reading but also Another, the incarnation of divinity, which will not be confined and about whom feminist women and men can speak in new ways.'

GOT INTO THE PARTY AFTER ALL:
WOMEN'S ISSUES AND THE FIVE FOOLISH VIRGINS[*]

Marie-Eloise Rosenblatt

I never liked the story of the ten virgins as it occurs in Matthew's Gospel. There are some projects we get 'bothered into'. The origin of this study has been my long-felt 'bother'. I like part of the parable better now, because I suspect that the story is really a composite of two distinct narratives, each with its own theological and social integrity. One is a parable of the kingdom focusing on women who wait for the bridegroom and the marriage feast. The other is a parable about wisdom and foolishness that is a corrective aimed at managing some disruptive women in the Matthean community. This is the one that's hard to take, and the source of my 'bother'.[1]

The division of any biblical text into multiple layers of composition is a staple of the historical-critical method. The parable of the ten virgins is not the only text in Matthew which illustrates the biblical literary convention of conflation—the combination of two separate stories into one. A typical example is the controversy-healing narrative of the man with a withered hand. At the base is the healing story say the form critics. Added to it is a dialogue or controversy about the question of what work may or may not be done on the Sabbath. The present form of the text intertwines the healing and controversy into one narrative (Mt. 12.9-14//Mk 3.1-5).

Artistic versions of the ten virgins support the suspicion that there are two separate pieces to the story. A poem of Thomas Merton, 'Les Cinq Vierges', for example, puts the emphasis on the celebration into which the women entered. However, the portals of two Gothic cathedrals, and a watercolor of William Blake omit a representation of the

---

[*] Originally published in *Continuum* 3 (1993), pp. 107-37. Reprinted by permission. The editor regrets that illustrations which were part of the original article could not be included for reason of copyright.

1. Another version of this study was presented as a paper in Washington, DC, at the annual meeting of the American Academy of Religion/Society of Biblical Literature in November 1993.

celebration and focus on the division of the women into two groups. The artistic renditions suggest that the polemical aspect overrides the reference to a wedding feast. Merton's poem, by way of contrast, resists the polemic and retrieves the spirit of a bridegroom parable favorable to women. A feminist reading points up the alienating features of the parable and raises suspicions about the purpose for it in Matthew's Gospel.

When compared with the trend of the treatment of women in the Gospels and women's overall relationships with Jesus, the polemical aspect of the parable stands out in relief. What is consistent with a gospel portrait of Jesus and women is the kingdom-bridegroom parable which presents women in an attractive and inspiring light. What is inconsistent with Matthew's own portrayal of women throughout the rest of the Gospel is the suggestion that the Lord rejects half the community of women in the wisdom-foolishness polemic. The hypothesis of a double dimension to the parable can account for the simultaneous presence of a friendly and an unfriendly portrayal of women.

The reader must ask what pastoral situation, historically, would account for the disguise of an appealing parable about women's inclusion in the kingdom, and its 'colonization' by a wisdom-foolishness polemic about women in the community. The New Testament hints in several places, especially the post-Pauline letters, about community situations in which intrusions of false prophets and teachers, or rival interpretations of doctrine, threatened the cohesion of the group. A 'redemptive reading' of the parable acknowledges the conflation of two pastoral interests integrated within the story.

Introduction

> Then the kingdom of heaven shall be compared to ten maidens who took their lamps and went to meet the bridegroom. Five of them were foolish and five were wise. For when the foolish took their lamps, they took no oil with them; but the wise took flasks of oil with their lamps. As the bridegroom was delayed, they all slumbered and slept. But at midnight there was a cry, 'Behold, the bridegroom! Come out to meet him.' Then all those maidens rose and trimmed their lamps. And the foolish said to the wise, 'Give us some of your oil, for our lamps are going out.' But the wise replied, 'Perhaps there will not be enough for us and for you; go rather to the dealers and buy for yourselves.' And while they went to buy, the bridegroom came, and those who were ready went in with him to the marriage feast; and the door was shut. Afterward the other maidens came also, saying, 'Lord, lord, open to us.'

But he replied, 'Truly, I say to you, I do not know you.' Watch therefore, for you know neither the day nor the hour.[2]

The common source-critical assumption is that Matthew's parable represents various stages of development, and its composition evidences a conflation of several earlier traditions. But exegetes are divided over where the dividing line between 'earlier' and 'later' composition lies.[3] The initial metaphor is joyful. The kingdom of heaven is like ten women who go forth to meet the bridegroom. The full count of ten, like a complete flock, whole measure, or complete monetary unit, is meant to enter into the feast.[4] The Christology is joyful and the arrival of the bridegroom is the consummation of a long-desired meeting.

The 'Bridegroom' Parable of Women Entering the Feast

> Then the kingdom of heaven shall be compared to ten maidens who took their lamps and went to meet the bridegroom. As the bridegroom

2. Translation is from the RSV.
3. The major contemporary study focused on this parable is the revised dissertation by Armand Puig i Tàrrech, *La parabole des dix vierges (Matt. 25.1-13)* (AnBib, 102; Rome: Biblical Institute Press, 1983). See his description of the context and themes on pp. 20-29. He posits and tries to retrieve the 'original parable' told by Jesus. He debates which parts of the parable are allegorical, and reviews the parable's context within the eschatological discourse, its thematic relation to other parables in the discourse, the theme of the delay of the parousia, and the adaptation of the parable to support a radical ethic to be lived out in the present time. The parables of Mt. 24 and 25 illustrate in multiple ways the same line of thought, he says. The unit of three parables in Mt. 24.45-51, 25.1-13 and 25.14-30 repeats a similar structure: two groups of characters and their behavior are proposed as a lesson. The contrast in each parable concerns the fate of one group vs. the fate of the others (26). Separation is the point in all three (28). For a summary of Tàrrech's study, see the review by Benedict T. Viviano, OP, in *RB* 94.3 (1987), pp. 425-28.
4. In the land of Israel, Jewish measures of wheat and of oil were divided in units of ten. A *homer* was ten times an *ephah*, and a *cor* was ten times a *bath*. In the Hellenistic and Roman period, the Romans adapted the Greek currency system to the Roman Empire, with a gold to silver value ratio of ten to one. Monetary units were also based on units of ten, such as the mina and the talent. See 'Measures and Money: Tables of Approximate Equivalents', in 'Supplements', *The Jerusalem Bible:* (New York: Doubleday, 1966). Matthew uses other units of ten to describe a concept of the whole, e.g., the hundred sheep whose full count is thrown off by the absence of one, Mt. 18.12-14. The ten thousand talents vs a hundred denarii in the parable of the unforgiving debtor also refer to monetary units of ten (18.24, 28). The most productive servant of the parable immediately following the story of the ten virgins receives five talents and makes five more (Mt. 25.15-16). This is the servant who has ten talents who receives an even greater 'bonus' at the end.

was delayed, they all slumbered and slept. But at midnight, there was a cry, 'Behold the bridegroom! Come out to meet him!' Then all those maidens rose and trimmed their lamps. The bridegroom came, and they went in with him to the marriage feast. Watch therefore, for you know neither the day nor the hour.

The second stratum of the parable has a very different tone and presents a rather harsh lesson about wisdom and foolishness. Naturally, the exact nature of the pastoral problem represented by the foolish women cannot be perfectly ascertained. Reasonable guesses can be made by looking at other New Testament passages in which problems with false prophets, heretical teachers and dissension within the community are addressed and linked with a wisdom-foolishness theme. This stratum of the parable is characterized by its emphasis on an eschatological theme of judgment between insiders and outsiders, and the division between those who are either wise or foolish. The joyful Christology competes with a warning to the community. The object of the address, 'Lord, lord', is a judgmental spokesperson behind the door and his severe and uncompromising voice rejects those who are unacceptable. A hypothetical breakdown of the parable looks like this:

The Polemic against Women, the Wisdom–Foolishness Parable

Five maidens were foolish and five were wise. When the foolish took their lamps, they took no oil with them; but the wise took flasks of oil with their lamps. And the foolish said to the wise, 'Give us some of your oil, for our lamps are going out.' But the wise replied, 'Perhaps there will not be enough for us and for you; go rather to the dealers and buy for yourselves.' And while they went out to buy [the bridegroom came] and those who were ready [went in with him to the marriage feast]. And the door was shut. Afterward the other maidens came also, saying, 'Lord, lord, open to us.' But he replied, 'Truly, I say to you, I do not know you.'

Conventional Readings

In arguing for the credibility of my division of the parable into these two themes, it is well to review briefly the standard approach to this parable. What shall account for the fact that the story of the ten virgins and their lamps doesn't receive major attention in recent books on parables? One of the major challenges to a reinterpretation of the parable is its liturgical invisibility, like other scriptural narratives about women which don't appear in the lectionary.[5] It is not

5. See a review of the presence and absence of biblical texts about women in the lectionary in Marjorie Proctor-Smith, 'Images of Women in the Lectionary', in

proclaimed very often or very visibly in the common liturgy. In the current Roman Catholic lectionary, for example, the parable is the assigned text for Friday of the Twenty-First Week of the Year, which means it is read as the gospel on a week-day once a year. If there are sufficient weeks in the fall before Advent, it is the A Cycle gospel for the Thirty-Second Sunday of the Year. This means it is read once every three years for the Sunday Eucharist, but may not be heard for six years.[6]

An academic answer for difficulties with the parable's interpretation is its oddness. Since it is a story unique to Matthew and his community, it doesn't fall into the set of parables treated as part of the corpus of the 'triple tradition', i.e., those teaching stories that occur in all three synoptics in one version or another. As a 'loner', it's also a puzzling, uncomfortable story, certainly having genetic resemblance to other 'unfriendly parables' in which guests and servants get thrown out of the house into the unwelcoming darkness. Luke has more attractive 'loner' stories, such as the Good Samaritan and the Prodigal Son, and these parables are consoling, inspiring and 'play well' to many audiences in a variety of pastoral situations. The Good Samaritan (Lk. 10.30-37) for example, can be used to inspire generosity toward those in need, compassion for the abandoned, identification of the goodness that resides in all people of good will. The Prodigal Son (Lk. 15.11-32) fosters trust in a waiting, forgiving God. It is ideal as a setting for the rite of reconciliation, adult conversion, and a return to the faith made after a long absence from religious practice.

However, the parable of the ten virgins has resisted all but the most conventional readings. Discussions typically revolve around interpretations which take their basic cue from the parable's eschatological end-note, 'Watch, therefore, for you know neither the day nor the hour' (Mt. 25.13). The parable has something to do with being alert and making sure you have enough oil with you. If you don't bring your oil, whatever it is you need to have for admission, chances are that you will be left out and not get 'into heaven'. The Bridegroom is Christ at the end of time and it is primarily a story about judgment and end-time. Unquestioned seems to be the equation made between

---

Elisabeth Schüssler Fiorenza and Mary Collins (eds.), *Women: Invisible in Church and Theology*, Concilium 182 (1985), pp. 51-62.

6. Bishops' Conference on the Liturgy, National Conference of Catholic Bishops (ed.), *The Roman Missal: Lectionary for Mass* (New York: Catholic Book Publishing, 1970).

176   *A Feminist Companion to Matthew*

'the bridegroom' all are awaiting, and the 'Lord, lord', addressed by the foolish women.[7]

The story of the ten virgins is generally read eschatologically as an illustration of the community's need to be prepared for the arrival of the bridegroom, with the wedding understood as an image of the messianic age and second coming of Christ. The placement toward the end of Matthew's Gospel in fact governs its assignment to the end of the liturgical year, just before Advent begins in late November or early December. Revision of this 'end-time' reading may have happened within the Matthean community itself as it acknowledged the unknown date and time of Christ's return.[8] Adjustment of its ethical perspective in light of a here-and-now reality turned on a theological resolution of the delay in Christ's return, the concept of 'realized eschatology'. According to this pastoral perspective, the qualities necessary for the last days, such as watchfulness, faithfulness, responsibility and attention, were essentially no different from those required for 'ordinary time'.[9] According to the standard reading of the parable, the five foolish virgins incarnate a failure to manifest those virtues or meet the requirements for either the last days or the present time. They didn't start off with what they needed, and by the time they catch up, it's too late.[10]

---

7. My suspicion about too easy an equation assumed between 'lord' and Jesus in the ten virgins parable is paralleled by notice of the ambiguity of the identity of 'the master' and Jesus in Luke's eschatological parable. See John S. Kloppenborg, 'The Dishonored Master (Luke 16.1-8a)', *Bib* 70 (1989), pp. 474-95.

8. The original parable, says Dodd, arose out of some crisis in the community. When that crisis was over, the parable was adapted to the second coming and the world crisis thought to be approaching. See C.H. Dodd, *The Parables of the Kingdom* (New York: Charles Scribner's Sons, 1969), pp. 136-39. An earlier discussion of the crisis theme proposes that the suddenness and unexpectedness of the coming of the groom, the thief and the master in Matthew's end-time parables are reflective of an earlier catastrophe. The crisis parable becomes later an allegory about Christ the bridegroom. See Joachim Jeremias, *The Parables of Jesus* (trans. S.H. Hooke; New York: Charles Scribner's Sons, 1955), pp. 41-43. Problematic is Jeremias's claim that the allegorical representation of the messiah as a bridegroom is foreign to the Old Testament. and the literature of late Judaism.

9. Midnight in the parable is an example of Christian allegorizing. The parable can be placed within a perspective of reflections on time: calendar time, memory, perceived time vs clock-time, societal time, the span of life to death, time of the race and ages of the world. See Frederick H. Borsch, *Many Things In Parables* (Philadelphia: Fortress Press, 1988), p. 88.

10. The foolish have failed because they weren't responsible. It was their job to give light at the feast and they didn't. The burning lamps stand for those good works in which the foolish didn't persevere. When things got difficult they didn't

Donahue outlines the issues in the parable in accord with this line of interpretation, noting the argument over Palestinian wedding conventions which occupies some exegetes.[11] Such issues concern the customs of first-century weddings, their length, and the sequence and location of the movements of the bride and her attendants and the groom and his attendants. From an historical point of view, does the parable describe a wedding which actually occupies several days and several nights with the women 'sleeping over' at the bride's house while they all wait for the groom and his attendants to show up at her house? Or is the destination of the festivities the groom's house, and do the women who take 'time off' to buy oil miss the procession through the streets with their friend who is the bride on her way to meet the groom?[12]

Donahue qualifies the real pastoral concern as an 'eschatological ethic' only insofar as the community is exhorted to consider the parousia as calling for attentiveness, preparedness, fruitfulness in good deeds and responsible discipleship in the present time which will determine the shape of the future. Watching is preparation for the present, not a passive expectation of future appearance of Jesus. The failure of the five foolish virgins is their 'sin of omission', or passivity and inactivity, suggested by the allegorical meaning of the lamp-oil as 'good deeds'. Donahue reflects the general trend of interpretation which lays light or heavy blame on the foolish women for their personal failures.[13]

---

keep their light going 'through the night'. So the judgment of David Wenham, 'The Wise and Foolish Girls' in *The Parables of Jesus* (Downers Grove, IL: Inter-Varsity Press, 1989), pp. 80-83. Or, in a more ultimate sense, the point of the parable is that there are some life situations for which one is either ready or not. Borsch, *Many Things in Parables*, p. 85.

11. John R. Donahue, *The Gospel in Parable: Metaphor, Narrative, and Theology in the Synoptic Gospels* (Philadelphia: Fortress Press, 1988), pp. 474-95.

12. See the discussion by Jean Pirot, 'Les dix vierges surprises par l'époux', in *Paraboles et allégories évangéliques* (Paris: P. Lethielleux, 1949), pp. 429-48. His material is based on a study of turn-of-the-century marriage customs in the land of Israel by a professor of the École Biblique in Jerusalem, J.A. Jaussen, OP *(Coutumes palestiniennes, Naplouse et son district* [Paris: Guethner, 1927]), pp. 50-84. The interpretive problem is whether Palestinian marriage conventions of the late 1800 and early 1900s replicate those of the first century, pre-Muslim era. In other words, it is a chancy anachronism to impose a centuries-later marriage scenario on the first-century text of Matthew's parable, as though marriage customs have been preserved unbroken through the centuries. In the last two decades, this line of historical investigation does not seem to attract commentators on the parable, with the notable exception of the fanciful reconstruction by Argyle. See below, n. 22.

13. The oil stands for grace, charity, or gifts of the Holy Spirit. Preparation has

'Artistic' Readings

Thomas Merton wrote a poem in French which amounts to his own interpretation of this end-time parable of the ten wise and foolish maidens with lamps in Mt. 25.1-13.[14] Entitled 'Les Cinq Vierges', the piece is dedicated to 'Jacques', presumably a man. This translation differs in several details from the English version by William Davis.

The Five Virgins (For Jacques)

There were five virgins
Rowdies
Who arrived for the Wedding of the Lamb

With their motor-scooters burned out
And their gas tanks
Empty

But since they knew how to
Dance
They were told to
Stick around anyhow.

So that's it: there were
Five rowdy virgins
Without gas
But really caught up
In the action.

There were then ten virgins
At the Wedding of the Lamb.[15]

Poets have a gift for synthesizing and distilling their intuitions. Merton's insight into the Matthean parable suggests a question. What is the 'real story' about? Is its subject truly the rejection of five women who didn't have enough oil, or about an entire band of ten women

---

to be personal and can't depend on religion, culture, social position, noble titles, or well-regarded civic reputation. The foolish should have had their own oil, not that of their companions. So Genesio da Gallarate, 'Le dieci vergini', in *Il regno dei cieli* (Brescia: Editrice Franciscanum, 1968), pp. 192-96.

14. The poem was called to my attention by Dr Mary Celeste Rouleau, RSM. A colleague at Santa Clara University, Dr Douglas Burton-Christie, located the source. See *The Collected Poems of Thomas Merton* (New York: New Directions, 1977). The poem in French is on p. 819, and the translation by William Davis on pp. 826-27.

15. The translation is by the present writer.

who gained entrance into a wedding feast? Is the parable about the rejection of women or about their inclusion in the end-time festivities? Merton specifies the nuptials as the wedding of the Lamb, an allusion to the 'lamb of God' in John's Gospel (Jn 1.36) and the book of Revelation (12.11). This image of Jesus alludes to the suffering servant of Isaiah who was like a lamb to be sacrificed, led to the slaughter and opened not his mouth (53.7).

By way of contrast, the exegetical masoners of Gothic cathedrals, no doubt conscious of death and the last things because of the plague, gave more attention to the Ten Virgins. The story forms part of the permanently featured 'visual aids' adorning the doors to cathedrals, for example, at the Church of St. Peter and Paul at Éguisheim in Alsace-Lorraine, and the Paradise portal of the Cathedral Magdeburg on the Elbe in Germany. These exegeses in stone are quite revealing of perceptions of the differences between the wise and the foolish women. At Éguisheim, the wise are standing in a quiet line, veiled and clothed in identical nun-like robes, holding their bowl-like lamps all at the same waist-height, eyes forward, silently and contemplatively awaiting the music by which they will, with great decorum, process into a worship service.[16] Christ stands at the open door, and bids them enter, beckoning them with forefinger raised in the classic gesture of teaching and proclamation. The foolish women are beautifully and fashionably dressed courtiers, with crowns and luxuriously wrought garments, clearly 'women of the world' who lack the modesty, conformity and decorum of the wise. The heads of two foolish women are turned to the one at their side. The five are in conversation, chattering with each other, in contrast to the silent attention of the wise. Above them in the tympanum, standing over the heads of them all, looms a larger figure of Christ, flanked by Peter holding an enormous key, and Paul holding a large book. This is the object lesson for women who would enter the church.

At the Cathedral of Magdeburg, five exuberantly joyful and laughing wise women stand at head-height on the left side of the portal as the entrant faces the door. They are holding their bowl-like lamps in their right hands above their waists. They are thin, graceful, simply garbed. Opposite them on the right side of the entry-way are similarly dressed, equally thin and probably once-as-beautiful women. But the foolish have now become weeping and disconsolate attendants who

---

16. Robert Will and Theodore Rieger, *Eglises et sanctuaires d'Alsace: Mille ans d'architecture sacrée* (Strasbourg: Edition des Derniteres Nouvelles, 1969), pp. 68-69.

180   *A Feminist Companion to Matthew*

have let their lamps fall to their sides below their waists.[17] They seem to address those who enter with two possibilities: joy, or sadness. Unlike the complexities of the Éguisheim tympanum, the drama of the parable at Magdeburg is focused on the women's emotional reactions after being either welcomed, or being rejected. It might be noted that such displays of emotional exuberance and joyful, smiling and laughing countenances are not found in French cathedrals, but are found in German iconography.[18]

For William Blake, the parable held a certain medieval-like fascination. He rendered a watercolor of the story at least five times.[19] Like the Gothic rendition at Éguisheim, Blake features prominently the behavioral differences between the two groups of women. Like the entry-way at Magdeburg with its attention on a single emotional contrast, Blake's watercolor dramatizes the emotional chasm that separates the two groups of women. Blake's wise women stand shoulder to shoulder, with lamps hanging suspended by a chain, like a censer. They serenely turn their heads and bodies away from the group opposite them. The foolish women are in emotional disarray, some crying out, some falling, one kneeling and beseeching the wise virgins, one tearing her hair, one stopping her ears, one covering her eyes. They are all dissimilar in posture and facial expression. Their unity—or conformity to a given posture—has given way to individualism of expression. Above them, an enormous angel blows a trumpet, signalling the 'last hour'. In the background, the light begins to break in the sky. There is no wedding feast. The scene emphasizes the

17. The tympanum above the entry-way, the Church of St. Peter Paul at Éguisheim. 'The Cathedral of Magdeburg', in Julius Baum, *German Cathedrals*, with an introduction by Julius Baum, photographs by Helga Schmidt-Glassner (New York: Vanguard Press, 1956), pp. 27-29. Photos of the ten virgins are featured on Plates 106, 107 and 108.

18. 'The Cathedral of Magdeburg', Plate no. 144, the smiling angel of the Münster at Freiburg-im-Breisgau, is an especially serene example. See Ingvild Saelid Gilhus, 'Religion, Laughter and the Ludicrous', *Rel* 21 (1991), pp. 257-77: 'Laughter signals the deconstruction of the reigning ideological system' (272); '...religious traditions with a weight on *gnosis* (both as an acute experience or as a process) are often accompanied by a jocular tradition filled with paradoxes and incongruities' (273).

19. *Blake: The Pitman Gallery* with an introduction by Geoffrey Keynest (New York: Pitman, 1949), 'The Wise and Foolish Virgins', Plate no. 2, p. 6. The watercolor is not signed or dated, but probably executed in 1805. The scene 'is generally regarded as one of the loveliest pictures that Blake ever painted. Its pale and delicate colouring is of exquisite quality, and the two groups of maidens are well characterized' (5).

rejection of one group of women by another, and the ultimacy of the moment which divides them into two disparate communities.

My own suspicions about the parable's troublesome tone have been reinforced by a choice to observe carefully the parable's artistic renditions and Merton's own poetic rebellion from the standard interpretive strategy. I observe that what assumes normative force in setting the parable's meaning is the wisdom-foolishness theme, not the bridegroom theme. The overriding shape, or final redaction of the story seems connected with a pastoral interest to separate women and distinguish community members from each other. I think the medieval artists, as well as William Blake, got the redactional interest right. The 'picture' the parable poses places the emphasis on a division between two groups of women. The imagery of the wedding feast is invisible in the stonework and in Blake. That's a thematic re-editing which accounts for the tension and the tragedy of the story. The joy of the wedding is submerged. Merton didn't like the 'last word' of the parable, so he rewrote the story by, perhaps, intuitively accessing the joyful spirit of the earlier layer of the bridegroom parable.

A Feminist Rereading

Merton's poem implies the sort of problems feminist readers have with this gospel story. The ten women in Matthew's parable have no voice of their own. They speak the lines 'written' for them by a moralistic male script-writer. This position—that women are being spoken to by men and lack their own voice—has become such a staple of the feminist critique of patriarchy in all fields that it approaches the status of a cliché. The rhetoric of the parable preserves a New Testament social and theological tradition in which women are primarily cast as the passive audience, and expected to enact the solutions to ecclesial problems defined from a masculine viewpoint. From a rhetorical point of view—i.e., the response to the question, 'Who is speaking to whom about what?'—the audience for the final version of Matthew's parable seems to have been women.

Reading from a feminist perspective which pays close attention to women's roles and sympathetically tries to reconstruct the scene with women's interests in mind, one notes that the story is clearly biased from the outset. The polarity between wisdom and foolishness constitutes the judgment of the teller of the parable at its opening (25.2), structures the characterization of the women, and determines their differing fates. The tragedy of what it means to be foolish is the real lesson for a community presumably better represented by the wise virgins. It is the wise, not the foolish, who succeed in joining the wedding celebration on time and enjoy a life 'on the inside' with the Lord. End-time, whether conceived as Christ's parousia or as a Christian's consciousness or alertness in daily life, is the moment which divides the community. The wise are gathered inside the house, while the foolish petitioners are left outside with the door shut in their faces. The behavior of the wise virgins is not really a victory celebration. The tragic loss of the foolish antiheroines defines the beginning and end of the story and ruins the wedding for the bride and her five other friends. The literal aspects of the story, five women trying to get at the oil five others possess, seems pathetic. The refusal of the wise women with the oil to help their companions makes them seem selfish, and their entrance into the feast seem unfair. If this is wisdom, it is unattractive. Is the kingdom of heaven about women at war with each other over oil?[20]

At the very least, one can observe that the denial of five women by the Lord and his refusal to open the door belongs to the genre of other 'unfriendly endings'. This series includes the death-sentence for some Jewish rejectors of Jesus in the vineyard parable (Mt. 21.41), the exclusion of the party-crasher who is not in conversation with the king in the parable of the marriage feast (Mt. 22.12-14), the sentencing to hell of the scribes, Pharisees and hypocrites (Mt. 23.32-33), the punishment of the wicked, unfaithful servant by putting him out where there is weeping and gnashing of teeth (Mt. 24.45-51), and the cursing of the uncompassionate into eternal fire with the devil and his angels (Mt. 25.41)

What is signal about the unfriendly ending in the Ten Virgins story, is that all five, half the group, are nameless women who exhibit either one of two types of behavior. They are wise or they are foolish. They are not servants or strangers in their relation to each other, but presumably friends of one another and honored friends of the bridal

20. This perspective is acknowledged in a sermon celebrating women's participation in church ministries by Nancy J. Duff, 'Wise and Foolish Maidens (Matthew 25:1-13)', *USQR* 40 (1985), pp. 55-58. However, Duff leaves off her feminist reading which identifies the trouble-spots in the wisdom–foolishness narrative, and adopts the conventional posture of blaming the foolish for not taking responsibility to take care of what they should have done themselves. In a creative turn on the convention, Duff interprets the foolish as the church itself which can leave responsibility for caring for the poor to the government or public agencies. Both women and the church can be 'foolish'. The alternative is to 'do what needs to be done' and women are showing their 'wisdom' in their readiness to assume responsibility for church-related tasks.

party. At a certain point, one group of women turns against the other group: 'Go to the dealers' (Mt. 25.9). The rejection is twofold. Not only do the wise women reject the other five, but the Lord does as well. The women's friendship with one another is compromised by the exclusion of half of them from the wedding and the Lord's denial of relationship with them.

The narrator of the parable seems intent on making the judgment upon five women clear from the beginning. The narration of the Ten Virgins is dissimilar to other parables in the immediate Matthean context whose outcome unfolds gradually. In other parables, a harsh judgment upon miscreants is reserved to the end. For the five women, however, the narrator determines a judgment on the foolish at the outset: 'Five were foolish and five wise' (Mt. 25.2). The notice defines the social relationship from the outset and names the foolish first. Within the story, wise women reject the foolish women by refusing to share their oil, and tell them to go away to the sellers (Mt. 25.8-9). The parable ends with the bridegroom's rejection of the foolish maidens (Mt. 25.12). The dynamic underlying the Ten Virgins parable is not external persecution, and its polemic does not seem directed at outsiders who are persecuting the virgins or the community. It is a story about women who failed the community itself, according to the perspective of the narrator. They were foolish at the beginning and throughout the story, so their end comes as no surprise.

Like the three servants entrusted with the master's property of five, two and one talents (Mt. 25.14-30) the matter of judgment concerns what the virgins have in hand and what they do with it left to their own devices. But what they have is not enough. Perhaps the significance of the oil has less to do with what oil 'equals' in the allegorical correspondence (good deeds), and more to do with the geographical notice about the market where goods such as oil are sold (πωλέω): 'Go rather to the dealers (πωλοῦντας) and buy (ἀγοράσατε) for yourselves' (Mt. 25.9). The five foolish women of the Ten Virgins are advised to buy from the market the oil they do not have in their possession, to supply what they did not bring with them. Does the 'market' refer to the smorgasbord of Hellenistic religious cults readily available to the 'buyer' or spiritual seeker?[21] The women are not sent home to their own residences or the homes of the other women, the

21. That there were a variety of approaches to religious doctrine and belief in the Greco-Roman world, even within Christian circles, is outlined by a useful summary of gnostic teaching and the early patristic polemic against it. See Elaine Pagels, *The Gnostic Gospels* (New York: Random House, 1979), p. 198.

normal place one would go to replenish supplies of oil late at night.[22] As soon as it is evident the foolish women lack something essential, they are shunned by the other women. This reinforces the sense that the five foolish women have been assigned the status of 'outsiders' within the larger community itself.

From a feminist perspective, the nonappearance of the bride is significant. She is also notable by her absence from Cathedral portals. The bride is apparently not needed for the action of the story to proceed, nor for the point of the story to be made. A story about a wedding, the one event which celebrated the life of a woman in Jewish society, is deflected by a focus on the bridegroom whose male identity has presumably already been celebrated at his *bris* and *bar mitzvah*. The imbalance of the focus is highlighted by the attention the women give to the bridegroom and even further, by the failure of half the women to live up to their role. The women as a group are not, apparently, waiting for the bride who has honored them.

Is the bride imagined to be already safe and secure inside the house where her women friends wait with her for the arrival of the groom's party which is late? One interpretation for the delay, favorable to the bride, has proposed that the delay concerns the complicated negotiations over the price of the bride, to be paid by the groom as compensation to the bride's family. She is very valuable in her father's eyes, so the bargaining is protracted.[23] But this perspective cuts both ways. It could also mean that the groom, ready to marry, is unwilling to pay the original price to the bride's family. They are all delayed because they are caught in a bind over his unwillingness to pay a price he doesn't think she's worth, and their desire to marry her off, even at a bargain price.

Women's passivity is underlined by the cry at midnight which arises from an anonymous quarter, 'Behold, the bridegroom! Come out to meet him' (Mt. 25.6). Since the women are all sleeping, someone else

---

22. One earnest exegete makes an amusing effort to de-allegorize the parable. He defends the literal and historical details of the story 'told by Jesus himself', proposing that catering shops stayed open 24 hours as a matter or course. They probably hired a day staff and a night staff to accommodate all-night wedding parties. Oil would likely have been sold in the same place as food. Thus, there is nothing unusual about the wise saying to the foolish to go out and buy oil in the middle of the night! See Aubrey W. Argyle, 'Wedding Customs in the Time of Jesus', *ExpTim* 86 (1975), pp. 214-15.

23. Juliana Casey, IHM, of Catholic Health Association in St. Louis, cited this interpretation in her address at the annual convocation of the Sisters of Mercy in Burlingame, California, 'The Spirituality of Commitment', 7 August, 1987.

has been keeping watch for them. William Blake's artistic solution to the problem of identifying the voice is to supply an enormous angel, gender indeterminate, who flies over the women blasting a trumpet. The artistic point is that a voice other than their own announces the timing for the women's activity and the direction for them to move, whether they be wise or foolish.

The women have no control over the moment of the groom's arrival, nor is any one of their number 'wise' enough to have assumed leadership or proven 'awake' enough to keep watch. The parable implies that they are essentially a leaderless group, and depend on the annunciatory voice rather than their own vision to 'wake them up' and determine where the bridegroom is and how distant his party is from the house. The request for oil and the refusal to give oil do not represent the initiative of any single woman. The women remain anonymous and corporate. Five speak as one, and their initiatives and responses reflect a common discernment and a common response, whether 'Give us some of your oil', or 'Go out and buy some'. The wise have no pity on the foolish even though their oil has diminished and their lamps are going out. 'Perhaps there will not be enough for us and for you; go rather to the dealers and buy some for yourselves'.

The women's powerlessness is underscored when the foolish women return from the market. They address a Lord/bridegroom whose coming they anticipated, but whose actual arrival they missed. 'Lord, Lord, open to us!' (Mt. 25.11). But the Lord behind the door gives to the women the same answer promised earlier to false prophets, 'Truly, I say to you, I do not know you' (Mt. 25.12). 'On that day many will say to me, "Lord, Lord, did we not prophesy in your name, and cast out demons in your name, and do many mighty works in your name?" And then will I declare to them, "I never knew you; depart from me, you evil-doers..." ' (7.22-23). The rejection is violent and uncompromising.[24]

It is not the bride who answers their pleas. She can do nothing for her foolish women friends who have apparently condemned themselves and guaranteed their exclusion from the community. Their repentance is useless, their rejection final. Women can no longer help their companions. The invited women who arrive late still do not qualify for entrance. The feelings of the bride and of the five wise

24. While the foolish suffer great social and emotional violence, this parable is not cited or its female characters treated by Marla J. Selvidge in 'Violence, Woman, and the Future of the Matthean Community: A Redactional Critical Essay', *USQR* 39 (1984), pp. 213-23.

women are of no consequence for the narrative. The wise women can offer no more help to their foolish female companions with whom they have dissolved relationships. The foolish must be left to bear the judgment of the Lord as though they have become strangers and aliens. 'I do not know you'. The foolish have been written out of the script the community is writing for its own future.

The Parable as Directive to Women

The harsh logic of the parable makes more sense when viewed as patriarchal instruction that women adopt 'stiff-upper-lip' behavior in facing a crisis situation over loss or exile of some of their members. The foolish women should have known the groom might be delayed, should have come prepared, and should have followed the lead of their wise women friends who had a habit of preparedness. But it is also apparent that even with a recovery of what they needed—the oil for their lamps—the foolish are unneeded, and unwelcome when they return. The foolish are caught in a double-bind. It's too late for them, even though they arrive at the right location and the right wedding party. Their fate has already been sealed by a judgment evident to the perspicacious narrator from the beginning: the wise took flasks of oil and the foolish didn't (Mt. 25.3-4).

Deep alienation between the two groups was made evident to the women only in the middle of the story when the differences between the wise and foolish were clarified by what the foolish demanded, 'Give us some of your oil, for our lamps are going out' (Mt. 25.8). If an ordinary community member had looked only at the deeds of the wise and foolish, the women's differences would have been indistinguishable. Even to their companions, the foolish succeed in remaining disguised up to a certain point. The wise and foolish had belonged to the same group of women. They had all been invited, all gone forth to meet the bridegroom, they all took lamps, they all slumbered and slept, they all awoke and all trimmed their lamps. This sameness among the women emphasizes the sense of tragedy and disillusion which must have erupted when some women eventually made choices or 'showed their colors' in ways most of the community never imagined they could have. Behind the naming of some women wise and others foolish is a deep sense of disillusionment. If all the women appeared to be so much alike, how could fully half prove to be radically different from the others?

The pastoral voice or 'lord' behind the narration of the parable assures women that the discernment between who was wise and who foolish did not require the wise women to exercise any special anticipatory intuition. That discernment was made evident by the self-selection of the foolish themselves. They themselves became aware of what they lacked. The threshold dividing outside from inside emerged at the moment when the wise women were asked to provide what no community could give such foolish women. If the foolish, after all the time spent in the community, have not yet acquired the means to light their own lamps, goes the logic of the parable, there comes a point when no one else in the community can do that for them. If some women have not found sophia-wisdom within the community, it is proof of their failure. The wise give a directive to the foolish which shows their wisdom enacted as a sense of personal responsibility and watchfulness over their own affairs in light of a long-term goal, meeting the bridegroom. 'Perhaps there will not be enough for us and for you'. The wise are justified in their refusal, even though it seems on the surface to be a betrayal of normal generosity and a spirit of sharing.

The wise women are rewarded for shunning their foolish companions and sending them away. Wisdom requires firm dividing lines and shut doors, like the 'great chasm' which divides compassionate from uncompassionate (Lk. 16.26). The proof is that the wise end up inside the wedding hall and the foolish outside. The fact that the celebration takes place without the foolish women proves that the enlightenment of their lamps and the oil supplying their inspired teaching are unneeded and ultimately irrelevant to the wedding festivities guarded over by the Lord of the door. The fact that they went to the market for oil and then tried to return only reinforces the rightness of the judgment that they are unacceptable as members of the community. While they may feel left out of the community, the community does not feel their loss.

The Lord's hostile verbal dismissal and his refusal to open the door to five women seems all the more frightening and confusing because the women who have left to buy oil now 'catch up' with the wedding party. They have returned from their trip to the market, presumably with enough oil to see them through the celebration. If they show up with their 'fault' corrected, why are they still refused entrance? The parable, of course, is mute on the point of the success or failure of the shopping trip in the middle of the night. As is often the case in parables, the final act of the story is left untold. We do not know whether the elder brother in the Prodigal Son story was ever reconciled to his younger brother's return. We do not know whether the woman who wanted to throw a party to celebrate having found her lost coin (Lk. 15.8-10) achieved the same joy as the angels in heaven in rejoicing over a sinner's return. We do not know whether the strangers railroaded into the king's party as his guests had a very good time, especially when one of their number was thrown out after he got there (Mt. 22.1-22).

The ending of the Matthean story is sufficiently disturbing to raise similar questions. Their faults seem puzzlingly trivial. They are rejected for their failure to bring oil for their lamps and for their tardiness in getting to the wedding feast. What is so blameworthy, either literally or allegorically, about the failures of these women? What merits so harsh a punishment? If this be the punishment, what is the real crime? What does their 'foolishness' actually mean? In the case of the five foolish women, it seems irrelevant that they have shown up with or without oil. Their very reappearance is unwelcome and intrusive. The mercy and kindness of Jesus the Lord during the public ministry toward sinners is noticeably absent in the parable's Lord. Its ending has no relation to the 'eleventh hour' generosity of the master of the vineyard who pays the same wage to those who worked one hour as to those who worked all day (Mt. 20.1-16)

Pastoral Situation Generating a Polemic Against Women

Donahue connects the bridegroom's rejection of half the women, 'I do not know you' with an earlier discourse of Jesus who will reject even people who claimed to do good deeds, 'I never knew you; depart from me, you evil-doers' (Mt. 7.21-23).[25] This is a major clue, I believe, which suggests the foolish virgins may also be rejected because they, too, are considered to be evil-doers. The discernment within the community happens only after a period of time. The persons rejected by Jesus earlier in the Gospel engaged in prophetic teaching, exorcisms and mighty works, but these public religious acts are not the equivalent of a tree bearing good fruit. Even good actions can have bad results. Even teachers, prophets, and exorcists may ultimately prove to the community that they are like trees bearing bad fruit. Such trees will be cut down and thrown into the fire (Mt. 7.16-23). Who are the bad trees with bad fruit? The immediate context suggests they are 'false prophets who come to you in sheep's clothing but inwardly are ravenous wolves' (Mt. 7.15). The harsh words of Jesus are addressed to false prophets—the gender is not specified—who are condemned at the outset, but show up before Jesus later, expecting admission to his circle of companions. They are rejected in spite of their impressive

25. Donahue, *The Gospel in Parable*, p. 104.

résumé of good deeds. According to Matthew, Jesus says he himself will condemn the evil doers, 'I never knew you' (Mt. 7.21-23).

The passage immediately following this condemnation is a parable which contrasts the outcome for the wise housebuilder who is grounded on rock, with the tragedy that befalls the foolish housebuilder who constructs on sand (Mt. 7.24-27). The wisdom-foolishness 'lesson' in contrast follows a condemnation of false prophets. By analogical and poetic transfer, false prophets are equivalent to ravenous wolves in sheep's clothing, to a tree that bears bad fruit, and to the foolish who build on sand. To such enemies of the community, those who address him as 'Lord, lord', the Lord in fact says 'I never knew you; depart from me, you evildoers' (Mt. 7.23).

Fruitfulness is a moral mandate for the community, as suggested by the metaphor of the good fruit, the outcome expected from members. The individual or the community which does not produce fruit has violated its own nature, like the servant who buried his talent. This failure brings on itself a death sentence in other parables, like the action attributed to Jesus, in which the 'master of the vineyard' curses the fig tree for not producing figs, and it dies immediately (Mt. 21.18-19). Is the failure of the five foolish virgins like that of the servant with one talent, or like the fig tree that does not produce? The interpretation of the five virgins' foolishness as failure to do good works seems on one hand a meaning 'borrowed' from the parable of the three servants, with the third not producing anything with his talent (Mt. 25.1-30). The foolish women didn't 'produce' either, at least temporarily. They do not have enough wherewithal to produce light for the wedding. Unanswered by the parable is the reason for refusing them readmittance even when they arrive with oil/good works after the shopping trip. Such a refusal might make sense if they had apostasized in a time of persecution (ran out of oil in the middle of the night), and then expected admission back into the community when they recovered their faith (succeeded in finding oil and were able to relight their lamps).

However, the real concern in the parable does not seem to involve welcoming back apostates or those convicted of sexual misconduct. The instruction about wisdom and foolishness sounded earlier in Matthew's Gospel is reinforced by the teaching on the same subject at the end. Members of the community must take a stand in light of the warning of Jesus. They are wise or foolish, depending on their discernment in the time of crisis, suggested by the rains, floods, and winds which beat on the houses (Mt. 7.25, 27). To reject false prophets and their utterances is to be wise and build on rock. Not to recognize who are the false prophets is to build on sand. I think a dispute over doctrine and the claim of some women to be teachers of wisdom is the most likely context for the telling of the parable condemning five foolish women. Do the five foolish virgins represent a current of prophesying, preaching, and teaching in the community that some men regarded as alien to the interests of the church?

To contextualize Matthew's concern over false prophets, it is well to be reminded that a perennial pastoral problem in first-century churches was the incursion of 'false teachers' and 'false prophets'. This implies a norm for determining 'true' from 'false' operating in the minds of the community leaders whose own positions must have been threatened by such competition. There are any number of passages in the New Testament which reflect this defensive posture toward 'outsiders' who may have for a time enjoyed inclusion as 'insiders'. The concern over false teachers was inseparable from the pastors' concern over the divisiveness and factionalism bred within a community whose loyalties were compromised by authority figures competing for the hearts and minds of the believers. Paul himself concludes his letter to the Romans by warning with vigorous dichotomies:

> Take note of those who create dissensions and difficulties, in opposition to the doctrine which you have been taught; avoid them. For such persons do not serve our Lord Christ, but their own appetites, and by fair and flattering words they deceive the hearts of the simple-minded. For while your obedience is known to all, so that I rejoice over you, I would have you wise as to what is good and guileless as to what is evil; then the God of peace will soon crush Satan under your feet (Rom. 16.17-20).

Paul's own meditation on wisdom and foolishness (1 Cor. 1.18-31; 2.1-16) immediately follows his appeal to the community to address the causes of its internal dissension, factionalism, and quarreling. Their doctrinal differences are reflected in their competitive social alliances, 'I belong to Paul', 'I belong to Apollos', 'I belong to Cephas', and 'I belong to Christ' (1 Cor. 1.10-12). Internal divisions over christological assertions are merely one cause for internal splits within the Corinthian community.

Ethical issues were complicated by the vulnerability within some communities to the appeal of gnostic doctrines and styles of interpretation. Thus, the pastor who writes 1 Timothy warns the community's leader to take some teachers in hand and actively direct some of them 'not to teach any different doctrine, nor to occupy themselves with myths and endless genealogies which promote speculations rather than the divine training that is in faith' (1 Tim. 1.3-4). It is probably not a future prediction but a crisis actually experienced in the community that: 'people will not endure sound teaching, but having itching ears they will accumulate for themselves teachers to suit their own likings, and will turn away from listening to the truth and wander into myths' (2 Tim. 4.14). The defensive posture of the speaker in 2 Peter is occasioned by the competitive voices of those claiming to speak prophetically according to their own interpretation. The warning is this:

> But false prophets also arose among the people, just as there will be false teachers among you, who will secretly bring in destructive heresies, even denying the Master who bought them, bringing upon themselves swift destruction. And many will follow their licentiousness, and because of them the way to truth will be reviled (2 Pet. 2.1-2).

The Johannine community, too, has known internal division over doctrinal disagreements. Its pastor has cut a clear division between the resident community and those who took the initiative to leave and abandoned the group. Pain has been inflicted on the community by accusations from the departed that those who stay 'do not know'. Very likely, the departed represent a break-away group that found the community insufficiently enlightened. The pastor tries to encourage and build up the confidence of those left behind:

> They went out from us, but they were not of us; for if they had been of us, they would have continued with us; but they went out, that it might be plain that they all are not of us. But you have been anointed by the Holy One, and you all know. I write to you, not because you do not know the truth, but because you know it, and know that no lie is of the truth. Who is the liar but he who denies that Jesus is the Christ?' (1 Jn 2.19-22).

When the causes for internal strife and division within the Matthean community are catalogued, they include defections as a result of persecution from Gentile and Jewish sources (Mt. 13.21), during which many fall away and betray one another (Mt. 24.10). Some prophets are wise, and should be supported by the community (Mt. 10.41), but many others are false and will lead the community astray by claiming to speak for Christ (Mt. 24.5).[26] One cause for the hostile tone in Matthew's community against Pharisees, e.g., the 'Woe to you scribes and Pharisees' section in Mt. 23, is attributed to post-70 CE friction between regional Jewish synagogues whose attitude toward Gentiles differed from the spirit of acceptance of Gentiles and God-fearers in

26. Raymond E. Brown, *The Churches the Apostles Left Behind* (New York: Paulist Press, 1984), pp. 131-32.

Matthew's church. At a time when both communities were struggling to maintain their identity and define their boundaries, it was inevitable that clashes over interpretation of Torah regulations and the identity of Jesus would polarize the two groups. Such hostility toward some Jewish groups is reflected in the painfully divisive and vengeful ending of the vineyard parable in which a terrible punishment is assigned the tenants who are judged to have killed God's servants and Jesus (Mt. 21.33-41).

Thus, even a brief survey of some of the causes for internal conflict in early Christian churches is enough to suggest that Matthew's community, as one typical of the times, was probably not immune to the divisive consequences of disputes over its relation to Jewish communities, over doctrine, ethics, endurance of persecution, and the setting of standards for discerning acceptable from unacceptable teachers. If Matthew's community had sociological similarities to other Christian groups, one can posit not only external synagogue-church conflicts, but also acknowledge sources of conflict arising from within the community. It seems consistent with first-century theological concerns to suggest that one source of conflict was a dispute over the behavior of women as spokespersons and the determination of their orthodoxy as prophetic teachers. This particular conflict might well explain the hostile tone and refocus of the parable about the ten virgins into a wisdom–foolishness diatribe.

A Redemptive Reading

Sandra Schneiders has proposed that even a biblical text oppressive of women can be reread in light of its liberating possibilities.[27] I think a 'split-level' reading of the Ten Virgins can both acknowledge its polemic against some women yet retrieve the vision which subverts that very patriarchal project. One really has a choice, I think, about determining the 'crime' of which those judged 'foolish' are guilty. The five foolish women may be understood variously as utterers of prophecies proved to be false, useless or disruptive; as teachers of unorthodox doctrine or oppositional interpreters of doctrine; as those who didn't conform to the standards set by the community leaders in manifesting those virtues attached to women's social roles; as those who claimed to have authority to lead and interpret even though they were not officially appointed by the Matthean pastors; as enlightened,

27. Sandra M. Schneiders, 'Feminist Ideological Criticism and Biblical Hermeneutics', *BTB* 19 (1989), pp. 3-9.

break-away defectors from the community who taunted those who stayed behind for their silliness in putting up with the situation as it was; or as those who were for any reason perceived as 'bad seed' or 'bad fruit', and exiled or excommunicated from the Matthean community by its leaders. Did some women defect from the community and leave on their own, causing pain and embarrassment to those who remained?

Were they gnostic teachers? Restless young women who sought new theological ideas in the market places? Syncretists whose novel formulations threatened the orthodox line of interpreting the gospel? Or were they powerful rivals to the men in exercising prophetic leadership? Was the community divided because some were nervous and others deeply inspired by these prophetic women? Did the unrest result from a community wounded by the scandal of what was perceived as outspoken women's betrayal of the spirit of unity? Were the women themselves divided, and the male pastors 'forced' to exercise 'authority' by exiling some of the recalcitrants from the community? Some women may have been adherents to 'outside' groups, even with other communities oriented to a stricter observance of Jewish customs. A group of women may have competed for authority roles and formal legitimation by the community's pastors. To whom should other women give their allegiance when their 'foolish' sisters were under attack?

That half the women were shut out suggests the crisis was a matter of consequence for the entire community. It was a significant rift. The historical situation may have involved a defection, such as that endured by the community of the first letter of John. In such case, the pastor might label the departed as foolish from the beginning. The parable is then an affirmation of those women of wisdom who remained. By such a parable, a pastor would assure all believers that such defection was both explainable and irreversible. Their foolishness, as seen from hindsight, would have continually undermined the community's spiritual integrity and clarity of vision. Thus, what happened to the foolish women was sad, but inevitable.

The wisdom–foolishness parable addressed to women is consistent in its polemical tone with other hostile polemics, such as the diatribes against Jewish leaders and teachers in Mt. 22.1-46. It is indeed uncomfortable to admit that a Matthean redactor 'has it in' for some women, as well as male Jewish leaders. The Gospel does not prepare readers to imagine that some women could be regarded as enemies of the community. That makes the preoccupation with gender in the ten virgins parable all the more interesting. Women, rather than men, seem to fulfill the conditions for being named evildoers, false prophets, false teachers, and those endangering the community's wellbeing. This implies that women were actually quite active in the community, rather than silent and passive.

The bridegroom parable is consistent with the positive portrayal of women elsewhere in Matthew's Gospel and is consistent with the exemplary roles of women in the genealogy (1.1-17), the woman with the hemorrhage (9.20-22), the Canaanite woman (15.21-28), and the women connected with the passion and resurrection accounts.[28] This 'lost story', embedded in the parable is the joyful image of endtime, anticipated not as judgment, but as a wedding feast to which all the women are admitted. This parable is a story about women waiting for a bridegroom who finally shows up, who kept them all waiting, including the bride. This level even has some humor to it, like Merton's poem. It is also possible to account for the historicity of this parable as representing the perspective of Jesus, because there is so much evidence of his positive treatment of women throughout the Gospels.

The original bridegroom parable may have belonged to the genre of other kingdom parables of future happiness which are optimistic and encourage the community. They include the assurance of the good fortune awaiting those who repent and are restored to the community, like the lost sheep (18.12-14), the happiness of the man who finds treasure in a field (13.44), the merchant who sells all to purchase a single pearl (13.45), and the ease and consolation which attend those who take up the yoke of Jesus (11.28-30).

The bridegroom parable emphasizes the liberating aspects of the kingdom to which women have access, and into which their light leads the whole community. Their accompaniment of the bridegroom departs from social convention, for it is the men who are the normal attendants to the groom. The parable suggests a new social role to women in their relation to the Lord. They have the same intimacy with the bridegroom as men. In fact, they are leaders of the community, for they bear their lighted lamps to meet him. They are the ones who have kept vigil for the bridegroom. It is their faithfulness, unabated even in the sleep of death, which is revived when the bridegroom appears and they relight their lamps. As a group of ten women, they represent

---

28. See Janice Capel Anderson, 'Matthew: Gender and Reading', *Semeia* 28 (1983), pp. 3-27 (reprinted in this volume, pp. 25-51). The article gives attention to the positive roles given by the evangelist to the female characters in the Gospel, even though they occupy roles subordinate to men. Anderson, like Selvidge, does not treat or refer to the parable of the ten virgins.

the wholeness of the community itself, like the monetary unit of ten talents produced by the fruitful steward, the whole measure of grain, or the entire flock of a hundred sheep. They all enter into the marriage celebration.

The parable, read as a double narrative, hints at a management strategy which ecclesial authorities once used to reinforce unity and squelch disruption within the community. The polemical level of the parable identifies the probable source of the disturbance as a good number of women. Some active and outspoken women were a source of disruption, and their behavior necessitated a firm hand. Disciplinary measures advocated their getting 'back into line', like the scene on the portal of the cathedral at Éguisheim with the wise veiled and robed like monastics in a well-ordered liturgical procession.

The two levels of the parable represent two theological moments, but also two strategies: encouragement of the community and correction of its deviation from official teaching. Acknowledging the two distinct narratives embedded there can have a positive effect. In identifying a kingdom parable which is sympathetic to women, those women who embody the hope of the entire community are endowed with dignity. The parable as it stands is also revelation: it is a mirror of the struggle churches presently face in dealing with issues of orthodoxy and authority. The question becomes: Is the polemical approach still an effective way for churches to confront these issues? A last question: Which tradition shall leaders of contemporary churches choose in dealing with dissent?[29]

---

29. I gratefully acknowledge helpful comments on the first draft of this manuscript from Dr Phyllis Brown and from Claudia McIsaac, both of the English Department at Santa Clara University. Important exegetical observations were raised by Professor Judith Schubert, RSM, of Georgian Court College, and Noel Keller, RSM, ThD. I am grateful for advice on the exegetical version of this study from Professor Joseph Grassi of Santa Clara University, and comments at the AAR/SBL meeting in Washington, DC, from Professor Elaine Wainwright, RSM, of Catholic Theological College, Queensland, Australia. This approach to Matthew's parable was influenced by Antoinette Clark Wire, *The Corinthian Women Prophets: A Reconstruction through Paul's Rhetoric* (Minneapolis: Fortress Press, 1990).

WHAT ARE THOSE WOMEN DOING AT THE TOMB OF JESUS?
PERSPECTIVES ON MATTHEW 28.1[*]

Thomas R.W. Longstaff

Because it tends to obscure themes and perspectives that are important in, and often unique to, the Gospel of Matthew,[1] it seems singularly unfortunate that in the twentieth century this Gospel has so often been studied with more attention given to the presumed Markan source than to the Matthean narrative itself.[2] Nowhere is this tendency more evident than in the account of the visit of the women to the tomb of Jesus (Mt. 28.1; Mk 16.1-2; Lk. 24.1). A survey of the commentaries on Matthew quickly reveals how pervasive this interest in the Markan narrative is.[3] Undoubtedly this focus on the Markan narrative is related

---

[*] This article is a revised version of an article entitled 'The Women at the Tomb: Matthew 28.1 Re-Examined', which appeared in NTS 27.2 (1981), pp. 277-82.

1. Many of these themes or perspectives are important ones for those interested in social justice and in particular for those concerned about issues of gender, race, or class (cf. William R. Farmer's comments in *The Gospel of Jesus: The Pastoral Significance of the Synoptic Problem* [Louisville, KY: Westminster/John Knox Press, 1994], pp. 10-11).

2. This statement remains true despite the excellent redaction-critical studies of Matthew that have contributed much to our understanding of that Gospel. Representative of this interest in the Matthean redaction are such studies as Günther Bornkamm, Gerhard Barth and Heinz Joachim Held, *Tradition and Interpretation in Matthew* (trans. Percy Scott; London: SCM Press, 1963); Reinhard Hummel, *Die Auseinandersetzung zwischen Kirche und Judentum im Mattäusevangelium* (Munich: Chr. Kaiser Verlag, 1963); W.D. Davies, *The Setting of the Sermon on the Mount* (Cambridge: Cambridge University Press, 1964); Krister Stendahl, *The School of St. Matthew* (Philadelphia: Fortress Press, 2nd edn, 1968); O. Lamar Cope, *Matthew: A Scribe Trained for the Kingdom of Heaven* (CBQMS, 5; Washington, DC: Catholic Biblical Association of America, 1976); and Jack Dean Kingsbury, *Matthew: Structure, Christology, Kingdom* (London: SPCK, 1976).

3. See, for example, W.C. Allen, *A Critical and Exegetical Commentary on the Gospel According to St. Matthew* (ICC; Edinburgh: T. & T. Clark, 1907), pp. 300-308; Philip A. Micklem, *St. Matthew* (Westminster Commentaries; London: Methuen, 1917), pp. 279-82; Theodore H. Robinson, *The Gospel of Matthew* (NTC; London: Hodder & Stoughton, 1928), pp. 234-37; A.W. Argyle, *The Gospel According to*

to the conclusion of many scholars that the Gospel of Mark is the earliest of the synoptic gospels, the source of Matthew and Luke, and the best source for information about the life and teaching of Jesus.[4] But while it is a reasonable exegetical procedure to compare one Gospel with another, the way in which the use of a preferred solution to the synoptic problem can also hinder an understanding of a work taken to be secondary is strikingly apparent in Michael D. Goulder's treatment of this passage. Goulder writes:

> The motive for the women's visit to the tomb is coherent in Mark. Joseph has rolled Jesus' body in linen, but it is not said that he anointed it: the women come to supply this need—they see where he is laid (xv.47), and come to anoint him (xvi.1). Matthew's story is incoherent: he does not mention the ointments throughout, and the women, having sat opposite the tomb (xxvii.61), come, weakly, to see the tomb (xxviii.1). On Markan priority this is easily understood: Matthew has introduced a guard on the tomb, so an anointing venture must seem impossible. But, on Matthean priority, what would they want to come and see the tomb for at first light?[5]

It would produce a better understanding of Matthew's Gospel to ask the question that closes the paragraph above, seriously seeking an answer, rather than rhetorically. The question then becomes an intriguing one: What *are* those women doing at the tomb of Jesus?

In this connection it is worth noting that in the introduction to his excellent redaction-critical study of Matthew, Lamar Cope observes that redaction criticism has often been too dependent upon source criticism and in particular on the widely accepted two-document hypothesis. He suggests that 'at least some of the redaction analysis of the Synoptic Gospels today should be free of any particular source

---

Matthew (Cambridge Bible Commentary: Cambridge: Cambridge University Press, 1963), pp. 220-22; W.F. Albright and C.S. Mann, *Matthew: Introduction, Translation and Notes* (AB, 26; Garden City, NY: Doubleday, 1971), pp. 358-59; and H. Benedict Green, *The Gospel According to Matthew* (The New Clarendon Bible; Oxford: Oxford University Press, 1975), p. 227. Cf. also the study by Benjamin W. Bacon, *Studies in Matthew* (London: Constable, 1930), pp. 250-61.

4. It should be stated that, in this article, the historicity of the events described in Mt. 28.1 is not at issue. Rather, this study is an attempt to understand the way in which the author of the Gospel envisioned the scene and intended that his readers envision it. If this can be accomplished, it will give us a window on the world of the author and the community that he addressed.

5. M.D. Goulder, 'Mark xvi.1-8 and Parallels', *NTS* 24 (1978), pp. 235-40 (235). Goulder presents his comments as one of three points intended to show that Matthew is dependent upon Mark. It seems to me, however, that his reasoning is circular, as the rhetorical question at the end of the paragraph shows.

theory'.⁶ In developing this methodological proposal Cope suggests that the critic should 'seek to show from internal evidence the basic strands of an author's thought processes and style of argument, his literary craft, and the theological purposes for which he writes', and then he concludes that 'this information, a factor which has not been fully taken into account in source criticism, ought then to be weighed in the light of source theories and either be corrected by them or serve as a corrective to them'.⁷ It is in this spirit, the determination to understand the author of Matthew on his own terms rather than to debate the synoptic problem in general, that we return to the intriguing question posed by Goulder: How shall we understand the visit of the women to the tomb as Matthew describes it in 28.1? Since the scene must be one that is credible both to Matthew and his audience, we may also learn a little more about the role of women in this early Christian community.

We may begin with the observation that Matthew's Gospel was written by an author and for an audience both of whom were thoroughly familiar with the customs and practices of Judaism.⁸ It is the thesis of this essay that for this reason neither Matthew nor his intended readers would have had any reason to wonder why the women had come to see the tomb. Their presence was part of a well-established ritual of mourning. Visits to tombs and burial grounds can be traced back to the Late Hellenistic period if not earlier.⁹ Indeed, in his discussion of Mt. 26.61 (where the two Marys are seated opposite the tomb) Sherman Johnson remarks that 'friends or relatives often watched at the tomb in case the apparently dead person should revive'.¹⁰ It is somewhat surprising that he does not follow up this line of interpretation in his comments on Mt. 28.1 where the custom of visiting the tomb is more precisely relevant, as we shall see.

6. Cope, *Matthew: A Scribe*, p. 5.
7. Cope, *Matthew: A Scribe*, p. 6.
8. This would be true even if their own observances were modified by their Christian faith.
9. See Kathleen E. Corley's careful study of the role of women in Jewish burial customs in 'Women and the Crucifixion and Burial of Jesus', *Forum* NS 1 (1998), pp. 190-96. A more extensive treatment of these themes will be available in her forthcoming book, where she concludes that 'the custom of tomb and graveyard visitation by women and family lamenting their loved ones and bringing them food and gifts had thousands of years of tradition on its side' [cited with permission of the author].
10. Sherman E. Johnson, *The Gospel According to St. Matthew: Introduction and Exegesis* (IB, 7; Nashville: Abingdon Press, 1951), p. 613.

It was very likely customary in early Judaism for loved ones (friends and relatives) to watch (i.e. to visit, פקד) the tomb until the third day after death in order to ensure that premature burial had not taken place. Usually, of course, these visits served as a confirmation of death. This function, like that of mourning or lamenting the dead, was more often done by women than men (although either, of course, could fulfill this customary duty). Indeed, these practices can even be described as 'stereotypical of women's behavior, not men's'.[11] The surprising thing, then, is not that the women are present at the tomb, but that they are silent. One would expect them to be publicly mourning the death of Jesus.[12] Since they are silent and since it is the third day, their presence and actions are consistent with the view that Matthew portrays them as coming to visit the tomb to confirm the death of Jesus.

Evidence for this custom may be found in *Sem.* 8.1.[13] Since this Talmudic passage is not widely known, a few words of introduction together with a citation of the relevant verse will be appropriate here.

Semahot ('Rejoicings', also known by the older title, *Ebal rabbati*, or 'Major Mourning') is one of the minor tractates of the Babylonian Talmud. It is described by Dov Zlotnick as 'the classic Rabbinic text on death and mourning'.[14] As such it collects together in one place a substantial number of regulations and customs concerning these topics. Zlotnick has considered the question of the date of this compilation in great detail and has concluded:

11. Corley, 'Women and the Crucifixion', p. 191.
12. Corley, 'Women and the Crucifixion', pp. 212-14.
13. I am indebted to Professor Eric M. Meyers for the suggestion (first made in a seminar at Hebrew Union College in Jerusalem in 1974) that *Sem.* 8.1 might explain the visit of the women to the tomb on the third day. In considering this possibility I have become convinced that it provides the key to understanding Mt. 28.1 but not the Markan and Lukan narratives, where it is clearly stated that the women came to anoint the body of Jesus. As an aside it may be noted here that according to the Mishnah (*Šab.* 23.5) it was permissible to anoint a body on the Sabbath, although the purchase of the necessary materials would not have been allowed.
14. Dov Zlotnick, *The Tractate 'Mourning' (Semahot) (Regulations Relating to Death, Burial, and Mourning)* (Yale Judaica Series, 27; New Haven: Yale University Press, 1966), I. Cf. also his comments in 'Semahot', *EJ* 14 (Jerusalem: Keter, 1971), col. 1138. Zlotnick's book is the most important and exhaustive modern study of this tractate known to me. Also important, however, are the translation and notes of R.J. Rabbinowitz, 'Ebal Rabbathi Named Masseketh Semahoth: Tractate on Mourning', in A. Cohen (ed.), *The Minor Tractates of the Talmud* (2 vols.; London: Soncino, 1971), I, pp. 325-400.

Most modern scholars favor a late date for this work, placing the time of final redaction at about the middle of the eighth century. There is nothing in the text, however, pointing clearly to a late date. The latest authorities cited are Judah ha-Nasi and his contemporaries in the third century. It is written in the language of the Mishnah; its style and structure throughout is that of the *tannaim*. It therefore seems preferable to follow the ancients in suggesting an early date—the end of the third century.[15]

Zlotnick's assessment of the evidence is thorough and convincing. Further, as Corley's research has shown, many of the traditions preserved in this tractate undoubtedly antedate (perhaps by centuries) the date of the compilation. Indeed, Rabbinowitz observes that:

The original *Semahoth* consisted of a collection of *Baraithoth* dealing with the laws of mourning for the dead prescribed by Judaism, compiled in Palestine by R. Eliezer b. Zadok (first cent. CE). Later it was amplified and embellished by R. Hiyya, a Babylonian of the second century. It took its present form probably in the middle of the eighth century.[16]

Although, as Zlotnick has shown, an eighth-century date for the final redaction of this tractate is probably too late, Rabbinowitz's description of the early history of the compilation is, I believe, basically accurate. The tractate represents the end process of a collection of tradition begun at least as early as the first century CE (in the age of the *tannaim*). Thus we may conclude that many of the customs described in this tractate can be assigned a date in the first century CE, if not earlier.[17] An early date for the practice of visiting the tomb described in *Sem.* 8.1 is also highly probable on archaeological grounds. The custom clearly presupposes a situation in which burial was in cave tombs (cf. the expression בית הקברות, below), a practice that was widespread in Palestine from the Chalcolithic Age well into the Byzantine period.[18] Although earth burials are found (as, for example, at Qumran) the practice of burial in cave tombs became very common throughout Palestine during the Hellenistic and Roman periods.[19] By

---

15. Zlotnick, 'Semahot', col. 1139. See the complete discussion in his *The Tractate 'Mourning'*, pp. 1-9.
16. Rabbinowitz, 'Ebal Rabbathi', p. v.
17. This conclusion seems consistent with the results of Corley's research.
18. J. Calloway, 'Burials in Palestine: From the Stone Age to Abraham', *BA* 26 (1963), pp. 74-91.
19. Perhaps the most important study of Jewish burial practices through the Roman period is Eric M. Meyers, *Jewish Ossuaries: Reburial and Rebirth. Secondary Burials in their Ancient Near Eastern Setting* (BibOr, 24; Rome: Biblical Institute

the middle of the first century CE a vast cemetery complex of such tombs partially encircled Jerusalem, stretching at least from Mt Scopus in the east to the Sanhedriya tombs in the northwest.[20] The fact that the use of stone ossuaries (an elaborate form of secondary burial associated with such tombs) reaches a peak in the period c. 50 BCE to 70 CE is further evidence of the importance of burial in cave tombs during this particular period.[21] The literary and archaeological evidence, considered together, allows us to conclude that it is virtually certain that the custom of visiting the tomb to ensure that premature burial had not taken place developed well before the first century CE and continued at least until the Byzantine period if not later.

We may now turn to the Talmudic text itself. Rabbinowitz provides the following translation of *Sem.* 8.1:

> Rule 1: We go out to the cemetery and examine the dead within three days and do not fear [being suspect of] superstitious practices. It once happened that [a man who was buried] was examined [and found to be living], and he lived for twenty-five years and then died. Another [so examined lived and] begat five children before he died.[22]

It is instructive to examine the crucial first sentence in Hebrew. It reads.[23]

Press, 1971). This book has an excellent and exhaustive bibliography. Also noteworthy is Meyers's more popular treatment of the topic in 'Secondary Burials in Palestine', *BA* 33 (1970), pp. 2-29. A clear picture of the type of tomb most common in Jerusalem and its environs in the Herodian Period may be obtained by reading L.Y. Rahmani, 'Jewish Rock-Cut Tombs in Jerusalem', *Atiqot* English Series 3 (1961), pp. 93-120; V. Tzaferis, 'Jewish Rock-Cut Tombs at and near Giv'at ha-Mivtar, Jerusalem', *IEJ* 20 (1970), pp. 18-32; and James F. Strange, 'Late Hellenistic and Herodian Ossuary Tombs at French Hill, Jerusalem', *BASOR* 219 (1975), pp. 39-67. It may be noted that the frequency with which oil lamps are found in such tombs (cf. Tzaferis's comment that Herodian lamps 'are found in nearly every Jewish tomb of the period between the rise of the Herodian dynasty and the destruction of the Second Temple' [p. 26]) is consistent with (although not proof of) the practice of periodic visitation and inspection that we are positing here.

20. See Strange, 'Late Hellenistic and Herodian Ossuary Tombs', p. 64 and Tzaferis, 'Jewish Rock-Cut Tombs', p. 30.

21. Cf. the discussion in Meyers, *Jewish Ossuaries*, and Rahmani, 'Jewish Rock-Cut Tombs'. Note especially the arguments presented by Rahmani in n. 4 (pp. 116-17) for his conclusion that ossuaries were not used in Jewish tombs prior to the reign of Herod I.

22. Rabbiniowitz, 'Ebal Rabbathi', p. 363.

23. This verse was copied from תלמוד בבלי (Wien: Jacob Schlossberg, 1867).

יוצאין לבית הקברות ופוקדי על המתים עד שלשה ימים ואין
חוששין משום דרכי האמורי:

> We go out to the burial caves and observe (visit; attend to) the dead until the third day and do not fear [being suspected of] superstitious practices.

The practice described here clearly entails going out to the burial caves (probably at intervals) to visit the dead *until* (עד) *the third day*.[24] If this practice was current when Matthew's Gospel was written (as we have argued that it was) then the scene which the author envisions becomes clear. When the Sabbath is over and the new day begins, the women are free to travel and they come again 'to see the tomb'. It is the third day and they come, as custom demands, for the final inspection to confirm that Jesus is really dead. This is a melancholy task! Therefore we suggest that the Matthean account is not as weak and deficient as Goulder suggests. On the contrary, it is a powerful and dramatic introduction to the account of Jesus' resurrection. The women who come (surely with sadness) to confirm Jesus' death become (with great joy) the first witnesses to his resurrection.[25]

This interpretation of Mt. 28.1 may also shed light on the way in which the author of this Gospel has incorporated the traditions about the sealing of the stone and the posting of a guard at the tomb of Jesus (Mt. 27.62-66; 28.11-15). It is generally argued that these stories had their origin in a controversy in which Christians were pressed to offer proof for the claim that Jesus had been raised from the dead. Matthew

---

24. While recognizing the strength of the reading 'until the third day', Zlotnick prefers to read 'for thirty days' (with some manuscripts of the Talmud). His arguments, however, are not convincing. It would not be at all likely that a person would survive for such a long period of time in a burial chamber without food, water, or the other necessities of life, especially in a weakened condition. A three-day period, however, is not excessive. Further, reference may be made to the tradition attributed both to R. Levi (*TJ M.K.* 3.5, 82b; *Yeb.* 16.1, 15c) and to Bar Kappara (*Mid. Rabbah*, Gen C.7) that the soul hovers about the body for three days hoping to be reunited with it. After three days there was no longer any hope of revival. Jn 11.17, 39 may reflect this belief and confirm our view that it is not a late development (see the notes on Jn 11.39 in Str-B, II, p. 544. Thus visiting the tomb 'until the third day' is to be preferred to the reading 'for thirty days'.

25. It could be asked whether this interpretation requires that the reader assume that the women either didn't hear or didn't believe Jesus' predictions about his resurrection. The portrayal of the women, however, including their need for reassurance both from the angel and from Jesus, seems to suggest that they are being depicted as acting according to custom rather than coming excitedly anticipating Jesus' resurrection.

is usually thought to have received these stories from the oral tradition current in his church.[26] Goulder, however, has recently rejected this view, arguing instead that these stories were created by the author of the Gospel. For Goulder they are *midrash*, a typically Matthean use of Josh. 10 and Dan. 6–12 to understand and describe the burial and resurrection of Jesus.[27] Goulder's position here is strong. Whether or not there are any pre-Matthean traditions behind these stories (a point which might be debated),[28] in their present form they have been shaped by the author of the Gospel and by his use of important biblical texts. But to what end? Here we may offer a very tentative suggestion. Perhaps the author has introduced a note of irony, but one with an important point. The guard at the tomb and the seal upon the stone present obstacles to the inspection of the tomb referred to above. Both of these obstacles are due to the initiative of the chief priests and the Pharisees (who also perpetrate the fraud of Mt. 28.11-15). That there is tension between the author of the Gospel of Matthew (and his community) and these Jewish leaders is clear to any careful reader of this Gospel. In many ways Matthew seems to believe that his community is more faithful to Jewish tradition than are the leaders of the Jewish community that he knows.[29] Thus, in this narrative, these particular leaders of the Jewish community make it difficult for the faithful followers of Jesus (for so the women are portrayed) to do what Jewish custom requires at the time of death and burial.

This essay began as a study in the synoptic problem, admittedly written by an advocate of Matthean priority. The intent was to show how too rigid an adoption of the theory of Markan priority could obscure the reading of the Gospel of Matthew. We rejected Goulder's view that the Matthean account of the visit of the women to the tomb is a weak and incoherent revision of the Markan narrative. Instead we

26. This line of interpretation is found in many of the commentaries on Matthew. See, by way of example, Claude J.G. Montefiore, *The Synoptic Gospels* (2 vols.; London: Macmillan, 1909), II, pp. 351-52; Johnson, 'Gospel According to Matthew', p. 613; Green, *Gospel According to Matthew*, p. 226.

27. M.D. Goulder, *Midrash and Lection in Matthew* (London: SPCK, 1974), pp. 447-48; 'The Empty Tomb', *Theology* 79 (1976), pp. 209-10.

28. The details of Mt. 28.11-15 make some element of controversy seem likely.

29. Thus Lamar Cope concludes that 'Matthew was written by a Jewish-Christian who belonged to a church which was already separated from Pharisaic Judaism and in sharp conflict with Pharisaism. The Christian fellowship probably included Gentiles (although precise evidence is lacking) but prided itself in being more faithful to the intent of the Torah (5.17-20; 12.1-21) than the Pharisees were' (*Matthew: A Scribe*, p. 130).

argued that it is an original and thoroughly comprehensible narrative, rooted deeply in Jewish custom and tradition, and developing theological motifs characteristic of the Gospel of Matthew. But what began as a study in the synoptic problem has become more than an exercise in source criticism. Our analyses have enabled us to see more clearly the central role of women in the practices associated with death, mourning, and burial[30] and the prominent role of certain women in the account of Jesus' resurrection. In Matthew's Gospel the women emerge as models of faithful discipleship. While the other disciples are conspicuously absent, these women are noticeably present, doing what should be done for a person who has just died. Amy-Jill Levine has put this particularly well. She comments that during the awesome effects of Easter morning the women:

> continue to act faithfully. They witness the empty tomb, and they follow precisely the instructions to report quickly the news of the resurrection. Although they are not included in the reference to 'his disciples' (28.7) or mentioned as present at the Great Commission (28.16-20), the angel's words (28.7) and the meeting with Jesus (28.9-10) indicate their substantive role in the Easter mission. Indeed, it is Jesus who first greets them, and they in turn are the first to worship him. Matthew records of the Eleven that 'some doubted' (28.17), but of the women only their legitimate fear and their joy are reported. These independent, motivated women are both the first witnesses to the resurrection and the first missionaries of the church.[31]

What are those women doing at the tomb of Jesus? They are doing exactly what one would expect faithful disciples to do in the face of death. They have come to see (to visit or to watch) the tomb.

---

30. For this I would like to express special appreciation to Kathleen Corley who graciously shared with me copies of her published work as well as sections of a manuscript shortly to be published. These were invaluable resources.

31. Amy-Jill Levine, 'Matthew', in C.A. Newsom and S. Ringe (eds.), *The Women's Bible Commentary* (London: SPCK, 1992), pp. 252-62 (262).

THE WOMEN AT THE TOMB: WHAT ARE THEY DOING THERE?[*]

Carolyn Osiek

This article will explore the role and function of the women in the empty tomb narratives of the gospel tradition. What purpose do they play in the resurrection kerygma of the early church? Why is the story of their first arrival at the tomb so persistent that it continues into the later apocryphal gospels? It has become an exegetical commonplace that women could not be legal witnesses in ancient Judaism, and thus these tomb narratives were not counted among official appearance stories. But if this is so, why were these narratives preserved at all? It is thought by some biblical scholars that the empty tomb stories are secondary to the appearance stories, and even perhaps invented by Mark. If this is so, why women? It would seem to have fit the kerygmatic purposes of early Christian preaching eminently better to have the male disciples come first to the tomb—or, if it be argued that, having fled at the arrest, according to the narrative they would not have known where the tomb was, then even Joseph of Arimathea, who surely could have come to check on his handiwork!

The discussion of this question will be in three parts. Part one will summarize the work on these passages done by scholars using redaction criticism. Part two will examine surrounding issues from the perspective of social history and social construction of meaning, especially with regard to women's subcultures, roles in burial customs, and public testimony. Part three will apply to these findings a feminist analysis using both a hermeneutic of suspicion and of remembrance.

Redactional Emphases

All four Gospels contain accounts of the women as first arrivals to the tomb on Easter morning, but they differ greatly in detail. The common thread to all four accounts is that at least one woman disciple of Jesus,

---

[*] Originally published in *Ex Auditu* 9 (1993), pp. 97-107. Reprinted by permission.

namely Mary Magdalene, came first to the tomb after the sabbath, found it empty, and went away again. Also common to the Synoptics is that they (Mary Magdalene and at least one other) received a message from someone(s) to interpret the meaning as the resurrection of Jesus. The number and names of the women are different in each case, as shown below.

Mk 16.1	Mary Magdalene, Mary mother of James, Salome
Mt. 28.1	Mary Magdalene and the other Mary
Lk. 24.10	Mary Magdalene, Joanna, Mary mother of James, and the others with them
Jn 20.1	Mary Magdalene

In addition:

Gos. Pet. 12.50 Mary Magdalene and her women friends

Epistula Apostolorum
| Ethiopic 9 | Sarah, Martha, Mary Magdalene |
| Coptic 9 | Mary, the daughter of Martha, Mary Magdalene |

Only the *Epistula Apostolorum* does not place the name of Mary Magdalene first.

Mark 16.1-8

One can now speak of a scholarly consensus that the original ending of Mark is at the end of v. 8. The same cannot be said for the questions surrounding the composition of those last eight verses. Some detect the presence of literary sources in the text itself. For others, 16.1-8 is an integral literary unit composed by Mark. For still others, this literary unity is sufficient indication that Mark not only composed the narrative, but invented it.[1] If one wants to discount all stories of

---

1. Examples of these three positions, in the same order, are: Reginald H. Fuller, *The Formation of the Resurrection Narratives* (New York: Macmillan, 1971), pp. 50-70; Frans Neirynck, 'Marc 16, 1-8 tradition et redaction', *ETL* 56 (1980), pp. 56-88; Adela Yarbro Collins, 'The Empty Tomb and Resurrection According to Mark', in eadem, *The Beginning of the Gospel: Probings of Mark in Context* (Minneapolis: Fortress Press, 1992), pp. 119-48. A summary of opinions on the historicity of the empty tomb to 1970 can be found in Edward Lynn Bode, *The First Easter Morning: The Gospel Accounts of the Women's Visit to the Tomb of Jesus* (AnBib, 45; Rome: Pontifical Biblical Institute, 1970), pp. 151-59. See also Pheme Perkins, *Resurrection: New Testament Witness and Contemporary Reflection* (Garden City, NY: Doubleday, 1984).

angelophany and search for the historical 'bare bones', the result is, not surprisingly, exactly what was given above as the line common to all four canonical Gospels: some women disciples arrived first at the tomb, found it empty, went away confused.

The women who came at sunrise were the same three who were present and witnessed the crucifixion along with other women disciples (15.40-41), and the two Marys saw the burial (v. 47), even though one of the sons of the second Mary is omitted alternately in 15.47 and 16.1. (To add to the confusion, Codex Vaticanus tries to make her into two people at 15.40: the wife of little James and the mother of Joses. See the conundrum posed by 6.3, where James and Joses are the brothers of Jesus, which would make this Mary the same as the mother of Jesus.) In spite of some confusion about the male relatives of the second Mary, there is a continuity in the women's experience. It is explicitly stated that they saw (θεωροῦσαι), even though at a distance (15.40), the crucifixion of Jesus and where he was buried (v. 47; Salome has disappeared for the burial, but has rejoined the two Marys at the tomb on Sunday morning). The usual interpretation of their distance from the scene is avoidance of the political danger that closer association would bring (also in Mt. 27.55 and Lk. 23.49, but contrast Jn 19.25).

The reason given for their return, the unfinished anointing of the body, is highly suspect. It occurs only in Mark and Luke. In Mark, the end of the passion narrative offers no explanation why they could not finish the task on Friday, so that their reason for returning seems artificial. Moreover, reopening the tomb to anoint the body nearly two days later has been seen by most commentators as incredible. It has been objected that what is envisioned is not complete anointing, but rather a general honorific sprinkling with aromatics around the corpse, as in 2 Chron. 16.14 or Josephus, *Ant.* 15.61, prophetically anticipated in Mk 14.8.[2] But when this anointing is to be done more than 36 hours after burial, it still strains credibility.

Those who would see an original, straightforward narrative behind the present text would see it composed of something like vv. 1, 2, 4, 8. Verse 3, the women's question to each other about how they will gain access to the tomb, is literary embellishment to heighten the sense of amazement in v. 4 when they find the stone already rolled back. The rather subdued angelophany (vv. 5-7), if indeed the modest account

---

2. Luise Schottroff, 'Mary Magdalene and the Women at Jesus' Tomb', in *eadem, Let the Oppressed Go Free: Feminist Perspectives on the New Testament* (Louisville, KY: Westminster/John Knox Press, 1993), pp. 168-203 (181 and 200 n. 42).

of a young man in a white robe can even be called that, introduces the kerygmatic message of Jesus' resurrection, and is therefore secondary. Verse 7 introduces yet another motif, return to Galilee in keeping with Jesus' own prediction in 14.28, and is perhaps inserted at an even later point.

The complex question of Mark's puzzling ending cannot be discussed here and is not relevant for this investigation, except inasmuch as the silence of the women affects their credibility as witnesses. This will be taken up in part three.

Matthew 28.1-10

Matthew's empty tomb narrative elaborates considerably the simple account of Mark. Two of Mark's three women remain, but they have company: the guards that have been stationed at the tomb (Mt. 27.62-66). The women came, not to finish anointing, but simply to 'see' (θεωρῆσαι) the tomb, to continue the faithful vigil they had been keeping at the time of burial (27.61). And there was plenty to see once they got there: an earthquake, and an angel who descended, rolled away the stone, and sat on it (28.2-3). Women and guards were witnesses to the shattering events immediately surrounding the actual resurrection. The contrasting reaction reveals the difference of response. While the guards accepted bribes to falsify what they witnessed (vv. 11-15), meanwhile back at the tomb, the women received the angelic message in approximately the same terms as in Mark, including the promise of seeing Jesus himself in Galilee (vv. 5-7). As contrasted with Mark, they fled the tomb not in fear and panic, but in fear and great joy to tell the other disciples (v. 8).

The subsequent appearance of Jesus cutting them off at the pass as they ran (vv. 9-10) is the most difficult part of the narrative and may be an addition. It adds nothing to the angel's message, but only repeats the message to go to Galilee. Moreover, it seemingly contradicts the angel, who had just told them to deliver the message that 'you will see him in Galilee'. Two verses later, they saw him at Jerusalem—and with nothing new to say. The Synoptic pattern of an angel(s) who sent women to male disciples who, in Matthew and Luke, are then sent to the world, is disrupted. This sudden and strange appearance of Jesus, however, serves to reinforce the essential message: he is risen. Other aspects of its significance include the following: it forges the first link between the empty tomb and appearance traditions; it is the first evidence of the tendency, to be developed in Lk. 24 and Jn 21, to relocate appearances in Jerusalem; and the women's response of worshipful grasping of Jesus' feet (v. 9) is evidence of the inevitable tendency to materialize the appearances.[3] In addition, for Matthew, the first appearance of the risen Jesus was to women disciples.

Luke 24.1-11
Only in Luke are the women disciples mentioned and partially named early on in Jesus' ministry (8.2-3). There with him in Galilee, in addition to the twelve, were women who had been healed and exorcised: Mary Magadalene, Joanna, and Susanna, who is never mentioned again. With them were 'many others', all of whom practiced διακονία with the twelve. Only here and in Mk 16.9 is Mary Magdalene a former demoniac—and nowhere in the New Testament is she a prostitute! Joanna may have been a woman of some status on the Herodian ladder, and inexplicably, traveled without her husband among a group of whom Herod did not approve.[4] The women reappear in 23.49-55 as part of the group of those who had followed Jesus (the language of discipleship) from Galilee to Jerusalem. According to Acts 13.31, they therefore form part of the group of witnesses to the events of Jesus' death and resurrection.

Luke is the first evangelist to imply that the male disciples were present at the crucifixion along with the women (23.49), even if at a distance. Only the women, however, witnessed the burial (v. 55), so that the textually uncertain visit of Peter to the tomb (24.12) must still presuppose the communication of its location by the women. They will remain nameless until 24.10. Here, in contrast to Mark, they have a reason to return Sunday morning to finish their anointing: the first sundown of sabbath was already beginning while Jesus was being buried (v. 54), and the women were observant of sabbath regulations (v. 56).

Though there is no mention in Luke's burial account of the stone being rolled over the tomb entrance, it is presupposed in 24.2, for there, it has already been rolled back. Luke, in common with Mark and against Matthew, does not narrate the actual movement of the stone. Only in Luke, the women first saw for themselves that Jesus' body was not there—before they were informed as to the meaning of its absence. Then they were instructed by the two men in dazzling

---

3. Fuller, *Formation of the Resurrection Narratives*, p. 79.
4. Compelling portraits of Mary Magdalene as one healed of mental illness and of Joanna as a well-to-do and independent lady are given by Elizabeth Moltmann-Wendel, *The Women around Jesus: Reflections on Authentic Personhood* (London: SCM Press, 1982), pp. 61-90, 131-44.

robes, not by means of kerygmatic statements, but two familiar Lukan devices. The first is a rhetorical question: 'Why do you look for the living one among the dead?' (v. 5; compare Acts 1.11). The second is a memory help: 'Remember how he told you about this in Galilee' (vv. 6-7), followed by their remembrance of his words, leading to understanding and proclamation. Even though, only in Luke, the women were not given a specific command to tell what they have seen, they did it anyway—but in vain, for they were not believed until Peter verified for himself (vv. 8-9, 11-12) and appearances of Jesus later in the day confirmed what had happened.

At 24.10, three of the women are finally named: Mary Magdalene, Joanna (see 8.2), and Mary mother of James (or wife, if Mk 15.40 is not to be presumed), but there were unnamed others with them. Joanna, the political question mark, has persisted from 8.2 along with Mary Magdalene.

For Luke, the women were certainly counted among the disciples. The angelic message to them at the tomb is not one of direct address, a statement to be repeated to the men. Rather, the message is directed to the women themselves. It is they who are to remember how Jesus, while still in Galilee, predicted his passion and resurrection. Only once in Luke's Gospel, at 9.22, are both passion and resurrection made part of a prediction that is not directed specifically to a closed group, but to the disciples in general. The women disciples, already mentioned in 8.2-3, are therefore part of the group of disciples who received the prediction in ch. 9,[5] as well as the disciple-witnesses from Galilee in Acts 13.31. In Luke's narrative, they form part of an inclusive pattern of women figures beginning with the prophets Mary and Anna in the infancy stories, through, among others, Martha and Mary (10.38-42), Mary and the women in the upper room at Pentecost (Acts 1.14), and the women prophets of Joel (Acts 2.18).

John 20.1-2, 11-18

With the first two verses of John, we may be once again very close to an original form of the story: a woman disciple goes early Sunday morning to the tomb; finds the stone rolled back; and runs to tell other disciples. The beloved disciple is of course a Johannine insertion, as is Mary's immediate assumption that the body has been stolen. John does not say explicitly that she noticed the body was not there

---

5. Maria-Luisa Rigato, '"Remember... Then They Remembered": Luke 24:6-8', in Gerald O'Collins and Gilberto Marconi (eds.), *Luke and Acts* (Mahwah, NJ: Paulist Press, 1993), pp. 93-101, 232-35.

(compare only Lk. 24.3), yet her message presupposes it. Mourning and preparation of a body for burial are social activities for women; the group of women is no doubt the earlier version. It has been reduced by John to Mary Magdalene alone for two reasons. First, the ensuing dialogue between her and Jesus in vv. 11-18 was composed as a private encounter, and it is possible that the original narrative continued from v. 1 to v. 11 without the intervening episode. Second, the focus on her prefigures her centrality in later apocryphal Easter stories as a major authority on communication from the risen Jesus. Some think that the plural 'we' in v. 2 is a remnant of the earlier version and implies other companions, who are not otherwise mentioned for the reasons just given.

In vv. 11-18, Mary Magdalene is mourner, lover, and momentarily uncomprehending foil for Jesus' revelation. Only in John is the mourning of the women at the tomb, women's special role at a funeral, made explicit: she stood outside the tomb weeping (v. 11). But looking in, she 'sees' (θεωρεῖ, cf. Mt. 28.1, etc.) two angels in white garments, one at the head and one at the foot of the place where the body of Jesus had been (v. 12).

> Ask an audience of ordinary Christians what Old Testament scene comes to mind as they picture two angels in a small dark space stationed one at the head and one at the foot of a shelf or slab, and almost immediately someone will respond, 'the ark of the covenant in the Holy of Holies'. That response is naive, uncomplicated, and correct.[6]

Mary's assumption of body snatchers in vv. 2, 13, 15 is portrayed as the raving of a distraught person, for who would steal the body except the disciples, to whom she first reported the loss? Yet it is a strange echo of the false explanation of the empty tomb in Mt. 27.62-66. The motif also prepares for the scene of teasing encounter and recognition that is a perennial favorite for those who ponder the scriptures. Jesus' gentle rebuke about her clinging to him in v. 17 recalls the women's grabbing hold of his feet in Mt. 28.9, the only other canonical account in which the risen Jesus appears to women at the tomb (with perhaps Mk 16.9, where the location of his appearance to Mary Magdalene is not specified). Like the women in the accounts of Mark and Matthew, she is given an explicit commission to tell the male disciples, not this time about a coming appearance in Galilee, but about Jesus' ascension/exaltation. The words of her message to

---

6. Robert H. Smith, *Easter Gospels: The Resurrection of Jesus According to the Four Evangelists* (Minneapolis: Augsburg, 1983), p. 161.

the disciples are the foundation text for later portrayals of Mary Magdalene as privileged recipient of revelation from the risen Jesus and 'apostle of the apostles': 'I have seen the Lord, and this is what he said to me' (v. 18; compare 1 Cor. 9.1).

Gospel of Peter
The persistence of the story of women at the tomb is demonstrated by the second-century redactor of this text, who found it necessary to include them, even though they arrive at the tomb after a plethora of witnesses—soldiers, scribes, and elders—have already seen the stone rolled back, two men of transcendent height enter the sepulcher and emerge with Jesus in the middle, with the talking cross behind them, and yet another angelic figure enters the tomb to guard it from the inside and wait for the women! (10.38–11.44).

After all these nocturnal events, Mary Magdalene, a woman disciple (μαθήτρια) of the Lord, set off for the tomb early in the morning with her women friends (τας φίλας). As in Mark and Luke, they had unfinished business there, but as in John, it is mourning, not anointing. Their reason for not doing it earlier was fear of the Jews. As in Mark, they wondered who will roll back the stone for them, but found the task already done and a young man who gave them the message of the resurrection. Why they had less fear of the Jews now, especially given the crowd that spent the night at the sepulcher, and why they needed the stone rolled back in order to mourn, are questions not entertained. Also as in Mark, they fled afraid, and it is not said that they told anyone (12.50–13.57). Here, however, they do not have to: half the world already knows! It is interesting to note, however, that the narrative does not provide a line of direct communication about the resurrection events to the male disciples.[7]

Here the story of women at the tomb is still thought important enough to keep in the narrative, even though it seems to serve no purpose, neither first witness nor medium of communication to the other disciples. It can only have been included because it was so much a part of the Easter story that the redactor could not leave it out.

A look at all five of these narratives leads to the conclusion that behind them lies a core version in which Mary Magdalene is the key figure who arrived first at the tomb, found it empty, and went away

---

7. While the *Gospel of Peter* contains invaluable information about the development of gospel traditions, I am not persuaded by the argument that its earliest core predated and influenced the canonical tradition; cf. John Dominic Crossan, *The Cross That Spoke: The Origins of the Passion Narrative* (San Francisco: Harper & Row, 1988).

confused. If this story is secondary to the appearance narratives and late in coming, then the question must again be asked, What purpose does it serve? Does the proclamation of the resurrection necessitate an empty tomb? It would seem not: as is well known, Paul does not allude to the empty tomb tradition—a fact usually put forth in support of the secondary character of the story—nor does the preaching in Acts, though Acts 2.29-31 and 13.34-37 perhaps presuppose it, both in reinterpretation of Ps. 16.10 (15.10 LXX).

An analysis of the relationship between resurrection beliefs and resuscitated body in the first-century Mediterranean world cannot be done here.[8] Most texts are ambiguous, but some, e.g., 2 Macc. 7.11, 23, seem to suggest a close connection, as does one Greco-Roman apotheosis story, that of Hercules by the first-century BCE historian, Diodorus Siculus (*Bib. hist.* 38.3-5). Hercules mounts the funeral pyre, which is consumed by a bolt of lightning. Those who come afterwards to gather up the remains find no bones, and conclude that Hercules has been translated to the realm of the gods. Paul's analogies to seed sown and astral bodies in 1 Cor. 15.35-44 are open to a variety of interpretations, but it does seem as if some continuity with the physical is supposed in the pneumatic transformation.

However, a close examination of the resurrection teaching of both Paul and Acts reveals that the core event is the appearances of the risen Christ. The allusions to Ps. 16.10 in Acts 2.29-31 and 13.34-37 are not offered as proofs, but as supporting scriptural arguments. Beyond these passages, the silence of Paul and of Acts about the empty tomb tradition cannot be taken as proof of its secondary nature, for the author of Acts of course knows that tradition. Rather, their silence is indication that the empty tomb tradition is not foundational to the kerygma of the resurrection. For the earliest Christian community, it served 'not as the origin and cause of their Easter faith, but as a vehicle for the proclamation of the Easter faith which they already held as a result of the appearances. It is as such that the Christian historian and the community of faith can accept the report of the empty tomb today'.[9]

If this is so, the question remains with even greater persistence: what purpose does the tradition of the women at the empty tomb serve? Why was it kept in this form at all?

8. See especially George W.E. Nickelsburg, *Resurrection, Immortality, and Eternal Life in Intertestamental Judaism* (Cambridge, MA: Harvard University Press, 1972).
9. Fuller, *The Formation of the Resurrection Narratives*, p. 70.

214 *A Feminist Companion to Matthew*

Sociological Issues

In this section, we will consider several aspects of women's cultural behavior in traditional Mediterranean societies and particularly in Judaism, as these considerations bear on the empty tomb narratives: the role played by women in funerals, women's subcultural narrative traditions, and the question of women as witnesses in rabbinic Judaism.

In many traditional societies including those of the eastern Mediterranean, it is women who prepare a body for burial, while men actually convey the body into the tomb. This fits well the gospel accounts: the women prepared the aromatic spices that were wrapped into the shroud and deposited around it, while Joseph of Arimathea (assisted by Nicodemus in John) made the public contact with the authorities, placed the body in the tomb, and secured it. Both men and women lament, often publicly (e.g. 2 Sam. 13.31; 18.33-19.8; Job 1.20; 2.12-13; Ezek. 29.30-36; Mk 5.38; Jn 11.33), but it is especially women who carry the tradition with their own particular and culture-specific customs.

The special role of women in mourning is often threatening to male familial and religious authorities, for it is perceived as giving them a power of contact with the dead. Thus woman, who is perceived by male society as having closer connection with birth, is also perceived as having closer contact with death, and that connection with the unclean and the unknown is terrifying and contaminating.[10] Perhaps the suspect motive of unfinished anointing attributed by Mark and Luke to the Gospel women for returning to the tomb is further from the actual situation than that provided by the other accounts. For Matthew, they returned simply to see the tomb (28.1); for the *Gospel of Peter*, to do what women do for their loved ones who die (12.50); and perhaps John is the most forthright and least threatened by women's presence, for Mary Magdalene is simply there, weeping (20.11).

The suggestion has been made that the empty tomb story was preserved (or originated) in women's groups, and finally made its way into the male 'mainstream' canonical tradition. Certainly many traditional cultures segregate male and female company in everyday social

---

10. The tradition of women's lament as a form of alternate social power still survives in rural Greece, but is rapidly disappearing. See especially Gail Holst-Warhaft, *Dangerous Voices: Women's Laments and Greek Literature* (London: Routledge, 1992); Anna Caraveli, 'The Bitter Wounding: The Lament as Social Protest in Rural Greece', in Jill Dubisch (ed.), *Gender and Power in Rural Greece* (Princeton, NJ: Princeton University Press, 1986), pp. 169-94.

interaction, and many eastern Mediterranean cultures yet today belong in this category. One need only be present in a village of Greece, Turkey, or an Arab country for the cycle of work and recreation in an ordinary day to be aware of this. In such a society, women have their own oral traditions and storytelling practices, passed on from generation to generation, that portray life and events from the women's point of view.[11] It has been frequently noticed that the apocryphal gospels and acts feature stories about women disciples and especially women leaders in unprecedented numbers when compared to their canonical counterparts. Indeed, the question is regularly asked whether this is one of the reasons for their noncanonical status.[12]

Cycles of stories that originate in women's storytelling circles presumably tell the women's side of an event. This is precisely what the empty tomb stories do, with appearances of the risen Jesus added to Matthew's and John's versions. A different light is shed on the original function of the empty tomb narrative if it can be seen as a 'private' version from the world of women, over against the 'public' version of appearances to the male disciples, like the very early list in 1 Cor. 15.5-7. This list includes no appearances to women. Could it be that the reason for Paul's silence about appearances to women, let alone the empty tomb, is not because the story is secondary, but because it has not yet made its way from the 'private' female kerygmatic tradition to the 'public' male kerygmatic tradition?

This brings us to the question of the ability or inability of women to be public witnesses according to Jewish law. It has become an unexamined scholarly commonplace in Christian exegesis that women's incapacity to serve as public witnesses is a major reason for the exclusion of appearances of the risen Jesus to women in the official testimonies of Acts and 1 Cor. 15. This judgment relies heavily on a statement by Josephus (*Ant.* 4.219) to the effect that Moses' legislation included a prohibition of women serving as legal witnesses because of their 'lightness and presumption' (διὰ κουφότητα καὶ θράσος, τοῦ γένους

---

11. See, e.g., Dubisch, *Gender and Power in Rural Greece*; Lila Abu-Lughod, *Veiled Sentiments: Honor and Poetry in a Bedouin Society* (Berkeley: University of California Press, 1986).

12. See, for example, Stevan L. Davies, *The Revolt of the Widows: The Social World of the Apocryphal Acts* (Carbondale: Southern Illinois University Press, 1980); Dennis R. MacDonald, *The Legend and the Apostle: The Battle for Paul in Story and Canon* (Philadelphia: Westminster Press, 1983); Virginia Burrus, *Chastity as Autonomy: Women in the Stories of the Apocryphal Acts* (Studies in Women and Religion, 23; Lewiston, NY: Edwin Mellen Press, 1987).

αὐτῶν), a prescription not included in the biblical law codes, but quite congruous with Josephus' valuation of women.

In fact, the inability of a woman to serve as witness in ancient Judaism is not so clear in Mishnaic law. Use of these sources to shed light on first-century Judaism must always be done with caution, since the compilations were done several centuries later. Nevertheless, several points may be relevant. First, women were disqualified from serving as witnesses in a case that necessitated bringing an accusation against another. This is an exemption, not an exclusion, since those not exempted are required to bear witness when necessary. Women were therefore exempted from being compelled to initiate public testimony of a crime committed. This situation does not apply to our case. Second, a woman could testify in matters of credibility: especially on questions that pertain particularly to women (e.g. virginity—including her own); when she was the only one present; in order to free herself or another from a legal obligation (e.g. the death of a husband); and in certain cases when men were not present or it would not be appropriate for them to be there. In business matters, a woman could take an oath of deposit and swear to her own honesty. Women's testimony was valued and drawn upon in the sphere of private affairs, but not in public, reaffirming a traditional distinction often made by modern scholars. That is, in domestic, family, and private law (including business contracts), women functioned as legal persons. But the general reluctance in ancient Mediterranean society to see women as public spokespersons or officeholders applies here as well.[13]

But how does all of this apply to the Gospel empty tomb narratives? In all four Gospels, Mary Magdalene and others are credibility witnesses, a credibility that is patently rejected by the male disciples in Lk. 24.11. In Mark, Matthew, and Luke, the women were the continuous witnesses to Jesus' death, burial, and empty tomb. In Matthew and John, as well as Mk 16.9, they were the first to have an appearance of the risen Christ. In Jn 20.18, Mary Magdalene gives testimony in formulaic language: 'I have seen the Lord, and these are the things he said to me' (cf. 1 Cor. 9.1). Credibility is exactly what is at stake in their witness, a witness that is variously received by the male disciples

---

13. Moshe Meiselman, *Jewish Woman in Jewish Law* (New York: Ktav, 1978), pp. 73-80; Judith Romney Wegner, *Chattel or Person? The Status of Women in the Mishnah* (New York: Oxford University Press, 1988), pp. 120-26, 188-89. Wegner's conclusion is that in matters of sexuality and reproduction, women are treated legally as men's property, while in all other aspects, they are legal persons in their own right.

until it is corroborated by their own experience. The silence of later preaching about the women's witness is not so surprising in the public speeches of Acts, located for the most part in public situations with unbelievers. Any respectable ancient eastern Mediterranean male would try to shield the women of his group from such public scrutiny and the risk of scorn. Paul's silence about the women in his enumeration of appearances in 1 Cor. 15.5-7, however, in the in-house environment of a group of Christian house churches, is more difficult to explain and will be discussed further below.[14]

A Feminist Analysis

We turn now to an analysis of our findings from the perspective of feminist hermeneutics. First, a hermeneutic of suspicion presupposes that a critical approach to the narratives is necessary in order to expose the androcentric bias operative in the selective transmission of the tradition.

Mark's silencing of the women in 16.8 is subject to many diverse interpretations. One effect, however, is to eliminate the women as witnesses and discredit their reliability. One way of reading the verse is that they did just the opposite of what they were commanded, creating the ultimate failure of discipleship and apostleship in Mark. While those earlier in the Gospel who were told not to proclaim what they had seen did so anyway (1.44-45; 7.36), now when proclamation is finally mandated, the women fail to do it.

What is far more serious, the denial of any historicity to the empty tomb stories completely dismisses the women's role in the original resurrection experience, for without the empty tomb, they play no part. Only the second ending of Mark, recognized by scholarly consensus as secondary and as late as the second century, does not explicitly locate the appearance of the risen Jesus to Mary Magdalene at the tomb (Mk 16.9).

Why did Paul and Acts pass over the empty tomb narratives, and therefore the role of the women, in complete silence? One of two alternative answers is usually given. First, the whole motif of the empty tomb is secondary and late, and Paul did not mention it because he did not know of it. Since it is not an apologetic story and offers no new proof on its own, it makes no difference whether there were men

---

14. At issue here is the symbolic location of the house church: a public gathering, as suggested by Paul's selection of the word ἐκκλησία, or a private, semi-household gathering, as suggested by its location in a private house.

or women at the tomb. This reason, of course, does not explain Luke's silence in Acts, for Luke surely knew the story and has already told it. Though the empty tomb seems presupposed twice in Acts (2.25-31; 13.34-37), it is never made an explicit part of the resurrection witness. The second reason offered, therefore, is that resurrection faith from the very beginning was based not on the empty tomb but on testimony to the appearances of the risen Christ, and it is to this that the earliest kerygma appealed. With this explanation the role of the empty tomb stories is moot; the empty tomb can stay, but it is simply not necessary. It enhances the meaning of the resurrection, but does not add further proof, for the simple reason that the explanation, without supernatural intervention, could just as well be that the body was stolen.

Still a third explanation offered is that Paul represents the combination of Luke's Jewish-Christian Jerusalem tradition with Paul's Hellenistic tradition that does not include the empty tomb, at the expense of others like the Johannine.[15] In this case, Mark and Matthew would represent a Galilean tradition that features the women who came from Galilee. Again, this is a possible explanation for Paul, but does not explain the silence regarding the empty tomb in the preaching of Acts. A fourth explanation, suggested above in part two, is that the empty tomb stories originated in women's circles, and had not yet made their way into the male kerygmatic tradition at the time of the writing of 1 Corinthians. Again, this does not explain the absence of the empty tomb motif in Acts.

However possible or probable some of the above explanations may be, none of them takes into account the effect of the elimination of the women's witness. Given the assumed androcentric bias of the accounts (which could have operated almost unconsciously and need not presume active misogyny), it is possible that the empty tomb stories are very old, but are passed over in silence by Paul and Acts precisely *because* they involve the testimony of women. That is, they are not considered as proof of the resurrection, not because faith is based on appearances, but rather the other way around: faith is based on appearances, not the empty tomb, because the empty tomb necessitates reliance on the credibility of women, whereas the abundant male experiences of appearances do not. It is significant for this argument that the appearances to women (Mt. 28.9-10; Jn 20.11-18) do not feature in 1 Cor. 15.5-7 either. Once the empty tomb is eliminated, it is

---

15. François Bovon, 'Le Privilège Pascal de Marie-Madeleine', *NTS* 30 (1984), pp. 50-62 (52).

not difficult to eliminate also the appearances to the women, which are tied to the tomb narratives and setting except in Mk 16.9.

Yet the empty tomb and the appearances to the women could not be completely eliminated, despite the evidence from Paul and Acts that this was tried. The authority of Mary Magdalene's testimony could not be so easily repressed in the memory of the early church, even if it did not develop until much later in orthodox circles. In other traditions, the tension between the developing authority of the twelve with Peter as their spokesman and that of Mary Magdalene as primary witness can be seen in such documents as *Gospel of Thomas* 114 and the fragmentary *Gospel of Mary*. In the former, a Coptic collection of Jesus' sayings from the gnostic Nag Hammadi library, Peter tried to dismiss Mary from the disciples as unworthy of eternal life. Jesus rebuked him by assuring that by becoming spiritual, that is, male, Mary too—and every female who makes herself male—will enter the kingdom of heaven. Whatever the symbolic meanings of female and male in this account, it is clear that the authority of Peter and that of Mary face off against each other, and Mary is included rather than rejected—but only at the expense of what modern interpreters would consider her integral feminine self.

The *Gospel of Mary*, preserved partially in Coptic from Nag Hammadi and partially in Greek from the early third century, includes Mary's communication to the disciples of the special revelation given her by the risen Christ, a frequent motif in gnostic gospels. But unlike most, here her testimony is followed by Peter's refusal to accept it, since he refused to believe that the Savior spoke to Mary rather than to him and the male disciples. He asked rather petulantly if Jesus preferred her to them. Peter was rebuked by Levi, who declared that the Savior knew her well and loved her more than them (*Gospel of Mary* 2-31). This time Mary is fully vindicated. These glimpses from the early church of traditions in competition, probably based on Jn 20.11-18, show how strong was the enduring memory of Mary Magdalene, and how much of a threat her memory was to those who would reject her authority.[16]

The stories of the events at the tomb from the experience and the memory of women erupt into the 'public' world and the public

---

16. See Gerald O'Collins and Daniel Kendall, 'Mary Magdalene as Major Witness to Jesus' Resurrection', *TS* 48 (1987), pp. 631-46; Martin Hengel, 'Maria Magdalena und die Frauen als Zeugen', in O. Betz, M. Hengel and P. Schmidt (eds.), *Abraham unser Vater: in Juden und Christen im Gespräch über die Bibel. Festschrift für Otto Michel zum 60. Geburtstag* (Leiden: E.J. Brill, 1963), pp. 243-56.

testimony of the written gospel accounts, prompting the celebration of a hermeneutic of remembrance. The empty tomb narratives mean that the least significant members of the community were entrusted with the first Easter encounter and the first mandate to proclaim it, reaffirming once more that the last shall be first and the poor shall be blessed. The women disciples who followed Jesus from Galilee to Jerusalem, even to his death on a cross, faithfully performed their *diakonia* of service, witness, and representation (Mk 15.40-41; Mt. 27.55-56; Lk. 8.1-3; 24.10). The empty tomb narrative is an epiphany story. It is the women's story, and they are the protagonists, for the story is about how they are changed, just as surely as Acts 9.1-19 is about how Paul is changed.[17]

The purpose of the empty tomb stories has less to do with proof than with meaning. The empty tomb indicates not the presence of Jesus (except in the two instances of appearances), but his absence: 'He is risen, he is not here'. Yet if the entire story is secondary, it surely would have disappeared, or at least the women would have vanished from it, for they and the story came to serve no kerygmatic purpose in the canonical tradition. But they remained because the memory of their role was so persistent that it could not be removed. Its very persistence must indicate that something actually happened that Sunday morning at the tomb.

17. Schottroff, *Let the Oppressed Go Free*, p. 183.

BIBLIOGRAPHY

Abel, E., 'Editor's Introduction', *Critical Inquiry* 8 (1981), pp. 179-84.
Abrams, M.H., *A Glossary of Literary Terms* (New York: Holt, Rinehart and Winston, 4th edn, 1981).
Abu-Lughod, L., *Veiled Sentiments: Honor and Poetry in a Bedouin Society* (Berkeley: University of California Press, 1986).
Albertz, R., *Persönliche Frömmigkeit und offizielle Religion* (CTM, 9; Stuttgart: Calwer Verlag, 1978).
Albright, W.F., and C.S. Mann, *Matthew: Introduction, Translation and Notes* (AB, 26; Garden City, NY: Doubleday, 1971).
Allen, W.C., *A Critical and Exegetical Commentary on the Gospel According to St. Matthew* (ICC, 26; Edinburgh: T. & T. Clark, 1907).
Anderson, J. Capel, 'Feminist Criticism: The "Dancing Daughter"', in J. Capel Anderson and S.D. Moore (eds.), *Mark and Method* (Minneapolis: Fortress Press, 1992), pp. 103-34.
—'Matthew: Gender and Reading', *Semeia* 28 (1983), pp. 3-27.
—'Over and Over and Over Again: Studies in Matthean Repetition' (PhD dissertation, University of Chicago, 1983).
—'Point of View in Matthew: Evidence' (paper delivered at SBL Symposium on the Literary Analysis of the Gospels and Acts, December, 1981).
Argyle, A.W., *The Gospel According to Matthew* (Cambridge Bible Commentary: Cambridge: Cambridge University Press, 1963).
—'Wedding Customs in the Time of Jesus', *ExpTim* 86 (April 1975), pp. 214-15.
Bach, A., *Women, Seduction, and Betrayal in Biblical Narrative* (Cambridge: Cambridge University Press, 1997), pp. 224-62.
Bacon, B.W., *Studies in Matthew* (London: Constable, 1930).
Baer, R.A., *Philo's Use of the Categories of Male and Female* (Leiden: E.J. Brill, 1970).
Baker, R., *Binding the Devil: Exorcism Past and Present* (New York: Hawthorn Books, 1974).
Balz, H., and G. Schneider (eds.), *Exegetical Dictionary of the New Testament* (3 vols.; Grand Rapids: Eerdmans, 1990).
Barth, G., 'Matthew's Understanding of the Law', P. Scott (trans.), in G. Bornkamm *et al.* (eds.), *Tradition and Interpretation in Matthew* (London: SCM Press, 1982), pp. 58-164.
Bauer, D.R., and M.A. Powell (eds.), *Treasures New and Old: Recent Contributions to Matthean Studies* (Atlanta: Scholars Press, 1996).
Baum, J., and H. Schmidt-Glasner, *German Cathedrals* (New York: Vanguard Press, 1956).
Begrich, J., 'Das priesterliche Heilsorakel', *ZAW* 52 (1934), pp. 81-92.
—'Das priesterliche Heilsorakel', in W. Zimmerli (ed.), *Gesammelte Studien zum Alten Testament* (Munich: Chr. Kaiser Verlag, 1964), pp. 217-31.

Berger, P., *The Sacred Canopy: Elements of a Sociological Theory of Religion* (Garden City, NY: Doubleday, 1969).
Beyer, H.W., 'θεραπαία, θεραπεύω, θεράπων', *TDNT*, III, pp. 128-32.
Bieber, M., '*Honos* and *Virtus*', *AJA* 49 (1945), pp. 25-34.
Bishops' Conference on the Liturgy, National Conference of Catholic Bishops (ed.), *The Roman Missal: Lectionary for the Mass* (New York: Catholic Book Publishing, 1970).
Black, M., *Models and Metaphors* (Ithaca, NY: Cornell University Press, 1962).
Böcher, O., 'γέεννα', in Balz and Schneider (eds.), *Exegetical Dictionary*, I, pp. 239-40.
Bode, E.L., *The First Easter Morning: The Gospel Accounts of the Women's Visit to the Tomb of Jesus* (AnBib, 45; Rome: Pontifical Biblical Institute, 1970).
Boers, H., *Neither on This Mountain nor in Jerusalem* (SBLMS, 35; Atlanta: Scholars Press, 1988).
Booth, W., *Critical Understanding* (Chicago: University of Chicago Press, 1979).
—*The Rhetoric of Fiction* (Chicago: University of Chicago Press, 1961).
Borg, M., *Jesus in Contemporary Scholarship* (Valley Forge, PA: Trinity Press International, 1994).
Bornkamm, G., 'End-Expectation and Church in Matthew', in Bornkamm, *et al.* (eds.), *Tradition and Interpretation in Matthew*, pp. 41-43.
Bornkamm, G., G. Barth, and H.J. Held, *Tradition and Interpretation in Matthew* (trans. P. Scott; London: SCM Press; Philadelphia: Westminster Press, 1963).
Borsch, F.H., *Many Things in Parables* (Philadelphia: Fortress Press, 1988).
Bovon, F., 'Le Privilège Pascal de Marie-Madeleine', *NTS* 30 (1984), pp. 50-62.
Boyarin, D., *Carnal Israel: Reading Sex in Talmudic Culture* (Berkeley: University of California Press, 1993).
Braidotti, R., 'What's Wrong with Gender?', in F. van Dijk-Hemmes and A. Brenner (eds.), *Reflections on Theology and Gender* (Kampen: Kok, 1994), pp. 49-67.
Brown, R.E., *The Birth of the Messiah: A Commentary on the Infancy Narratives in Matthew and Luke* (Garden City, NY: Doubleday, 1977).
—*The Churches the Apostles Left Behind* (New York: Paulist Press, 1984).
—*The Death of the Messiah: A Commentary on the Passion Narratives in the Four Gospels*, II (New York: Doubleday, 1994).
Brueggemann, W., *Israel's Praise: Doxology Against Idolatry and Ideology* (Philadelphia: Fortress Press, 1988).
—*The Message of the Psalms* (Minneapolis: Augsburg, 1984).
Bultmann, R. *History of the Synoptic Tradition* (trans. J. Marsh; Oxford: Basil Blackwell; New York: Harper & Row, 1963; 2nd edn, 1968).
—'Der religionsgeschichtliche Hintergrund des Prologs zum Johannes-Evangelium', in H. Schmidt (ed.), *Eucharisterion: Studien zur Religion und Literatur des Alten und Neuen Testaments* (Göttingen: Vandenhoeck & Ruprecht, 1923), pp. 1-11.
Burrus, V., *Chastity as Autonomy: Women in the Stories of the Apocryphal Acts* (Studies in Women and Religion, 23; Lewiston, NY: Edwin Mellen Press, 1987).
Bynum, C. Walker, 'Women's Stories, Women's Symbols: A Critique of Victor Turner's Theory of Liminality', in R.L. Moore and F.E. Reynolds (eds.), *Anthropology and the Study of Religion* (Chicago: Center for the Scientific Study of Religion, 1984), pp. 104-25.

Cady, S., M. Ronan, and H. Taussig, *Sophia: The Future of Feminist Spirituality* (San Francisco: Harper & Row, 1986).
—*Wisdom's Feast: Sophia in Study and Celebration* (San Francisco: Harper & Row, 1989).
Calloway, J., 'Burials in Palestine: From the Stone Age to Abraham', *BA* 26 (1963), pp. 74-91.
Cameron, R., *The Other Gospels: Non-Canonical Gospel Texts* (Philadelphia: Westminster Press, 1982).
Camp, C., 'The Female Sage in Ancient Israel and in the Biblical Wisdom Literature', in Gammie and Perdue (eds.), *The Sage in Israel and the Ancient Near East*, pp. 185-203.
—'Understanding a Patriarchy: Women in Second Century Jerusalem through the Eyes of Ben Sira', in Levine (ed.), *Women Like This*, pp. 1-39.
—*Wisdom and the Feminine in the Book of Proverbs* (Bible and Literature, 11; Sheffield: Almond Press, 1985).
Canterella, E., *Pandora's Daughters: The Role and Status of Women in Greek and Roman Antiquity* (trans. M.B. Fant; Baltimore: The Johns Hopkins University Press, 1987).
Caraveli, A., 'The Bitter Wounding: The Lament as Social Protest in Rural Greece', in J. Dubisch (ed.), *Gender and Power in Rural Greece* (Princeton, NJ: Princeton University Press, 1986), pp. 169-94.
Carter, W., *Households and Discipleship: A Study of Matthew 19–20* (JSNTSup, 103; Sheffield: JSOT Press, 1994).
Chesnutt, R.D., 'Revelatory Experiences Attributed to Biblical Women in Early Jewish Literature', in Levine (ed.), *Women Like This*, pp. 107-25.
Christ, C., 'Women's Studies in Religion', *CSRBull* 10 (1979), pp. 3-5.
Cohen, S.J.D., 'Menstruants and the Sacred in Judaism and Christianity', in S.B. Pomeroy (ed.), *Women's History and Ancient History* (Chapel Hill, NC: University of North Carolina Press, 1991), pp. 273-99.
—'Purity and Piety: The Separation of Menstruants from the Sancta', in S. Groomsman and R. Haute (eds.), *Daughters of the King/Women and the Synagogue: A Survey of History and Contemporary Localities* (Philadelphia: Jewish Publication Society, 1992), pp. 103-15.
Collins, A.Y., 'The Empty Tomb and Resurrection According to Mark', in eadem, *The Beginning of the Gospel: Probings of Mark in Context* (Minneapolis: Fortress Press, 1992), pp. 119-48.
Conkey, M.W., and J.M. Gero, 'Tensions, Pluralities, and Engendering Archaeology: An Introduction to Women and Prehistory', in J.M. Gero and M.W. Conkey (eds.), *Engendering Archaeology: Women and Prehistory* (Oxford: Basil Blackwell, 1991), pp. 3-30.
Conrad, E., *Fear Not Warrior: A Study of 'al tira' Pericopes in the Hebrew Scriptures* (Chico, CA: Scholars Press, 1985).
—'Second Isaiah and the Priestly Oracle of Salvation [Reply to J. Begrich]', *ZAW* 93 (1981), pp. 234-46.
Conzelmann, H., 'The Mother of Wisdom', in J.M. Robinson (ed.), *The Future of Our Religious Past* (trans. C.E. Carlston and R.P. Scharlemann; London: SCM Press, 1971), pp. 230-43.
Cope, O.L., *Matthew: A Scribe Trained for the Kingdom of Heaven* (CBQMS, 5; Washington, DC: Catholic Biblical Association of America, 1976).

Corley, K.E. 'Women and the Crucifixion and Burial of Jesus', *Forum* NS 1 (1998), pp. 190-96.
Coser, L., *The Functions of Social Conflict* (Glencoe, IL: Free Press, 1956).
Countryman, L.W., *Dirt Greed and Sex: Sexual Ethics in the New Testament and Their Implications for Today* (Philadelphia: Fortress Press, 1988).
Crossan, J.D., *The Cross That Spoke: The Origins of the Passion Narrative* (San Francisco: Harper & Row, 1988).
—*Who Killed Jesus? Exposing the Roots of Anti-Semitism in the Gospel Story of the Death of Jesus* (San Francisco: HarperSanFrancisco, 1995).
Cummings, J.T., 'The Tassel of his Cloak: Mark, Luke, Matthew—and Zechariah', in E.A. Livingstone (ed.), *Studia Biblica 1978. II. Papers on the Gospels* (JSNTSup, 2; Sheffield: JSOT Press, 1980).
Da Gallarate, G., 'Le dieci vergini', in *Il regno dei cieli* (Brescia: Editrice Franciscanum, 1968), pp. 192-96.
D'Angelo, M.R., 'Abba and "Father": Imperial Theology and the Jesus Traditions', *JBL* 111.4 (1992), pp. 611-30.
—'Gender and Power in the Gospel of Mark: The Daughter of Jairus and the Woman with the Flow of Blood', in J.C. Cavadini (ed.), *Miracles in Jewish and Christian Antiquity: Imagining Truth* (Notre Dame: Indiana University Press, 1999).
—'Women Partners in the New Testament', *JFSR* 6 (1990), pp. 65-86.
Davies, S.L., *The Revolt of the Widows: The Social World of the Apocryphal Acts* (Carbondale, IL: Southern Illinois University Press, 1980).
Davies, W.D., *The Setting of the Sermon on the Mount* (Cambridge: Cambridge University Press, 1964).
Davies, W.D., and D.C. Allison, Jr, *A Critical and Exegetical Commentary on the Gospel According to Matthew* (3 vols.; ICC, 26; Edinburgh: T. & T. Clark, 1988, 1991, 1997).
De Groot van Houten, C., 'Pondering the Word', *Perspectives* (August/September 1994), pp. 13-47.
Derrett, J.D.M., 'Law in the New Testament: The Syrophoenician Woman and the Centurion of Capernaum', *NovT* 15 (1973), pp. 162-73.
Deutsch, C., *Hidden Wisdom and the Easy Yoke: Wisdom, Torah and Discipleship in Matthew 11.25-30* (JSNTSup, 18; Sheffield: Sheffield Academic Press, 1987).
—*Lady Wisdom, Jesus, and the Sages; Metaphor and Social Context in Matthew's Gospel* (Valley Forge, PA: Trinity Press International, 1996).
—'The Sirach 51 Acrostic: Confession and Exhortation', *ZAW* 94 (1982), pp. 400-409.
—'The Transfiguration: Vision and Social Setting in Matthew's Gospel (Matthew 17.1-9)', in V. Wiles *et al.* (eds.), *Putting Body and Soul Together: Essays in Honor of Robin Scroggs* (Valley Forge, PA: Trinity Press International, 1997), pp. 124-37.
—'Wisdom in Matthew: Transformation of a Symbol', *NovT* 32 (1990), pp. 13-47.
Dibelius, M., *From Tradition to Gospel* (New York: Charles Scribner's Sons, 1965).
Dodd, C.H., *The Parables of the Kingdom* (New York: Charles Scribner's Sons, 1969).
Donahue, J., *The Gospel in Parable: Metaphor, Narrative, and Theology in the Synoptic Gospels* (Philadelphia: Fortress Press, 1988).
Dube, M.W., 'Readings of *Semoya*: Batswana Women's Interpretations of Matt. 15:21-28', *Semeia* 73 (1996), pp. 111-30.

Dubisch, J., *Gender and Power in Rural Greece* (Princeton: Princeton University Press, 1986).
Duff, N.J., 'Wise and Foolish Maidens (Matthew 25.1-13)', *USQR* 40 (1985), pp. 55-58.
Duling, D.C., 'The Eleazar Miracle and Solomon's Magical Wisdom in Flavius Josephus's *Antiquitates Judaicai* 8.42-49', *HTR* 78 (1985), pp. 1-25.
—'The Matthean Brotherhood and Marginal Scribal Leadership', in P.F. Esler (ed.), *Modelling Early Christianity: Social Scientific Studies of the New Testament in Its Context* (London: Routledge, 1995), pp. 159-82.
—'Matthew's Plurisignificant "Son of David" in Social Scientific Perspective: Kinship, Kingship, Magic and Miracle', *BTB* 22 (1992), pp. 99-116.
—'Solomon, Exorcism, and the Son of David', *HTR* 68 (1975), pp. 235-52.
—'The Therapeutic Son of David: An Element in Matthew's Christological Apologetic', *NTS* 24 (1978), pp. 392-410.
Engelsman, J.C., *The Feminine Dimension of the Divine* (Philadelphia: Westminster Press, 1979).
Farmer, W.R., *The Gospel of Jesus: The Pastoral Significance of the Synoptic Problem* (Louisville, KY: Westminster/John Knox Press, 1994).
Fears, J.R., 'The Cult of Virtues and Roman Imperial Ideology', *ANRW*, II, pp. 827-948.
Fetterley, J., *The Resisting Reader: A Feminist Approach to American Fiction* (Bloomington: Indiana University Press, 1978).
Fineman, J., 'The History of the Anecdote: Fiction and Fiction', in H.A. Veeser (ed.), *The New Historicism* (New York: Routledge, 1989), pp. 49-76.
Fiorenza, E.S., *In Memory of Her: A Feminist Theological Reconstruction of Christian Origins* (New York: Crossroad, 1985).
—*Jesus: Miriam's Child, Sophia's Prophet: Critical Issues in Feminist Christology* (New York: Continuum, 1994).
—'Luke 2:41-52', *Int* 36 (1982), pp. 399-403.
—'Toward a Feminist Biblical Hermeneutics: Biblical Interpretation and Liberation Theology', in B. Mahan and L.D. Richesin (eds.), *The Challenge of Liberation Theology: A First World Response* (Maryknoll, NY: Orbis Books, 1981), pp. 91-112.
Fitzmyer, J., *The Gospel According to Luke I-IX* (AB, 28; New York: Doubleday, 1981).
Frankenmölle, H., 'λαός', in Balz and Schneider (eds.), *Exegetical Dictionary*, II, pp. 339-44.
Fredriksen, P., 'Did Jesus Oppose the Purity Laws?', *BR* 11 (1995), pp. 18-25, 42-47.
—*From Jesus to Christ* (New Haven: Yale University Press, 1988).
Frye, N., *The Great Code: The Bible and Literature* (San Diego, CA: Harcourt, Brace, Jovanovich, 1982).
Frymer-Kensky, T., *In the Wake of the Goddesses: Women, Culture and the Biblical Transformation of Pagan Myth* (New York: Free Press, 1992).
Fuller, R.H., *The Formation of the Resurrection Narratives* (New York: Macmillan, 1971), pp. 50-70.
Gammie, J.G., and L.G. Perdue (eds.), *The Sage in Israel and the Ancient Near East* (Winona Lake, IN: Eisenbrauns, 1990).
Garland, D., *Reading Matthew: A Literary and Theological Commentary on the First Gospel* (New York: Crossroad, 1993).

Garrett, S.R., *The Demise of the Devil: Magic and the Demonic in Luke's Writings* (Minneapolis: Fortress Press, 1989).
Geertz, C., *The Interpretation of Cultures: Selected Essays by Clifford Geertz* (New York: Basic Books, 1973).
Gench, F.T., *Wisdom in the Christology of Matthew* (Lanham, MD: University Press of America, 1997).
Gerstenberger, G., *Der bittende Mensch* (Neukirchen–Vluyn: Neukirchener Verlag, 1980).
Gibbs, J.M., 'Purpose and Pattern in Matthew's Use of the Title "Son of David"', *NTS* 10 (1963–64), pp. 446-64.
Gilhus, I.S., 'Religion, Laughter and the Ludicrous', *Rel* 21 (1991), pp. 257-77.
Gnilka, J., *Das Matthaüsevangelium* (Freiburg: Herder, 1988).
Goodblatt, D., 'The Beruriah Traditions', *JJS* 26 (1975), pp. 68-85.
Goodfriend, E.A., 'Prostitution', *ABD*, V, pp. 505-10.
Goulder, M.D., 'The Empty Tomb', *Theology* 79 (1976), pp. 206-14.
—*Midrash and Lection in Matthew* (London: SPCK, 1974).
—'Mark xvi.1-8 and Parallels', *NTS* 24 (1978), pp. 235-40.
Green, H.B., *The Gospel According to Matthew* (The New Clarendon Bible; Oxford: Oxford University Press, 1975).
Greimas, A.J., and J. Cortes, *Semantics and Language* (Bloomington: Indiana University Press, 1982).
Guardiola-Saenz, L.A., 'Borderless Women and Borderless Texts: A Cultural Reading of Matthew 15.21-28', *Semeia* 78 (1997), pp. 69-81.
Gundry, R., *Matthew: A Commentary on His Literary and Theological Art* (Grand Rapids: Eerdmans, 1982).
Gunkel, H., *Einleitung in die Psalmen* (Göttingen: Vandenhoeck & Ruprecht, 1933).
Hagner, D., *Matthew 1–13* (WBC, 33a; Dallas, TX: Word Books, 1993).
Hamerton-Kelly, R., *Pre-existence, Wisdom and the Son of Man: A Study of the Idea of Pre-existence in the New Testament* (SNTMS, 21; Cambridge: Cambridge University Press, 1973).
Harrington, D.J., *The Gospel of Matthew* (Sacra Pagina, 1; Collegeville, MN: Liturgical Press, 1991).
Harris, W.V., *Ancient Literacy* (Cambridge, MA: Harvard University Press, 1989).
Hawkins, J.C., *Horae Synopticae* (Oxford: Clarendon Press, 2nd edn, 1968).
Held, H.J., 'The Miracle Stories as Witnesses for Matthew's Christology', in G. Bornkamm, G. Barth, and H.J. Held (eds.), *Tradition and Interpretation in Matthew*, pp. 246-75.
—'The Retelling of Miracle Stories', in G. Bornkamm, G. Barth, and H.J. Held, *Tradition and Interpretation in Matthew*, pp. 165-211.
Hengel, M., 'Jesus als messianischer Lehrer der Weisheit und die Anfänge der Christologie', in *Sagesse et Religion; Colloque de Strasbourg, 1976* (Paris: Presses Universitaires de France, 1979), pp. 147-88.
—*Judaism and Hellenism: Studies in their Encounter in Palestine during the Early Hellenistic Period* (trans. J. Bowden; Philadelphia: Fortress Press, 1974).
—'Maria Magdalena und die Frauen als Zeugen', in O. Betz, M. Hengel, and P. Schmidt (eds.), *Abraham unser Vater: Juden und Christen im Gespräch über die Bibel. Festschrift für Otto Michel zum 60. Geburtstag* (Leiden: E.J. Brill, 1963), pp. 243-56.

Henle, P., 'Metaphor', in P. Henle (ed.), *Language, Thought, and Culture* (Binghamton, NY: Vail-Ballou, 1958), pp. 173-95.
Henry, M.M., 'The Edible Woman: Athenaeus's Concept of the Pornographic', in A. Richlin (ed.), *Pornography and Representation* (New York: Oxford University Press, 1992), pp. 250-68.
Hiers, R.H., 'Satan, Demons, and the Kingdom of God', *SJT* 27 (1974), pp. 35-47.
Hill, D., *The Gospel of Matthew* (NCB; Grand Rapids: Eerdmans, 1972).
Hoffmann, P., *Studien zur Theologie der Logienquelle* (NTAbh, 8; Münster: Aschendorff, 1972).
Holst-Warhaft, G., *Dangerous Voices: Women's Laments and Greek Literature* (London: Routledge, 1992).
Horsley, R.A., 'Spiritual Marriage with Sophia', *VC* 33 (1979), pp. 30-54.
Humphries-Brooks, S., 'Indicators of Social Organization and Status in Matthew's Gospel', in E.J. Lovering (ed.), *SBLSP* 30 (Atlanta: Scholars Press, 1991), pp. 31-49.
—'Matthew', in W.E. Mills and R.F. Wilson (eds.), *Mercer Commentary on the Bible* (Macon, GA: Mercer University Press, 1995).
—'Spatial Form and Plot Disruption in the Gospel of Matthew', *Essays in Literature* 20 (1993), pp. 54-59.
Hummel, R., *Die Auseinandersetzung zwischen Kirche and Judentum im Mattäusevangelium* (Munich: Chr. Kaiser Verlag, 1963).
Irigaray, L., 'Questions to Emmanuel Levinas on the Divinity of Love', in R. Bernasconi and S. Critchley (eds.), *Re-Reading Levinas* (trans. M. Whitford; Bloomington: Indiana University Press, 1991), pp. 109-18.
Iser, W., *The Act of Reading* (Baltimore: The Johns Hopkins University Press, 1978).
—*The Implied Reader* (Baltimore: The Johns Hopkins University Press, 1974).
Jaussen, J.A., *Coutumes palestiniennes, Naplouse et son district* (Paris: Guethner, 1927).
Jeremias, J., *The Parables of Jesus* (trans. S.H. Hooke; New York: Charles Scribner's Sons, 1955).
Johnson, L.T., 'The New Testament's Anti-Jewish Slander and the Conventions of Ancient Polemic', *JBL* 108 (1989), pp. 419-41.
Johnson, M.D., 'Reflections on a Wisdom Approach to Matthew's Christology', *CBQ* 36 (1974), pp. 44-64.
Johnson, S.E., 'The Gospel According to St. Matthew: Introduction and Exegesis', (IB, 7; Nashville: Abingdon Press, 1951).
Kelly-Gadol, J., 'The Social Relations of the Sexes: Methodological Implications of Women's History', *Signs* 1 (1976), pp. 809-24.
Keynest, G., *Blake: The Pitman Gallery* (New York: Pitman Publishing Corporation, 1949).
Kingsbury, J.D., *Matthew: Stucture, Christology, Kingdom* (Philadelphia: Fortress Press, 1975; London: SPCK, 1976).
—'The "Miracle Chapters" of Matthew 8-9', *CBQ* 40 (1978), pp. 559-73.
—'The Title "Son of David" in Matthew's Gospel', *JBL* 95 (1976), pp. 591-602.
—'The Verb *Akolouthein* ("to Follow") as an Index of Matthew's View of His Community', *JBL* 97 (1978), pp. 56-73.
Kleinman, A., *Patients and Healers in the Context of Culture: An Exploration of the Borderland between Anthropology, Medicine and Psychiatry* (Comparative Studies

of Health Systems and Medical Care; Berkeley: University of California Press, 1980).

Kloppenborg, J.S., 'Collegia and *Thiasoi*: Issues in Function, Taxonomy and Membership', in J.S. Kloppenborg and S.G. Wilson (eds.), *Voluntary Associations in the Graeco-Roman World* (London: Routledge, 1996), pp. 16-30.

—'The Dishonored Master (Luke 16. 1-8a)', *Bib* 70 (1989), pp. 474-95.

—*The Formation of Q: Trajectories in Ancient Wisdom Collections* (Studies in Antiquity and Christianity; Philadelphia: Fortress Press, 1987).

—'Wisdom Christology in Q', *LTP* 34 (1978), pp. 139-47.

Kohler, K., '"Abba", Father; Title of Spiritual Leader and Saint', in H.Z. Dimitrovsky (ed.), *Exploring the Talmud*. I. *Education* (New York: Ktav, 1976), pp. 150-63.

Kolodny, A., 'A Map for Re-Reading: Or, Gender and the Interpretation of Literary Texts', *New Literary History* 11 (1980), pp. 329-45 (345).

—'Turning the Lens on "The Panther Captivity": A Feminist Exercise in Practical Criticism', *Critical Inquiry* 8 (1981), pp. 329-45.

Kosky, B., *Barrie Kosky's King Lear by William Shakespeare* (Queensland Theatre Company, nd).

Kraemer, R.S., *Her Share of the Blessings: Women's Religions among Pagans, Jews, and Christians in the Greco-Roman World* (New York: Oxford University Press, 1992).

Lee, B.J., *Jesus and the Metaphors of God: The Christs of the New Testament* (New York: Paulist Press, 1993).

Lefkowitz, M.R., and M.B. Fant, *Women's Life in Greece and Rome: A Source Book in Translation* (Baltimore: The Johns Hopkins University Press, 2nd edn, 1992).

Levenson, J., 'Is There a Counterpart in the Hebrew Bible to New Testament Antisemitism?', *JES* 22 (1985), pp. 243-60.

Levine, A.-J., 'Discharging Responsibility: Matthean Jesus, Biblical Law, and Hemorrhaging Woman', in D.R. Bauer and M.A. Powell (eds.), *Treasures New and Old: Contributions to Matthean Studies* (Altanta: Scholars Press, 1996), pp. 379-97.

—'Matthew', in C.A. Newsom and S.H. Ringe (eds.), *The Women's Bible Commentary* (London: SPCK; Louisville, KY: Westminster/John Knox Press, 1992), pp. 252-62.

—'Matthew's Advice to a Divided Readership', in D. Aune (ed.), *The Gospel of Matthew in Current Study* (Grand Rapids: Eerdmans, 2000), pp. 22-41.

—*The Social and Ethnic Dimensions of Matthean Salvation History: "Go Nowhere among the Gentiles..." (Matt 10:5b)* (Studies in the Bible and Early Christianity, 14; Lewiston, NY: Edwin Mellen Press, 1988).

—'Who's Catering the Q Affair? Feminist Observations on Q Paraenesis', *Semeia* 50 (1990), pp. 145-61.

—(ed.), *'Women Like This': New Perspectives on Jewish Women in the Greco-Roman World* (Atlanta: Scholars Press, 1991).

Longstaff, T., 'The Women at the Tomb: Matthew 28.1 Re-Examined', *NTS* 27.2 (1981), pp. 277-82.

Luz, U., 'The Disciples in the Gospel According to Matthew', in G. Stanton (ed.), *The Interpretation of Matthew* (Issues in Theology and Religion, 3; Philadelphia: Fortress Press, 1983), pp. 98-128.

___ 'Die Jünger im Matthäusevangelium', *ZNW* 62 (1971), pp. 141-71.
___ *Matthew 1-7* (Minneapolis: Augsburg, 1989).
MacDonald, D.R., *The Legend and the Apostle: The Battle for Paul in Story and Canon* (Philadelphia: Westminster Press, 1983).
Mack, B.L., 'Wisdom Myth and Mythology', *Int* 24 (1970), pp. 46-60.
Mack, B.L., and V.K. Robbins, *Patterns of Persuasion in the Gospels* (Sonoma, CA: Polebridge, 1989).
Malbon, E.S., 'Narrative Criticism: How Does the Story Mean?', in J.C. Anderson and S.D. Moore (eds.), *Mark & Method* (Minneapolis: Fortress Press, 1992), pp. 23-49.
Malbon, E.S., and E.V. McKnight (eds.), *New Literary Criticism and the New Testament* (JSNTSup, 109; Sheffield: Sheffield Academic Press, 1994), pp. 145-63.
Malina, B.J., 'Humility', in J.J. Pilch and B.J. Malina (eds.), *Biblical Social Values and their Meaning: A Handbook* (Peabody, MA: Hendrickson, 1993), pp. 107-108.
McKane, W., *Proverbs: A New Approach* (Philadelphia: Westminster Press, 1970).
McNeile, A.H., *The Gospel According to St. Matthew* (Grand Rapids: Baker Book House, 1980 [1915]).
Meeks, W., 'The Image of the Androgyne: Some Uses of a Symbol in Earliest Christianity', *HR* 13 (1974), pp. 165-208.
Meiselman, M., *Jewish Woman in Jewish Law* (New York: Ktav, 1978).
Mendilow, A.A., *Time and the Novel* (New York: Humanities Press, 1965).
Merton, T., *The Collected Poems of Thomas Merton* (trans. W. Davis; New York: New Directions, 1977).
Metzger, B.M., *A Textual Commentary on the Greek New Testament* (London: United Bible Societies, 1971; Stuttgart: United Bible Societies, 1975).
Meyers, E.M., *Jewish Ossuaries: Reburial and Rebirth. Secondary Burials in their Ancient Near Eastern Setting* (BibOr, 24; Rome: Biblical Institute Press, 1971).
—'Secondary Burials in Palestine', *BA* 33 (1970), pp. 2-29.
Micklem, P.A., *St. Matthew* (Westminster Commentaries; London: Methuen, 1917).
Milgrom, J., *Leviticus I-XVI* (AB, 3; New York: Doubleday, 1991).
Minear, P.S., 'The Disciples and the Crowds in the Gospel of Matthew', *ATRSup* 3 (1974), pp. 28-44.
Moi, T., *Sexual/Textual Politics: Feminist Literary Theory* (London: Routledge, 1991).
Moltmann-Wendel, E., *The Women around Jesus: Reflections on Authentic Personhood* (London: SCM Press, 1982).
Montefiore, C.J.G., *The Synoptic Gospels*, II (London: Macmillan, 1909).
Mowery, R., 'The Disappearance of the Father: The References to God the Father in Luke-Acts' (SBL paper, San Francisco, CA, November 1992).
—'God, Lord and Father: The Theology of the Gospel of Matthew', *BibRes* 33 (1988), pp. 24-36.
Muilenburg, J., 'Form Criticism and Beyond', *JBL* 88 (1969), pp. 1-18.
Mulack, C., *In Anfang war die Weisheit; feministische Kritik des männlichen Gottesbildes* (Stuttgart: Kreuz Verlag, 1988).
Murray, O. (ed.), *Sympotica: A Symposium on the Symposion* (Oxford: Clarendon Press, 1990).
Neirynck, F., 'Marc 16, 1-8 tradition et redaction', *ETL* 56 (1980), pp. 56-88.
Nel, P., 'The Concept "Father" in the Wisdom Literature of the Ancient Near East', *JNSL* 5 (1977), pp. 53-66.

Newman, B., 'The Pilgrimage of Christ-Sophia', *Vox Benedictina* 9 (1992), pp. 9-18.
Newsom, C.A., 'A Maker of Metaphors—Ezekiel's Oracle Against Tyre', *Int* 38 (1984), pp. 151-64.
—'Woman and the Discourse of Patriarchal Wisdom: A Study of Proverbs 1-9', in P. Day (ed.), *Gender and Difference in Ancient Israel* (Minneapolis: Fortress Press, 1989), pp. 142-60.
Neyrey, J.H., *Honor and Shame in the Gospel of Matthew* (Louisville, KY: Westminster/John Knox Press, 1998).
Nickelsburg, G.W.E., 'The Apocalyptic Message of 1 Enoch 92-105', *CBQ* 39 (1977), pp. 309-28.
—'Enoch, Levi, and Peter: Recipients of Revelation in Upper Galilee', *JBL* 100 (1981), pp. 575-600.
—*Resurrection, Immortality, and Eternal Life in Intertestamental Judaism* (Cambridge, MA: Harvard University Press, 1972).
O'Collins, G., and D. Kendall, 'Mary Magdalene as Major Witness to Jesus' Resurrection', *TS* 48 (1987), pp. 631-46.
O'Day, G.R., *Revelation in the Fourth Gospel* (Philadelphia: Fortress Press, 1986).
Oepke, A., 'ἰάομαι', TDNT, III, pp. 194-215.
Orton, D., *The Understanding Scribe: Matthew and the Apocalyptic Ideal* (JSNTSup, 25; Sheffield: JSOT Press, 1989).
Overman, J.A., *Matthew's Gospel and Formative Judaism: The Social World of the Matthean Community* (Minneapolis: Fortress Press, 1990).
Padel, R., 'Women: Model for Possession by Greek Daemons', in A. Cameron and A. Khurt (eds.), *Images of Women in Antiquity* (London: Croom Helm, 1983), pp. 3-19.
Pagels, E., *The Gnostic Gospels* (New York: Random House, 1979).
Perkins, P., *Resurrection: New Testament Witness and Contemporary Reflection* (Garden City, NY: Doubleday, 1984).
Perkinson, J., 'A Canaanitic Word in the Logos of Christ: or the Difference the Syro-Phoenician Woman Makes to Jesus', *Semeia* 75 (1996), pp. 61-85.
Perrin, N., *The Resurrection According to Matthew, Mark and Luke* (Philadelphia: Fortress Press, 1977).
Perrine, L., *Sound and Sense: An Introduction to Poetry* (San Diego, CA: Harcourt Brace Jovanovich, 6th edn, 1982).
Petersen, N., *Literary Criticism for New Testament Critics* (Philadelphia: Fortress Press, 1978).
___ 'Point of View in Mark's Narrative', *Semeia* 12 (1978), pp. 97-121.
Pilch, J.J. 'Understanding Biblical Healing: Selecting the Appropriate Model', *BTB* 18 (1988), pp. 60-66.
—'Understanding Healing in the Social World of Early Christianity', *BTB* 22 (1992), pp. 26-33.
Pirot, J., 'Les dix vierges surprises par l'époux', in *Paraboles et allegories evangeliques*, (Paris: P. Lethielleux, 1949), pp. 429-48.
Pomeroy, S.B., *Goddesses, Whores, Wives and Slaves: Women in Classical Antiquity* (New York: Schocken Books, 1975).
—*Women in Hellenistic Egypt from Alexander to Cleopatra* (New York: Schocken Books, 1984).
Proctor-Smith, M., 'Images of Women in the Lectionary', *Concilium* 182 (1985), pp. 51-62.

Puig i Tàrrech, A., *La parabole des dix vierges (Matt. 25.1-13)* (AnBib, 102; Rome: Biblical Institute Press, 1983).

Rabbinowitz, R.J., '"Ebal Rabbathi Named Masseketh Semahoth: Tractate on Mourning', in A. Cohen (ed.), *The Minor Tractates of the Talmud* (London: Soncino, 1971), I, pp. 325-400.

Rahmani, L.Y., 'Ancient Jerusalem's Funerary Customs and Tombs', *BA* 44 (1981), pp. 171-77.

—'Jewish Rock-Cut Tombs in Jerusalem', *Atiqot* English Series 3 (1961), pp. 93-120.

Ricoeur, P., *The Rule of Metaphor* (trans. R. Czerny; Toronto: University of Toronto Press, 1977).

Rigato, M.-L., '"Remember... Then They Remembered": Luke 24:6-8', in G. O'Collins and G. Marconi (eds.), *Luke and Acts* (Mahwah, NJ: Paulist Press, 1993), pp. 93-101, 232-35.

Ringgren, H., *Word and Wisdom* (Lund: Haken Ohlssons, 1947).

Robinson, J.M., 'Jesus as Sophos and Sophia', in R.L. Wilken (ed.), *Aspects of Wisdom in Judaism and Early Christianity* (SJCA, 1; Notre Dame: University of Notre Dame Press, 1975), pp. 1-16.

—'Very Goddess and Very Man: Jesus' Better Self', in K. King (ed.), *Images of the Feminine in Gnosticism* (Philadelphia: Fortress Press, 1988), pp. 115-23.

Robinson, T.H., *The Gospel of Matthew* (London: Hodder & Stoughton, 1928).

Rosaldo, M. Zimbalist, 'Woman, Culture, and Society: A Theoretical Overview', in M.Z. Rosaldo and L. Lamphere (eds.), *Woman, Culture, and Society* (Stanford, CA: Stanford University Press, 1974), pp. 17-42.

Ruether, R.R., 'Feminist Theology: Methodology, Sources, and Norms', in *eadem*, *Sexism and God-Talk: Toward a Feminist Theology* (Boston: Beacon Press, 1983), pp. 1-46.

Sakenfeld, K.D., 'Response to Ruether's "Christology and Feminism: Can a Male Savior Help Women?"' (paper circulated to SBL/AAR Liberation Theology Working Group, April, 1981), pp. 3-7.

Saldarini, A.J., 'Delegitimation of Leaders in Matthew 23', *CBQ* 43 (1992), pp. 659-80.

—'The Gospel of Matthew and Jewish Christian Conflict in Galilee', in L. Levine (ed.), *Studies on Galilee in Late Antiquity* (New York: Jewish Theological Seminary, 1992), pp. 23-38.

—*Matthew's Christian-Jewish Community* (Chicago Studies in the History of Judaism; Chicago: University of Chicago Press, 1994).

Sanders, E.P., *Jesus and Judaism* (Philadelphia: Fortress Press, 1985).

—'Jesus and the Sinners', *JSNT* 19 (1983), pp. 5-36.

Sapir, J.D., 'The Anatomy of Metaphor', in J.D. Sapir and J.C. Crocker (eds.), *The Social Use of Metaphor: Essays on the Anthropology of Rhetoric* (Philadelphia: University of Pennsylvania Press, 1977).

Schnackenburg, R., *The Gospel According to John*, III (New York: Crossroad, 1982).

Schneiders, S.M., 'Feminist Ideology Criticism and Biblical Hermeneutics', *BTB* 19 (1989), pp. 3-9.

Schottroff, L., *Let the Oppressed Go Free: Feminist Perspectives on the New Testament* (Louisville, KY: Westminster/John Knox Press, 1993).

—'Maria Magdalena und die Frauen am Grabe Jesu', *EvT* 42 (1982), pp. 3-25.

Schweizer, E., *The Good News According to Mark* (trans. D.H. Madvig; Richmond, VA: John Knox Press, 1970).

—*The Good News According to Matthew* (trans. D.E. Green; Atlanta: John Knox Press, 1975).
Scott, J.C., 'Matthew 15.21-28: A Test-Case for Jesus' Manners', *JSNT* 63 (1996), pp. 21-44.
Selvidge, M.J., 'Mark 5:24-34 and Leviticus 15:19-20: A Reaction to Restrictive Purity Regulations', *JBL* 103 (1984), pp. 619-23.
—'Violence, Woman, and the Future or the Matthean Community: A Redactional Critical Essay', *USQR* 39 (1984), pp. 213-23.
—*Woman, Cult and Miracle Recital: A Redactional Critical Investigation of Mark 5:24-34* (Lewisburg, PA: Bucknell University Press, 1990).
Senior, D., *The Gospel of Matthew* (IBT; Nashville: Abingdon Press, 1997).
Setzer, C., 'Excellent Women: Female Witness to the Resurrection', *JBL* 116 (1997), pp. 259-72.
Sheridan, M., 'Disciples and Discipleship in Matthew and Luke', *BTB* 3 (1973), pp. 235-55.
Sly, D., *Philo's Perception of Women* (BJS, 209; Atlanta: Scholars Press, 1990).
Smith, M., 'Ascent to the Heavens and the Beginnings of Christianity', *Eranosjahrbuch* 50 (1981), pp. 403-24.
—*Clement of Alexandria and the Secret Gospel of Mark* (Cambridge, MA: Harvard University Press, 1973), pp. 237-49.
—'The Origin and History of the Transfiguration Story', *USQR* 36 (1980), pp. 39-44.
Smith, R.H., *Easter Gospels: The Resurrection of Jesus According to the Four Evangelists* (Minneapolis: Augsburg, 1983).
Stanton, G.N., *A Gospel for a New People: Studies in Matthew* (Edinburgh: T. & T. Clark, 1992).
Stendahl, K., 'Quis et Unde?, An Analysis of Mt 1-2', in W. Eltester (ed.), *Judentum – Urchristentum – Kirche*, BZNW 26.2 (1964), pp. 19-105.
—*The School of St. Matthew* (Philadelphia: Fortress Press, 2nd edn, 1968).
Strange, J.F., 'Late Hellenistic and Herodian Ossuary Tombs at French Hill, Jerusalem', *BASOR* 219 (1975), pp. 39-67.
Suggs, M.J., *Wisdom, Christology and Law in Matthew's Gospel* (Cambridge, MA: Harvard University Press, 1970).
Tannehill, R., 'The Gospel of Mark as Narrative Christology', *Semeia* 16 (1979), pp. 57-95.
Theissen, G., *The Gospels in Context: Social and Political History in the Synoptic Tradition* (trans. L.M. Maloney; Minneapolis: Fortress Press, 1991).
—'The Sociological Interpretation of Religious Traditions: Its Methodological Problems as Exemplified in Early Christianity', in N.K. Gottwald (ed.), *The Bible and Liberation: Political and Social Hermeneutics* (Maryknoll, NY: Orbis Books, 1983), pp. 38-58.
Thompson, W.G., *Matthew's Advice to a Divided Community* (AnBib, 44; Rome: Biblical Institute Press, 1970).
—'Reflections on the Composition of Matthew 8:1–9:34', *CBQ* 33 (1971), pp. 365-88.
Trible, P., 'Exegesis for Storytellers and Other Strangers', *JBL* 114 (1995), pp. 1-19.
—'Feminist Hermeneutics and Biblical Studies', *Christian Century* 99 (1982), pp. 116-18.
Trilling, W., 'Amt und Amtverständnis bei Matthäus', in A. Descamps and R.D.

A. de Halleux (eds.), *Mélanges bibliques en hommage au R.P. Béda Rigaux* (Gembloux: Duculot, 1970).

—*Das wahre Israel: Studien zur Theologie des Matthäus-Evangeliums* (SANT, 10; Munich: Kösel, 1964).

Turner, V., *The Ritual Process: Structure and Anti-Structure* (Ithaca, NY: Cornell University Press, 1969).

Twelftree, G.H., *Jesus the Exorcist: A Contribution to the Study of the Historical Jesus* (Peabody, MA: Hendrickson, 1993).

Tzaferis, V., 'Jewish Rock-Cut Tombs at and near Giv'at ha-Mivtar, Jerusalem', *IEJ* 20 (1970), pp. 18-32.

Uspensky, B., *A Poetics of Composition* (Berkeley: University of California Press, 1973).

Van Tilborg, S., *The Jewish Leaders in Matthew* (Leiden: E.J. Brill, 1972).

Vermes, G., *The Religion of Jesus the Jew* (Minneapolis: Fortress Press, 1993).

Viviano, B.T., 'Review', *RB* 94 (1987), pp. 425-28.

Waetjen, H.C., 'The Genealogy as the Key to the Gospel According to Matthew', *JBL* 95 (1976), pp. 205-30.

Wainwright, E.M., 'The Gospel of Matthew', in E.S. Fiorenza (ed.), *Searching the Scriptures*, II (New York: Crossroad, 1994), pp. 637-77.

—*Shall We Look For Another? A Feminist Rereading of the Matthean Jesus* (Maryknoll, NY: Orbis Books, 1998).

—*Towards a Feminist Critical Reading of the Gospel According to Matthew* (BZNW, 60; Berlin: W. de Gruyter, 1991).

—'A Voice from the Margin: Reading Matthew 15:21-28 in an Australian Feminist Key', in F.F. Segovia and M.A. Tolbert (eds.), *Reading from this Place. II. Social Location and Biblical Interpretation in Global Perspective* (Minneapolis: Fortress Press, 1995), pp. 132-53.

—'"Your Faith Has Made You Well": Jesus, Women and Healing in the Gospel of Matthew', in I.R. Kitzberger (ed.), *Transformative Encounters: Jesus and Women Re-viewed* (Leiden: E.J. Brill, 1999), pp. 224-44.

Wegner, J. Romney, *Chattel or Person? The Status of Women in the Mishnah* (New York: Oxford University Press, 1988).

—'Philo's Portrayal of Women—Hebraic or Hellenic?', in Levine (ed.), *Women Like This*, pp. 41-66.

Wenham, D., *The Parables of Jesus* (Downers Grove, IL: InterVarsity Press, 1989).

Westermann, C., *Praise and Lament in the Psalms* (Atlanta: John Knox Press, 1981).

Whybray, R.N., *Wisdom in Proverbs: The Concept of Wisdom in Proverbs 1–9* (SBT; Naperville, IL: Alec R. Allenson, 1965).

Wilcox, M., 'Peter and the Rock: A Fresh Look at Matthew 16.17-19', *NTS* 22 (1975), pp. 73-88.

Will, R., and T. Rieger, *Eglises et sanctuaires d'Alsace: Mille ans d'architecture sacrée* (Strasbourg: Edition des Dernieres Nouvelles, 1969).

Wire, A.C., 'Gender Roles in a Scribal Community', in D.L. Balch (ed.), *Social History of the Matthean Community: Cross-Disciplinary Approaches* (Minneapolis: Fortress Press, 1991), pp. 87-121.

Witherington III, B., *Women in the Ministry of Jesus: A Study of Jesus' Attitudes to Women and their Roles as Reflected in his Earthly Life* (SNTSMS, 51; Cambridge: Cambridge University Press, 1984).

Wolfson, E.R., 'Female Imaging of the Torah: From Literary Metaphor to Religious Symbol', in J. Neusner, *et al.* (eds.), *From Ancient Israel to Modern Judaism: Intellect in Quest of Understanding* (BJS, 173; 4 vols.; Atlanta: Scholars Press, 1989), II, pp. 271-307.

—'Woman—The Feminine as Other in Theosophic Kabbalah: Some Philosophical Observations on the Divine Androgyne', in L. Silberstein and R. Cohn (eds.), *The Other in Jewish Thought and History* (New York: New York University Press, 1994), pp. 166-204.

Zeller, J., 'Zu einer jüdischen Vorlage von Mt 13, 52', *BZ* 20 (1976), pp. 223-26.

Zlotnick, D., 'Semahot', *EJ* XIV, col. 1138.

—*The Tractate 'Mourning' (Semahot): (Regulations Relating to Death, Burial, and Mourning)* (Yale Judaica Series, 27; New Haven: Yale University Press, 1966).

Zumstein, J., 'Matthieu 28.16-20', *RTP* 105 (1972), pp. 14-33.

INDEX

INDEX OF REFERENCES

OLD TESTAMENT

Genesis		Deuteronomy		21.8-16	153
2.24	163	4.6	92	21.23	154
18.22-33	124	22.12	83		
38.6-30	68	23.2	141	2 Kings	
		24.1	163	1.8	149
Exodus				2.1-12	154
1-2	86	Joshua		4.32-37	77
		2	138, 139	9.30-37	154
Leviticus		2.1-21	68	10.11	154
15	34	2.9-13	139		
15.10	79	6.25	68, 139,	2 Chronicles	
15.13-15	78		153	16.14	207
15.18	79	6.26	153		
15.19-33	77	10	203	Esther	
15.19-20	74	12.20	142	3.19	103
15.19	75				
15.25-33	72	Ruth		Job	
15.25-27	73	3.1-14	68	1.20	214
15.25	75			2.12-13	214
15.28-30	78	1 Samuel		28	91
15.31	76	16.14-23	131	28.1-28	91
15.33	75	16.14	131	28.27	92
18.16	148	28	131		
18.19	78, 79			Psalms	
19.29	141	2 Samuel		13	120, 121
20.18	75, 78, 79	13.31	214	13.1	120
20.21	148	18.33-19.8	214	13.2	120
21.7	141			13.3	120
21.14	141	1 Kings		13.4	120
27.29	139	1.11-31	68	13.5	120, 121
		16.31	153	13.6	121
Numbers		16.34	153	15.10	213
11.11-15	124	17.17-24	77	16.10	213
15.38-41	83	21.1-28	153	22	122
		21.4	153	22.1-2	122

Psalms (cont.)		4.3	94	Isaiah	
22.3-5	122	4.6-9	91	23	115
22.6-8	122	6.20	94	53.7	179
22.9-10	122	8.1-31	91		
22.11	122	8.1-8	91	Jeremiah	
22.12-18	122	8.2-3	91, 98	31.15	86
22.19-21	122	8.14-16	91	38.15	86
86.16	119	8.15-16	92		
88.11	123	8.17	109	Ezekiel	
109.26	119	8.22-31	93	1.28	105
		8.22-30	92	26–28	115
Proverbs		8.23-24	91	29.30-36	214
1–9	88, 96	8.27	91, 92	36.17	73
1.2-19	94	8.30	92		
1.8	94	8.32-36	91, 98	Daniel	
1.20-33	91, 93, 98	8.32-33	94	6–12	203
1.20-21	91, 98	9.1-6	91, 110	8.17-18	105
1.22	91	9.3	91, 98	10.9-12	105
1.28	91	9.10-12	91		
2.1-19	93	15.20	94	Joel	
2.1-8	94	16.16	91, 102	3.4	115
3.13-18	91	23.22	94		
4.1-9	94	23.25	94	Zechariah	
4.1	94	31.1-9	94	8.20-22	83

APOCRYPHA

Tobit		Sirach		24.7	98
6.14-18	131	1.1-10	91	24.19-22	91, 98, 100, 110
		1.1	92		
Wisdom of Solomon		1.4	92	24.30-34	94
1.15	102	1.10	92	24.33	95
6–9	92	1.15	91	39.6	95
6.1–9.18	93	3.1-11	94	39.12–43.33	95
6.12-11.1	91	4.11-28	91	51.13-30	91, 93
7.8-9	91	4.11	91	51.13-14	109
7.11	91	4.17	91	51.23	94
7.22	92	6.18-31	91	51.25	94
7.27	91, 100	6.20-31	91	51.26	100
8.1-2	91	6.25	100	51.27	91
8.2	91, 109	14.20–15.10	91		
8.3	92	14.20–15.8	91	Baruch	
8.6	92	14.22	109	3.9–4.4	91
8.8	91	14.24-25	91	4.1-4	92
8.9-14	91	15.2-3	91		
9.1-18	95	15.5	91	2 Maccabees	
9.10	92	24	92	7.11	213
10.1–11.14	100	24.1-34	91, 93	7.23	213
11.1	91	24.3	92		

Index of References

NEW TESTAMENT

Matthew		4.21-22	60, 61	7.22	129
1-2	68	4.23-24	34	7.23	189
1.1-17	29, 51, 108, 194	4.23	46	7.24-27	189
		4.24	81, 129	7.25	189
1.2	30	4.25	143	7.27	189
1.3	31	5.1	161	8-9	34, 98, 130, 136, 137, 143
1.5	31, 138	5.2	49		
1.6	30, 31	5.3-10	103		
1.11	30	5.8	57, 58	8	37, 85
1.12	30	5.9	49, 57, 58, 147	8.1-17	35
1.16	30, 31			8.1	83
1.17	30	5.15-16	54	8.2-9.35	72
1.18-2.23	50	5.16	53, 55	8.2-17	35
1.18-25	29, 50	5.17-20	203	8.2-3	72
1.18	32, 109	5.18	77	8.2	38, 39, 133
1.20-25	68	5.27-32	152	8.4	83
1.20	32, 109	5.27-30	51	8.5-14	109
1.23	32	5.27-28	149	8.5-13	37, 64, 116, 133, 143
2	147, 149	5.28	29, 147		
2.1-12	37	5.31-32	29, 51, 149		
2.2	38, 85	5.32	29, 148	8.5-7	72
2.3	147	5.33-37	147	8.5-6	133
2.4	147	5.33	57	8.7	85, 133
2.8	38	5.34	57, 58	8.8	135
2.9-11	147	5.45	53, 55, 64	8.9	85
2.10-12	68	5.48	55, 64	8.10-13	144
2.11	38, 39	6.1	53, 55, 64	8.13	135
2.13-15	68	6.4	53, 58, 64	8.14-17	50
2.13	50, 63	6.6	53, 58, 64	8.14-15	108, 166
2.16	86	6.8	53, 64	8.15	42, 136
2.18	51, 86	6.9	55, 56	8.16-17	34
2.19-23	68	6.14-15	54	8.16	129
2.19-21	50	6.14	55	8.18-9.17	35
2.20	63	6.15	53	8.18-34	35
2.21	63	6.18	53, 58, 64	8.19-22	98, 99
2.22-23	63	6.24	57, 58	8.19	40, 98
2.22	48, 63	6.26	53, 55, 64	8.21-22	63, 76
3.1-17	147, 149, 152	6.29	56	8.23-27	37
		6.30	57, 58	8.23	161
3.3-4	147	6.32	55	8.25	76
3.7-10	58	6.33	57, 58	8.28-34	136
3.7	59	7.9-10	64	8.28	129
3.12	59	7.9	63	9	37, 85, 86
4.4	57	7.11	55	9.1-17	35
4.7	57	7.15	188	9.1-8	36
4.10	57	7.16-23	188	9.1	79
4.11	42	7.21-23	188, 189	9.2-22	37
4.14-16	37	7.21	53-55, 64	9.3	36
4.18-22	110	7.22-23	185	9.8	36

Matthew (cont.)		10.29	53, 54	12.28	56, 57		
9.9-13	36	10.32-33	55	12.38-42	37, 99, 109		
9.9	98, 110	10.32	53, 55	12.42	51		
9.10	109	10.33	53, 55	12.46-50	44, 50, 51,		
9.11	98	10.35-39	51		65, 69		
9.12	135, 161	10.35-37	65	12.48-49	109		
9.14-17	36, 98	10.35-36	76	12.50	53-55, 65,		
9.18-34	35	10.35	65		109		
9.18-31	35, 36	10.37	65, 76	13	100, 156		
9.18-26	64, 70, 73,	10.41	191	13.3	49		
	74, 81, 83,	11.1-14	155	13.11	100		
	86, 144,	11.2-13.58	100	13.15	135		
	151	11.2-13.54	99	13.21	191		
9.18-19	35, 50	11.2-30	89	13.33	29, 51, 108		
9.18	35, 36, 38,	11.2-19	99	13.43	53, 54		
	39, 76, 133	11.2-14	149	13.44	194		
9.19	84	11.2	99	13.45	194		
9.20-22	29, 34, 35,	11.4-16	34	13.52	43, 104		
	50, 108,	11.4-6	99	13.53-58	50		
	194	11.5	77	13.54	46		
9.20	34, 72, 83	11.13	56	13.55	63		
9.22	34-36, 109,	11.14	152	14	86		
	136	11.16-19	98, 99	14.1-13	145		
9.23-26	35, 50	11.16-17	51	14.1-12	44, 50, 86		
9.24-25	86	11.17	48	14.1	146		
9.25	35, 86, 136	11.18	48	14.2	86, 149		
9.26	35	11.19	48, 51, 98-	14.3-11	69		
9.27-31	35, 37		100, 109,	14.8	146		
9.27	38, 40, 133		112	14.11	86		
9.28	38	11.20–13.58	100	14.12	43		
9.29	36, 38	11.20-24	99, 143	14.13-34	149		
9.31	35	11.25-30	89, 98-100,	14.13-21	37		
9.32-34	35, 37		103	14.13	146, 149		
9.32	129	11.25-27	99	14.21	29, 50, 51,		
9.33	35, 36	11.25	57		108		
9.34	36, 98	11.27	55	14.22-23	37		
9.35	34, 36, 46,	11.28-30	98, 99,	14.33	38, 39		
	98		101, 194	14.34-36	83		
9.37	98	12.1-21	203	15	19		
9.38	83	12.1-8	100	15.1-20	38		
10	36, 98	12.1	161	15.1-19	51, 116		
10.1	161	12.4	57	15.1-9	115		
10.2	61, 161	12.7	129	15.3	57		
10.5-6	85	12.9-14	100, 171	15.4-9	65, 66		
10.5	49, 143,	12.9	46	15.4-7	65		
	144	12.15	132	15.4	57		
10.6	37, 143	12.18-21	37	15.5	66		
10.8	129, 137	12.22-37	37	15.6	57, 67		
10.17	46	12.22-32	142	15.10-20	115		
10.20	53, 54	12.22	129, 132,	15.13	53-55		
10.21-22	65		135	15.21-28	18, 29, 34,		
10.21	51, 65	12.23	142		50, 68, 85,		

	108, 109,	16.21	166	19.11-12	164
	114-19,	16.23	57, 58	19.13-15	159, 161,
	121, 123-	16.27	55		164
	27, 129,	17	105	19.16-31	164
	130, 133,	17.1-9	105, 111	19.16-22	65, 66
	137, 142,	17.1	56, 61	19.16	165
	194	17.6	105	19.17-20	165
15.21	115, 132	17.7	105	19.19	51, 65
15.22-28	37	17.14-21	64	19.20-22	40
15.22-23	117	17.15	135, 136	19.21	165
15.22	34, 38,	17.18	129, 135,	19.22	164, 165
	115, 119,		136	19.23-30	165
	121, 125,	17.22-23	166	19.24	57, 58
	127, 132,	17.22	104	19.26	57, 58
	133, 135,	18–20	20, 21,	19.28	165
	136, 143		158, 159	19.29	51, 65
15.23-24	117	18	20, 158-62,	19.31	164
15.23	39, 117,		166, 167	20	158, 162,
	122, 133,	18.1-2	159		168
	142	18.2-5	161, 164	20.1-16	164, 166,
15.24	37, 39, 85,	18.4-5	159		188
	133, 134	18.4	160	20.14-15	164
15.25-28	117	18.6	161	20.16	164
15.25	38, 39,	18.10	53-55, 161	20.17-19	44, 166
	119, 121,	18.11	54	20.19	104
	122, 133,	18.12-14	173, 194	20.20-28	61, 108,
	134, 143	18.12-13	54		166
15.26-27	125	18.12	162	20.20-24	60, 68
15.26	122, 133,	18.14	53-55, 161	20.20-21	162
	144	18.15-20	47	20.20	38, 43, 50,
15.27	121, 122,	18.15-17	161, 162		167
	125, 134,	18.19	53-55, 64	20.21	62
	143	18.21	162	20.22-28	168
15.28	34, 51,	18.23-34	162	20.22-23	68
	109, 118,	18.23	162	20.22	167, 169
	132, 135,	18.24	173	20.23	53, 54, 62
	136	18.25	51, 162	20.25-28	42, 47
15.29-31	125	18.26	38, 39, 162	20.27-28	164
15.30-31	34	18.28	173	20.28	110
15.32-39	125	18.32	162	20.29-34	36, 37
15.32-38	37	18.35	53-55	20.30	38
15.38	29, 50, 108	19	158, 162,	20.31	39
15.40-41	68		166	20.34	39, 40, 42
15.47	197	19.1–20.28	163	21.5	51
16.1-8	197	19.1–20.16	162	21.18-19	189
16.1-4	37	19.1-12	29, 51	21.22-43	29
16.1	197	19.3	163	21.23	102
16.5-12	38	19.5	163	21.28-32	51
16.17-19	104	19.6-7	163	21.31-32	109
16.17	53-55, 64	19.6	57	21.31	51, 57
16.18-19	47	19.8-9	163	21.32	51
16.21-22	104	19.9	163	21.33-41	192

Matthew (cont.)		24.8	51	27.25	33, 59, 60
21.41	182	24.9	51	27.46	57, 58
21.42	57, 58	24.10	191	27.53-55	168, 169
21.43	57	24.19	51, 108	27.54	40
21.45	48	24.36	55	27.55-56	29, 40, 41,
22.1-46	193	24.41	51		43, 68, 220
22.1-22	188	24.45-51	173, 182	27.55	50, 109,
22.1-14	144	25	173		166, 168,
22.12-14	182	25.1-30	189		207
22.21	57	25.1-13	21, 51,	27.56	43, 50, 60,
22.23-33	29, 51		108, 144,		62, 158,
22.29	57		173, 178,		168
22.32	57		182	27.57	42, 43
22.37	57	25.2	181, 183	27.61	29, 40, 41,
22.41-46	48	25.3-4	186		50, 158,
22.41-42	49	25.6	184		197, 208
22.44	48, 57	25.8-9	183	27.62-66	202, 208,
22.45	48	25.8	186		211
23	49, 101,	25.9	183	28.1-10	29, 40, 50,
	105, 191	25.11	185		110, 169,
23.8-12	47	25.12	183, 185		208
23.1-12	101, 160,	25.13	175	28.1-7	41
	161	25.14-30	173, 183	28.1	158, 196-
23.1-2	49	25.15-16	173		98, 202,
23.5	83	25.26	123		206, 211,
23.8-12	103	25.27	123		214
23.9	53-55, 63,	25.28	123	28.2-3	208
	102	25.31-46	51	28.2	110, 111
23.12	160	25.34	51-54	28.3	110
23.13	101	25.41	182	28.4	110
23.15	101	25.44	42	28.5-7	208
23.22	57	26.2	41	28.5	110
23.23	101	26.6-13	29, 40, 50	28.7	44, 110,
23.25	101	26.7	40		204
23.27	101	26.10	41	28.8-10	41
23.28	101	26.13	41	28.8	44, 110,
23.29	101	26.18	48		208
23.30-32	59	26.25	48	28.9-10	110, 204,
23.30	59	26.27	62		208, 218
23.31	59	26.29	53, 54	28.9	38, 39, 41,
23.32-33	182	26.36-46	62		209, 211
23.33	59	26.37	60	28.10	44
23.34-36	98, 100-	26.39-42	54	28.11-15	202, 203,
	102, 104	26.39	55		208
23.34	46, 100,	26.42	53	28.16-20	105, 109,
	161	26.53	53, 54		170, 204
23.37-39	51, 98,	26.56	110, 169	28.16	41, 44
	100, 101	26.58	161	28.17	38, 39, 41,
23.37	29, 51, 101	26.61	198		204
23.39	57	26.69-75	169	28.19-20	47, 111
24	173	26.69	50	28.19	43, 53, 54
24.1	102	27.19	50, 51, 108	28.20	105
24.5	191				

Index of References

241

Mark		15.6-14	108	10.28	57
1.19-20	60	15.34	58	10.30-37	175
1.19	61	15.40-41	207, 220	10.38-42	210
1.44-45	217	15.40	168, 207, 210	11.11	63
3.1-5	171			11.12	55
3.17	61	15.41	109, 168	11.13	55, 56
3.31-35	67	15.47	207	11.29-32	109
3.35	54	16	22	11.33	54
4.21	54	16.1-8	110, 206	11.49-51	98
4.35	76	16.1-2	196	11.49	100
5.21-43	64, 81	16.1	206, 207	12.6	54
5.22	151	16.2	207	12.8-9	54
5.24-34	74	16.3	207	12.12	54
5.25-34	108	16.4	207	12.24	54
5.25	75	16.5-7	207	12.30	55
5.38	214	16.5	110	13.20-21	108
6.3	63, 207	16.6-7	111	13.34-35	98, 101
6.17-28	69	16.6	110	15.3-7	54
6.19	150	16.7	208	15.8-10	187
6.20	148	16.8	206, 207, 217	15.11-32	175
6.44	108			16.1-8	176
6.56	83	16.9	209, 211, 216, 217, 219	16.26	187
7.6-13	65, 66			21.23	108
7.24-30	68, 108, 115			22.16	54
				22.18	54
7.24	115	Luke		22.41-46	54
7.26	142	2.41-52	29	22.42	55
7.31-37	85	3.7-9	58	22.43-44	54
7.31	115	6.36	55, 64	23.17-23	108
7.36	217	6.46	54, 64	23.34	57
8.9	108	7.18-35	99	23.46	57
8.38	55	7.35	98, 99	23.49-55	209
9.2	61	8.1-3	220	23.49	169, 207, 209
9.14-27	64	8.2-3	169, 209, 210		
10.12	163			23.54	209
10.35-45	61, 108	8.2	210	23.55	169, 209
10.35-41	60	8.16	54	23.56	209
10.35-36	68	8.19-21	67	24	22, 208
10.35	167	8.21	54	24.1-11	209
10.40	54	8.40-56	64, 81	24.1	196
11.25	54-56	8.44	83	24.2	209
11.26	54	9	210	24.3	211
12.34	57	9.22	210	24.5	210
13.17	108	9.26	55	24.6-8	210
13.32	55	9.28	61	24.6-7	210
14.8	207	9.37-43	64	24.8-9	210
14.25	54	9.38	57	24.10	206, 209, 210, 220
14.28	208	9.57-60	76, 98		
14.33	60, 62	10.1-42	57	24.11-12	210
14.36-40	54	10.21-22	98, 99	24.11	216
14.36	55	10.22	55	24.12	209

John		Acts		Colossians	
1.36	179	1.11	210	3.18–4.1	162
3.9	58	1.14	210		
4	118	2.18	210	1 Timothy	
9.38	38	2.25-31	218	1.3-4	190
11.17	202	2.29-31	213		
11.33	214	7.11	116	2 Timothy	
11.39	202	9.1-19	220	4.14	191
12.27	54, 55	13.19	116		
15.14	54	13.31	209, 210	Hebrews	
18.39-40	108	13.34-37	213, 218	11.31	138, 141
19.25	168, 207				
20	22	Romans		James	
20.1-2	210	16.17-20	190	2.25	138, 141
20.1	206, 211				
20.2	211	1 Corinthians		1 Peter	
20.11-18	210, 211,	1.10-12	190	2.11–3.12	162
	218, 219	1.18-31	190		
20.11	211, 214	2.1-16	190	2 Peter	
20.12	211	9.1	212, 216	2.1-2	191
20.13	211	15	215		
20.15	211	15.5-7	215, 217,	1 John	
20.17	211		218	2.19-22	191
20.18	212, 216	15.35-44	213		
21	208			Revelation	
		Ephesians		1.17	105
Q		5.22–6.9	162	12.11	179
11.13	56				

PSEUDEPIGRAPHA

1 Enoch		94.6-11	95	Apoc. Abr.	
14.14-15	105	98.9-16	95	17.8-21	95
15.7–16.1	131	99.1-2	95	48.36	98
37.2	95	99.11-16	95		
39.11-14	95	100.7-9	95	Jos. Asen.	
40.7	131			14–17	96
42	91, 93, 98	2 Bar.			
48–49	98	8.47-49	103	Jub.	
53.3	131	48.36	98	4.22	131
56.1	131			5.1	131
69.4-6	131	4 Ezra		25.14	96
72–82	95	5.9-12	91, 93	35.6	96
84.3	91, 93	7.1	105		
92-105	95	11.41-42	103	T. Job	
94.5	98			46–53	96

QUMRAN

11QTemple		9.20–11.22	95	11QPsa	
48.15-17	73	10.26	95	18.8	91
1QH				18.12	91
1.35-36	95	1QSa		21.11-17	91
4.2-6	95	1.4-11	96	22.1	91
5.16	95				
5.18	95	1QSb		CD	
5.21-22	103	5.22	95, 103	4.12–5.17	73
7.20-22	94			6.16	95, 103
7.21-22	103	4Q171		6.21	95, 103
		2.8-11	103	9–10	158
1QM				13.9-10	94
14.7	95, 103	4Q185			
		1.13-14	94	1Q (Gen.Apoc)	
1QS				20.16-32	131
5.24–6.3	158				

RABBINIC

MISHNAH		b. 'Erub.		y. Mo'ed Katan	
Ber.		53–54	96	3.5	202
2.12	80	73	94	3.82	202
Nid.		b. Hag.		y. Šebu.	
7.4	80	14	95	9.1	95
				9.37	95
Šab.		b. Ket.		9.38	95
23.5	199	61	78		
				y. Sot.	
Yeb.		b. Men.		1.4	95
16.1	202	44	84	1.16	95
16.15	202			1.45	95
Zab.		b. Nid.		9.17	95
4.1	73	66	75	9.24	95
5.1	81			9.29	95
5.6	81	b. Pes.			
		62	96	TOSEFTA	
TALMUDS				t. B. Qam.	
b. 'Abod. Zar.		b. Šab.		1.6	96
18	96	110	73	4.17	96
		119	103		
b. B. Meṣ.				t. Hag.	
83–85	78	b. Sanh.		2.2	95
		101	91, 92		
				t. Pes.	
b. Ber.		b. Ta'an.		1.27	95
10	96	23	84		
22	80			t. Sot.	
		y. Hag.		13.3	95
		2.1	95	13.4	95

MIDRASH		30.2	103	10	139
ARN		Lam. R.		Sem.	
25	103	3.6	96	8.1	199-201
31	91, 92				
35	103	Mek.		Sifre	
Gen. R.		9.130-31	94	34	94
1.1	92	9.99-116	95	48	92, 95, 103
7	202				
		Pes. R.		95	103
Lev. R.		167	139	305	94
1.5	95			307	96
20.10	92	Qoh. R.		321	103
21.8	95	8	139	335	94

OTHER ANCIENT REFERENCES

EARLY JEWISH AND CHRISTIAN		PHILO		JOSEPHUS	
Acts of Pilate		Cher.		Ant.	
7	74	27.2	95	3.261	80
				4.219	215
Epistula Apostolorum		Conf. Ling.		5	141
9	206	49	91	7	141
				8.42-49	131
Gospel of Mary		Congr.		15.61	207
2-31	219	9	92, 106	18.109-15	148
				18.11	149
Gospel of Peter		Det. Pot. Ins.		18.136	148
10.38-11.44	212	115-116	91		
12.50-13.57	212	225-26	92	Apion	
12.50	206, 214			2.103-104	73
		Ebr.			
Gospel of Thomas		30-31	92	Life	
90	99			5.227	73
114	219	Fug.		CLASSICAL	
		52	106	Cicero	
Isodore of Seville		62	92	Sest.	
Etimologias		109	91	38	91
11.1.141	82				
		Spec. Leg.		Diodorus Siculus	
LAB		3.6	95	Bib. hist.	
30.2	96			38.3-5	213
31.1	96	Vit. Cont.			
33.1	96	12	96	Pliny	
		32-33	96	Natural History	
		68-69	96	7.15.64	82
		83-88	96		

INDEX OF AUTHORS

Abel, E. 25, 26
Abrams, M.H. 28, 30
Abu-Lughod, L. 215
Albertz, R. 119
Albright, W.F. 197
Allen, W.C. 196
Allison, D.C., Jr 59, 73-75, 81, 127, 160-62,
    164, 168, 169
Anderson, J. Capel 37, 46, 48, 72, 108,
    145, 149, 152, 194
Argyle, A.W. 184, 196

Bach, A. 145, 156
Bacon, B.W. 197
Baer, R.A. 92
Baker, R. 131
Barth, G. 34, 105, 196
Bauer, D.R. 70
Baum, J. 180
Begrich, J. 121
Berger, P. 94
Beyer, H.W. 135
Bieber, M. 90
Black, M. 89
Böcher, O. 59
Bode, E.L. 206
Boers, H. 118
Booth, W. 30, 34, 46
Borg, M. 71
Bornkamm, G. 34, 35, 196
Borsch, F.H. 176, 177
Bovon, F. 218
Boyarin, D. 78, 81
Braidotti, R. 130
Brown, R.E. 30-33, 109, 138, 139, 141, 161,
    169, 191
Brueggemann, W. 119, 120, 123
Bultmann, R. 93, 101, 116, 117
Burrus, V. 215
Bynum, C.W. 95

Cady, S. 88

Calloway, J. 200
Cameron, R. 74
Camp, C. 88, 89, 94, 96
Caraveli, A. 214
Carter, W. 158-60, 162, 163, 165
Chestnutt, R.D. 96
Christ, C. 25, 27
Cohen, S.J.D. 75, 79-82
Collins, A.Y. 206
Conkey, M.W. 129
Conrad, E. 121
Conzelmann, H. 93
Cope, O.L. 104, 106, 196, 198, 203
Corley, K.E. 198, 199
Cortes, J. 118
Coser, L. 102
Countryman, L.W. 82
Crossan, J.D. 71, 74, 212
Cummings, J.T. 83

D'Angelo, M.R. 56, 74, 79, 82
Da Gallarate, G. 178
Davies, S.L. 81, 215
Davies, W.D. 59, 73-75, 127, 160-62, 164,
    168, 169, 196
Derrett, J.D.M. 122
Deutsch, C. 89, 91, 93, 98-100, 102, 103,
    105, 109, 111, 112
Dodd, C.H. 176
Donahue, J. 177, 188
Dube, M.W. 127
Dubisch, J. 215
Duff, N.J. 182
Duling, D.C. 34, 131, 134, 161, 167

Engelsman, J.C. 88

Fant, M.B. 111
Farmer, W.R. 196
Fears, J.R. 91
Fetterley, J. 26
Fineman, J. 150

Fiorenza, E.S. 27, 29, 72, 88, 144
Fitzmyer, J. 64
Fredriksen, P. 71, 78
Frunkenmölle, H. 60
Frye, N. 90, 93
Frymer-Kensky, T. 88, 93, 97
Fuller, R.H. 206, 209, 213
Furman, N. 26

Garland, D. 72, 73
Garrett, S.R. 130
Geertz, C. 94
Gench, F.T. 89
Gero, J.M. 129
Gerstenberger, G. 119
Gibbs, J.M. 36, 39
Gilhus, I.S. 180
Gnilka, J. 98, 99, 101, 102, 104, 105
Goodblatt, D. 96
Goodfriend, E.A. 140
Goulder, M.D. 197, 203
Green, H.B. 197, 203
Greimas, A.J. 118
Groot van Houten, C. de 144
Gundry, R. 42, 114
Gunkel, H. 120

Hagner, D. 72, 75
Hamerton-Kelly, R. 98
Harrington, D.J. 63, 127
Harris, W.V. 111
Hawkins, J.C. 48
Held, H.J. 34, 35, 108, 116, 196
Hengel, M. 90, 98, 219
Henle, P. 90
Henry, M.M. 140
Hiers, R.H. 128
Hill, D. 100
Hoffmann, P. 101
Holst-Warhaft, G. 214
Horsley, R.A. 96
Hummel, R. 196
Humphries-Brooks, S. 138, 142, 143, 149

Iser, W. 30

Jaussen, J.A. 177
Jeremias, J. 176
Johnson, L.T. 102, 105
Johnson, M.D. 89
Johnson, S.E. 198, 203

Kelly-Gadol, J. 25
Kendall, D. 219
Keynest, G. 180
Kingsbury, J.D. 33-36, 39, 40, 42, 84, 87, 169, 196
Kittel, G.W. 68
Kleinman, A. 130
Kloppenborg, J.S. 99, 101, 158, 176
Kohler, K. 94
Kolodny, A. 26, 28, 29
Kosky, B. 126
Kraemer, R.S. 112

Lee, B.J. 107
Lefkowitz, M.R. 111
Levenson, J. 115
Levine, A.-J. 65, 73, 85, 88, 89, 107, 112, 128, 133, 144, 204
Longstaff, T. 196
Luz, U. 33, 43, 52, 62

MacDonald, D.R. 215
Mack, B.L. 93
Malina, B.J. 160
Mann, C.S. 197
McKane, W. 94
McNeile, A.H. 42, 43
Meeks, W. 92
Meiselman, M. 216
Mendilow, A.A. 48, 49
Metzger, B.M. 56, 58
Meyers, E.M. 200, 201
Micklem, P.A. 196
Milgrom, J. 73, 78, 80
Minear, P.S. 33, 43
Moi, T. 112
Moltmann-Wendel, E. 209
Montefiore, C.J.G. 203
Mowery, R. 53, 58
Muilenburg, J. 28
Mulack, C. 88

Neirynck, F. 206
Nel, P. 94
Newman, B. 88
Newsom, C.A. 73, 88, 89, 115
Neyrey, J.H. 165
Nickelsburg, G.W.E. 95, 104, 105, 213

O'Collins, G. 219
O'Day, G.R. 114, 122

Index of Authors

Oepke, A. 135
Orton, D. 89, 104
Osiek, C. 205
Overman, J.A. 101, 157

Padel, R. 132
Pagels, E. 183
Perkins, P. 206
Perkinson, J. 127
Perrin, N. 40
Perrine, L. 90
Petersen, N. 46, 50
Pilch, J.J. 129, 134
Pirot, J. 177
Pomeroy, S.B. 75
Powell, M.A. 70
Proctor-Smith, M. 174
Puig i Tàrrech, A. 173

Rabbinowitz, R.J. 199-201
Rahmani, L.Y. 201
Ricoeur, P. 90
Rieger, T. 179
Rigato, M.L. 210
Ringe, S.H. 73
Ringgren, H. 90
Robinson, J.M. 99, 107
Robinson, T.H. 196
Ronan, M. 88
Rosaldo, M.Z. 91
Rosenblatt, M.-E. 171
Ruether, R.R. 27

Sakenfeld, K.D. 25
Saldarini, A.J. 93, 100-102, 104, 105, 157
Sanders, E.P. 78
Sapir, J.D. 90
Schneiders, S.M. 192
Schottroff, L. 169, 207, 220
Schweizer, E. 42, 68, 119
Scott, J.C. 127
Selvidge, M.J. 74, 185
Senior, D. 127
Setzer, C. 109, 110
Sheridan, M. 33, 43

Sly, D. 92
Smith, M. 105
Smith, R.H. 211
Stanton, G.N. 53
Stendahl, K. 68, 196
Stern, E. 140
Strange, J.F. 201
Suggs, M.J. 89, 101

Tannehill, R. 39
Taussig, H. 88
Theissen, G. 95
Thompson, W.G. 35, 38, 43, 48
Tolbert, M.A. 25
Trible, P. 25, 152, 154, 155
Trilling, W. 104
Turner, V. 95
Twelftree, G.H. 128
Tzaferis, V. 201

Uspensky, B. 45, 46, 48

Van Tilborg, S. 33
Vermes, G. 83
Viviano, B.T. 173

Waetjen, H.C. 32
Wainwright, E.M. 72, 73, 76, 81, 83, 88, 89, 110, 126, 128, 130, 132-34, 137, 157, 168, 170
Wegner, J.M. 92, 216
Wenham, D. 177
Westermann, C. 119, 120
Whybray, R.N. 94
Wilcox, M. 104
Will, R. 179
Wire, A.C. 103, 105, 108, 195
Witherington III, B. 75
Wolfson, E.R. 97, 112
Wright, N.T. 71

Zeller, J. 104
Zimmerli, W. 121
Zlotnick, D. 199, 200
Zumstein, J. 105

Printed in Great Britain
by Amazon